JOSEPH CONRAD
THE WAY OF DISPOSSESSION

JOSEPH CONRAD

THE WAY OF DISPOSSESSION

by

H. M. Daleski

FABER AND FABER
3 Queen Square London WC1

First published in 1977
by Faber and Faber Limited
3 Queen Square London WC1
Printed in Great Britain by
Western Printing Services Ltd Bristol

ISBN 0 571 10816 4

To SHIRLEY

In order to arrive at what you do not know
  You must go by a way which is the way of ignorance.
In order to possess what you do not possess
  You must go by the way of dispossession.

T. S. ELIOT:
'East Coker', *Four Quartets*

Contents

Acknowledgements

A shortened version of Chapter Two has appeared in *The Hebrew University Studies in Literature*, Autumn 1974; and an essay based on parts of Chapters One and Seven in *The Critical Quarterly*, Autumn 1975. I am grateful to the editors for permission to use this material.

I wish to thank the Hebrew University for a grant towards the cost of typing.

I am glad to acknowledge a debt to graduate students at both the Hebrew University and Tel-Aviv University: in recent years I have benefited greatly from discussions on Conrad with them. I am particularly indebted to Mr. James Warner, who taught me a salutary lesson about dark powers in Conrad; and to Mrs. Pamela Schwed, who in spirited argument led me to change my mind about a considerable number of important issues.

I should like to express my thanks to two friends and colleagues: to Professor Baruch Hochman, with whom I had many rewarding talks about Conrad, and whose penetrating and constantly challenging criticism of the typescript has led to its improvement in countless ways; and to Professor Ruth Nevo, who has now been a guide and mentor for a long time. She has an infallible capacity for detecting a weakness in an argument, and showed me there were other 'soft spots' in the typescript than those I was talking about in Conrad's characters. She coupled this, moreover, with happy advice for resolving apparently intractable problems, and has once again left me inestimably indebted to her.

I am most grateful to my wife, Shirley, for many extremely helpful suggestions, and for her discernment in matters of style.

H.M.D.

NOTE ON TEXTS

Page references to Conrad's works are to the
Dent twenty-one volume Collected Edition,
London, 1946–1955.

A Literary Compass

PERHAPS the most widely quoted passage in the whole of Conrad is that in which he refers to the 'ideas' in his work: 'Those who read me know my conviction that the world, the temporal world, rests on a few very simple ideas; so simple that they must be as old as the hills. It rests, notably, among others, on the idea of Fidelity.'[1] One can well understand the allure of this statement: simple and succinct, offering a *Weltanschauung* in a sentence, it is authoritatively reductive of the complexities of a great writer. It is a statement that by now has had a long run in Conrad criticism. The editor of the first major collection of essays on Conrad, for instance, subscribes to it without reservation: 'Fidelity is the crux of Conrad's artistic code as well as of his moral code. And fidelity is also the theme upon which almost all his imaginative works pivot.'[2] Though other critics have been more circumspect in their responses to the passage, it is regularly reflected in generalizing statements about the nature of Conrad's distinctive preoccupations. In their own way, two of the finest Conrad critics, Thomas Moser and Albert J. Guerard, endorse a similar view. Moser writes:

> On the surface, Conrad's ethic seems very simple indeed. Humanity is important; fidelity is the highest virtue. When we come to consider this ethic in relation to the actions of the characters, we shall see that Conrad's interests are much more subtle and complex than these two simple ideas suggest. But we should be misreading him if we failed to appreciate the strength of his intellectual and emotional allegiance to a stoic humanism.[3]

Guerard maintains that 'the success or failure of . . . attempted communications between individuals (and the ensuing acts of loyalty or betrayal) is the subject and central preoccupation of Conrad's greatest books, most obviously of *Lord Jim* and *Under Western Eyes*'.[4] Some ten years after Moser and Guerard, John A. Palmer declares that 'critical indignation over the famous passage in *A Personal Record*' is 'usual', but he also insists that the passage is nonetheless fundamental: 'Conrad's perception of what is involved in a commitment to [the] "few very simple ideas" – their psychological, social, and philosophical implications – is of course complex, and the narrative and symbolic superstructure he builds upon that commitment cannot be understood by looking at the foundation alone. But this is not the same as denying that the foundation exists.'[5]

With so much attention having been paid to the Familiar Preface to *A Personal Record*, it is surprising that the importance of what seems to be a far more revealing statement in the preface has not been stressed. Having commented on the need to 'surrender oneself to occult and irresponsible powers' in order to be 'a great magician', and on the phenomenon of 'simple men selling their souls for love or power to some grotesque devil', Conrad asserts that 'anything of the sort is bound to be a fool's bargain':

> I don't lay claim to particular wisdom because of my dislike and distrust of such transactions. It may be my sea training acting upon a natural disposition to keep good hold on the one thing really mine, but the fact is that I have a positive horror of losing even for one moving moment that full possession of myself which is the first condition of good service. And I have carried my notion of good service from my earlier into my later existence. (p. xvii)

It has been remarked that Conrad gives very little away in his ostensibly personal record, but the sudden note of self-revelation that is sounded, apparently involuntarily, in this prefatory passage is significantly repeated in the reminiscences that follow, and in a way that again relates it not only to his service at sea but also to his art: 'I have tried to be a sober worker all my life – all my two lives. I did so from taste, no doubt, having an instinctive horror of losing my sense of full self-possession, but also from artistic conviction' (p. 112). It is of no more than biographical interest that Conrad should have felt that his two very different lives were linked by the same sort of demand that each made of himself, and that the artist met the seaman in the common self-command necessitated by a craft; but I believe we can only begin to come to grips critically with the Conrad who repeatedly writes in his letters of the anguish of composition when we realize that for him the terrors and perils of a life at the desk were as actual as those encountered at sea. Or in the jungle – since to be an artist, for Conrad, is to be a Kurtz set loose in a heart of darkness, as the following passage from the same preface strikingly suggests: 'In that interior world where [the artist's] thought and his emotions go seeking for the experience of imagined adventures, there are no policemen, no law, no pressure of circumstance or dread of opinion to keep him within bounds. Who then is going to say Nay to his temptations if not his conscience?' (p. xviii). If conscience thus enjoins that the artist be kept within bounds by an unremitting self-possession, his self-possession is conceived as a *sine qua non* of art.

Self-possession is also the primary 'article of creed' in Conrad. Being 'the first condition of good service', it is necessarily anterior to all that is subsumed by that ideal, to the effective deployment of the characteristic Conradian virtues of fidelity, solidarity, duty, discipline, courage, endurance – to compliance, in short, with the code of the Merchant Marine, to which Conrad subscribed in his first life and used as an initial moral marker in his second. If the world rests on a few simple ideas, those ideas or values are dependent for their realization on a prior condition of being.

It is a condition about which Conrad clearly felt very strongly, and in a directly personal way which adds a further dimension to its importance in his life and work. That he should declare he has 'a positive horror' of losing his self-possession 'even for one moving moment', and again admit to 'an instinctive horror' of such a loss, is indicative not only of the supreme value accorded the quality but also, in the unexpected excess of the sense of horror, of a personal insecurity, a radical uncertainty as to the tenure of his hold on the one thing really his. And indeed in ordinary, everyday life, if not under the pressure of stresses encountered at sea or at his desk, Conrad was on occasion revealingly unable to live up to his ideal. Richard Curle, an intimate friend, has suggestively described the 'paroxysms of fury' into which he could be plunged by people who, for one reason or another, had angered him: 'These paroxysms of fury happened but seldom. But after one of them Conrad would sometimes smoulder for hours. It was very curious. He seemed like a man coming slowly back to life out of some hideous nightmare, and I am sure that he underwent at such times a kind of mental suffocation.'[6] Bernard C. Meyer, equally suggestively, has commented on Conrad's obsessive sense of loss: 'Throughout his adult life, and presumably earlier, Conrad was obsessed by the idea of loss, which included not only the loss of persons but of material objects as well, of things often of insignificant importance. He was forever misplacing or losing objects, often insisting that they were irretrievably lost simply because he could not recall where he had put them. Once he had reconciled himself to the idea that they were gone he would become resentful if they were recovered.'[7] With reference to clearly autobiographical elements which link 'Falk', 'The Secret Sharer', and *The Shadow-Line*, Bruce Johnson states that Conrad underwent a personal 'crisis' in his seafaring days in the Far East, and concludes that 'it appears quite vividly that Conrad's fear in Singapore and Bangkok was of losing identity'.[8] Most revealingly of all, Meyer, a professional psychoanalyst, has decided from his examination of Conrad's work that he had only a tenuous sense of self, declaring 'it would appear certain that the tenuousness of the sense of self and the reparative reliance on fetishism pervading Conrad's fiction was a projection of identical elements in his own personality' (p. 321).

Following the completion of *Under Western Eyes* in 1910 Conrad suffered a major nervous breakdown: ' . . . the memories of "Under Western Eyes" are associated,' he wrote, 'with the memory of a severe illness which seemed to wait like a tiger in the jungle on the turn of a path to jump on me the moment the last words of that novel were written.'[9] He had penetrated as far as he could go, it would seem, into the 'interior world' of which he wrote in the preface to *A Personal Record* – and actually experienced that loss of the full possession of himself which seems to have haunted him. Citing letters written in 1896, Meyer maintains that Conrad's 'fear of mental illness' must have been of 'long duration': 'I have long fits of depression that in a lunatic asylum would be called madness. I do not know what it is. It springs from nothing. It is ghastly. It lasts an hour or a day and when it departs it leaves a fear'; 'I ask myself whether I am breaking up mentally. I am afraid of it.'[10] Meyer points out that during this period Conrad's friends were concerned about him, Sir William Rothenstein, for instance, observing that Conrad's 'morbid fear of breaking down and leaving his wife and boy penniless is really tearing his nerves to shreds', and, later, directly proclaiming a fear 'for his reason'.[11] When Conrad began to emerge from his illness in 1910, he characteristically expressed a determination to keep a firm hold on himself – 'I am keeping a tight hold on myself for fear my nerves go to pieces' – and Meyer states that the 'psychological defenses' he thereafter adopted in order to 'insure himself against a recurrence of that frightening experience' had 'a profound and unfelicitous effect upon him as an artist, and, as some might believe, as a person too'.[12]

In view of Conrad's breakdown and of the kind of perilous foray into the interior which characterizes his best work, the question arises how he managed to maintain the self-possession which he believed was the necessary condition of artistic excellence. The answer, one may hazard, lies in the paradox which was implicit in the first of Conrad's two lives. Self-possession, he held, was the first condition of good service, yet he also wrote: 'Subjugated but never unmanned I surrendered my being to that passion [i.e. his 'great passion for the sea'] which various and great like life itself had also its periods of wonderful serenity which even a fickle mistress can give sometimes on her soothed breast, full of wiles, full of fury, and yet capable of an enchanting sweetness.'[13] What is implicit in such abandon, however, as D. H. Lawrence was vividly to show in the directly sexual terms which Conrad could only laboriously use as metaphor, is that one must lose the self to find it. And indeed Conrad was aware that 'the imperishable sea', to which he had surrendered his being, was, together with the ships and the 'simple men' who sailed them, 'the ultimate shaper' of his 'character, convictions, and, in a sense, destiny' (p. viii). Conrad's second life, too, I take it, was characterized in its finest moments by the finding that is dependent on letting go – as he seems tacitly to admit in the 'Author's Preface' (1920) to *The Secret Agent*: 'I have no doubt, however, that there had been moments during the writing of the book when I was an extreme revolutionist, I won't say more convinced than they but certainly cherishing a more concentrated purpose than any of them had ever done in the whole course of his life. I don't say this to boast. I was simply attending to my business. In the matter of all my books I have always attended to my business. I have attended to it with complete self-surrender. And this statement, too, is not a boast. I could not have done otherwise. It would have bored me too much to make-believe' (p. xiv).

*　　*　　*

Given the artistic, moral and psychological ramifications of the issue of self-possession in Conrad's life, it might well be expected that it constitute a steady nuclear complex in his work. I believe this to be the case, and, confining myself to the literary aspects of the question, wish to trace the development of the theme of self-possession in Conrad through a critical analysis of his major fiction. Which individual works precisely should be included within that category is still a matter of critical controversy, particularly in regard to the merits of *Chance* and *Victory*. I believe, with Thomas Moser, that Conrad's best work was done in the period that began with the writing of *The Nigger of the 'Narcissus'* and ended with that of *Under Western Eyes*;[14] and since, in my view, Moser has conclusively exposed the weaknesses of the work that falls outside this period (and that includes both *Chance* and *Victory*), I propose to limit myself to work that I think can be shown to be important. Conrad's distinctive weaknesses as a writer, as Moser has brilliantly demonstrated, are revealed in his treatment of sexual love; and it is on the theme of love that Conrad concentrated both in the callow work that preceded *The Nigger* and in the inferior productions that followed *Under Western Eyes* – and his breakdown. When he recovered from his illness, he would seem to have eschewed further journeys into the interior and to have turned to safer and more superficial explorations of love. Moser is I think overstating the case when he says that love 'had no place in . . . the important early Conrad', for I shall seek to show that it is crucial in *Under Western Eyes* and of no little consequence in *Nostromo* and *The Secret Agent*, but he is right to stress the fact that 'of the seven novels [Conrad] wrote after 1912, all but one are centered in love affairs'.[15]

19

I propose to confine myself to the significant early Conrad, furthermore, because I believe it was in the writing of *The Nigger of the 'Narcissus'* that Conrad first discovered his central theme, and that this continued to claim him in work after work until it was finally exhausted in *Under Western Eyes*. I shall argue that he failed for some time to apprehend the full nature and scope of his theme, and so was led, first, to uncertainties of effect and even blanknesses of incomprehension, and then, as he pushed forward, to an apparently sharp change of direction; but the work of this period nevertheless has a unity which sets it off from the earlier *Almayer's Folly* and *An Outcast of the Islands*, in which there are only scant adumbrations of the theme, and from the later compositions, such as *Chance* and *Victory*, in which there are no more than perfunctory reminiscences of it. I have chosen to discuss only this limited body of work, that is to say, because it seems to me that in Conrad studies there is now a need not so much for further demolition – or idiosyncratic reconstruction – as for a concern with the design of the main structure.

If self-possession may be seen as Conrad's obsessive preoccupation, it is at once striking that the obsession should manifest itself in repeated depictions of loss of self. The ways in which self may be lost are varied, there being, I believe, four main variations which interest Conrad. There is, first, abandon, the letting go or surrender of self in passion; then there is panic, the losing of one's head in a situation which demands physical self-possession; third, there is nullity or vacancy, the loss of self that is a concomitant of spiritual disintegration; and finally there is suicide, the deliberate destruction of self. These, I suggest, are the four points of Conrad's literary compass.[16]

The question of self-possession figures in Conrad's earliest work in relation to that of passion. Sexual abandon was not a subject which Conrad was psychologically equipped to handle successfully, as Meyer has indicated in his psychoanalytic study, but it usurped his energies, at first covertly, and then openly, in his first two novels, the main productions of what he referred to as 'the Malayan phase' of his work. *Almayer's Folly* (1895) is about the steady deterioration of Almayer, 'the only white man on the east coast', until his ultimate deliverance from 'the trammels of his earthly folly' (p. 208); but the pivot of the action is the passion of his daughter Nina and Dain Maroola. Willems's passion for Aïssa stands firmly and clearly at the centre of *An Outcast of the Islands* (1896). Neither of these novels seems to me to be worth detailed consideration, but in their treatment of passion there are interesting pointers to motifs in the work that was to follow them.

In *Almayer's Folly* passion is seen as a matter of unrestraint, and freedom from trammelling inhibition is equated with savagery. When Dain declares his love to Nina in 'burning words', he is said to give up to her 'the whole treasure of love and passion his nature [is] capable of with all the unrestrained enthusiasm of a man totally untrammelled by any influence of civilized self-discipline' (p. 64); and he continues to speak to her 'with all the rude eloquence of a savage nature giving itself up without restraint to an overmastering passion' (p. 69). The uninhibited self, indeed, is a lost self, for while Dain speaks, Nina '[abandons] herself to a feeling of dreamy happiness' (p. 64); and Dain, in turn, feels 'himself carried away helpless by a great wave of supreme emotion' (p. 68). Conrad may be describing the love of a man and a woman, but the stakes are civilization and savagery. The implicit view here of a self-possessed restraint as a mark, almost an index, of civilization is one that Conrad will be led to modify somewhat in his presentation of Marlow's cannibal crew in 'Heart of Darkness', but it nonetheless remains the basis of his judgement of inhabitants of moral as well as actual jungles.

In *An Outcast of the Islands* the relationship of the white and 'civilized' Willems and the dark and 'savage' Aïssa concretizes what was implicit in the earlier novel; and Willems's abandoned fall, an outcast from his kind, is the subject of the book. Conrad's presentation of Willems perhaps throws some light on his own horror of abandon, for Willems's loss of self is insistently depicted as an experience of death[17] – and this not in a context of sexual intercourse, where the apprehension is familiar enough, but in situations anterior to it. When Aïssa parts from him, he feels 'in the sudden darkness of her going' as though he has been 'despoiled violently of all that [is] himself', that 'his very individuality' has been 'snatched from within himself by the hand of a woman', and that all that has 'been a man within him' is 'gone'; but when, on another occasion, she takes his hand in hers, 'all his life' seems 'to rush into that hand leaving him without strength, in a cold shiver, in the sudden clamminess and collapse as of a deadly gun-shot wound' (p. 77). Willems has an analogous experience while he is sitting opposite Almayer during dinner: he believes that he is 'keeping a tight hand on himself', but at the same time he has an illusion 'of being in charge of a slippery prisoner' and feels 'a growing terror of escape from his own self'; now and then he grasps the edge of the table and sets his teeth 'in a sudden wave of acute despair, like one who, falling down a smooth and rapid declivity that ends in a precipice, digs his finger-nails into the yielding surface and feels himself slipping helplessly to inevitable destruction' (p. 78). Finally, as he leaves Almayer and makes his way to Aïssa, his loss of self becomes irrevocable and the threatened 'death' is accomplished:

The novelty of the sensations he had never experienced before in the slightest degree, yet had despised on hearsay from his safe position of a civilized man, destroyed his courage. He was disappointed with

himself. He seemed to be surrendering to a wild creature the unstained purity of his life, of his race, of his civilization. He had a notion
of being lost amongst shapeless things that were dangerous and
ghastly. He struggled with the sense of certain defeat – lost his footing
– fell back into the darkness. With a faint cry and an upward throw of
his arms he gave up as a tired swimmer gives up: because the
swamped craft is gone from under his feet; because the night is
dark and the shore is far – because death is better than strife. (pp.
80–81)

The passages I have quoted have an urgency and immediacy that are
generally lacking in most of the novel, and would therefore suggest
Conrad's own deep engagement in this aspect of his tale. But more
important than the biographical implications of these passages is their
paradigmatic significance in the development of Conrad's art. In imaginatively exploring this particular feature of Willems's loss of self, though
apparently still keeping to the terms established in *Almayer's Folly* as the
reference to the civilized Willems's surrender to the wild creature
emphasizes, Conrad perceived that a letting go may also be a giving up,
a hopeless and despairing acceptance of sliding finger-nails or exhausted
and sinking limbs, that death may be 'better than strife'. It is an intuition
that permeates the rest of his work, and that he returns to with notable
effect when Jim, for instance, far from exotic jungles and wild women,
stands on the deck of the *Patna* or when Decoud is left alone on the island
and prepares to take his own life. If Shakespeare links the lover with the
lunatic and the poet, Conrad connects him ultimately – via panic and
emptiness – with the suicide.

Nostromo will exemplify such emptiness when he sits in the dinghy
that is stained with Decoud's blood, sitting immobile, as if the soul has
taken flight from his 'untenanted body' – and Willems is linked to him too.
With a look Aïssa draws 'the man's soul away from him through his immobile pupils', and it is 'an ecstasy of the senses' that '[takes] possession
of his rigid body' (p. 140). Nature, Conrad makes clear, abhors a vacuum,
and loss of self is compensated for by a counter-possession. Willems is
said, somewhat clumsily, to have 'an expression of being taken possession
of' (p. 141), and by the end of his adventure he is made to assent to
Lingard's assertion that he has been 'possessed of a devil' (p. 273); he
himself finally concludes that he is 'a lost man' (p. 340). It is through
more than the chance coincidence of a word that we may trace Nostromo's
genealogy back to the outcast of the islands, but it is 'an outcast soul' that
stealthily 'takes possession' of his untenanted body in the dinghy.

Conrad's Malayan phase, accordingly, should not be thought of as an
altogether false start, for he was already moving towards the insights that

were to inform his treatment of more congenial subjects than passion. With the clarifications that followed in the writing of *The Nigger of the 'Narcissus'* (1897), he was ready to launch the sustained explorations that, together with *The Nigger*, constitute the great central body of his work: 'Heart of Darkness' (1899), *Lord Jim* (1900), 'Typhoon' (1901), *Nostromo* (1904), *The Secret Agent* (1907), 'The Secret Sharer' (1909), and *Under Western Eyes* (1910). These works, listed and dated according to the order of their completion, are the ones I wish to study at length. If it is these works which constitute Conrad's right to be regarded as one of the greatest English novelists of the twentieth century, it is notable that he produced no single unquestionable masterpiece, and that his many virtues as a writer are most effectively deployed in three separate novels. Though *Nostromo* is clearly his most substantial achievement, and readily affords the most striking example of his range and profundity, it is in *The Secret Agent* that his technique is most assured and his writing at its best, while it is *Under Western Eyes* that contains his finest piece of characterization.

In the works I have selected for analysis Conrad strenuously asserts the necessity for self-possession, but is led to a sympathetic and constantly deepening apprehension of panic and nullity and suicide. The works may be divided into two groups. From *The Nigger of the 'Narcissus'* to 'Typhoon' Conrad is primarily concerned with the question of physical self-possession, though in his portrayal of Kurtz in 'Heart of Darkness' he makes his first (largely unsuccessful) attempt to analyse a case of nullity. In the storm scenes in *The Nigger of the 'Narcissus'* and 'Typhoon' and in the journey up the river in 'Heart of Darkness', Conrad succeeds in depicting men who are endowed with a saving self-possession; but his imagination would appear to be most strongly seized by varied manifestations of panic and of abandon, both physical and spiritual. This phase culminates in *Lord Jim*, in which he arrives at a definitive account of the nature of the inner weakness that may make a man fall to pieces; and in 'Typhoon', in which he shows how a potential Jim may acquire inner strength and be braced into indomitability. Conrad would seem to have exhausted the theme of physical self-possession by the time he had completed 'Typhoon' – it is notable that a capacity for such self-possession is simply taken for granted in *Nostromo* – but he unexpectedly recurs to the subject in 'The Secret Sharer', where it undergoes a crucial development.

In the next phase, from *Nostromo* to *Under Western Eyes*, Conrad's interests are generally thought to have turned to the political, and the three major novels in this group are usually linked together as 'the political novels'. It is clear that in this period the setting is affairs of state rather than the whirl of typhoons, but the essential drama, it seems to me, is unchanged. I believe, that is, that Conrad is still fundamentally concerned with the problem of selfhood, though he now explores new ways in which a man may lose the full possession of himself. In this phase he is concerned with manifestations of spiritual nullity and with suicide rather than with physical panic. The nullity, he shows time and again, is the product of abandon, of the surrender of the self to a non-sexual but consuming passion, which is most often represented as a fixed idea or obsession. The state of nullity is conceived as a condition of spiritual vacancy, and it manifests itself outwardly in a pervasive moral nihilism. The phenomenon of obsession, moreover, is shown to have self-destructive implications, and, in the case of Martin Decoud in *Nostromo* and Winnie Verloc in *The Secret Agent*, to lead in the end to suicide.

The two phases are unified by more than a common concern with the loss of self. When a man loses possession of himself in Conrad, he lays himself open – as I have already indicated with reference to Willems in *An Outcast of the Islands* – to a counter-possession. Such a man, whether he abandons himself to passion or to panic, to obsession or despair, is conceived in almost legendary terms as a man possessed. This, we shall see, is the case with both Kurtz and Jim in the first group of works, and – cutting across the division between the two phases – it is equally shown to be the case with Gould and Nostromo and Decoud and Dr. Monygham, with Winnie Verloc, and with Razumov. Men possessed, it would seem to follow, may be saved only by dispossession; but, though this would appear to be an obviously logical development, it was not until *Under Western Eyes* that Conrad could comprehensively and centrally portray it. I assume he was inhibited by the corollary that, in order to be dispossessed, a man must be ready to let go – for such a conception, as I have pointed out, was anathema to him. His art, however, soon began to confront him with situations in which it was clearly necessary for a character to let go, and also to pose the need for an authorial acceptance of the fact of unrestraint. Conrad's reluctance to follow the drive of his own art led, first, to the blurring of a crucial aspect of *The Nigger of the 'Narcissus'*, and then to the botching of the end of 'Heart of Darkness'.

Conrad took a significant step forward in this regard, however, in his portrayal of Dr. Monygham in *Nostromo*. Possessed by a sense of his own earlier disgrace but impelled by a love which he knows will remain unrequited, Monygham lets go customary restraints and risks his life for Mrs. Gould. The effacement of self that he demonstrates tacitly emerges at this point as a further necessary preliminary to dispossession. He is the first character in Conrad to move beyond a state of possession, and may in this respect be viewed as a forerunner of the more complex Razumov in *Under Western Eyes*. Razumov's self-effacement at the moment of dispossession is so radical that he envisages it as a surrendering of the self to destruction. Risking himself with abandon, he too is impelled by love, though he knowingly renounces the object of his passion when he lets go. Ultimately it is this kind of renunciation, with its concomitant self-effacement, that is set against the inability of self-centred men like Gould and Nostromo to renounce that which possesses them. To be dispossessed, that is, a man possessed must be ready to give up what is most precious to him. Since such self-effacement is worked by love, however, it would appear (in a manner that is analogous to the sexual loss and finding of self referred to earlier) to lead paradoxically to the re-establishment of self – as proves to be the case with both Dr. Monygham and Razumov. What Conrad's art finally insists on – and the captain-narrator in 'The Secret Sharer' (whose climactic risking of his ship parallels an experience of the young Captain Korzeniowski) is a further striking instance of this – is that true self-possession is based on a capacity for abandon.

CHAPTER TWO

The Nigger of the 'Narcissus'

I

IT WAS only after completing *The Nigger of the 'Narcissus'* that Conrad finally decided his life at sea was at an end. In a note which he wrote later for an American edition of the novel, he said it was when the last words of *The Nigger* were written that he 'understood' he 'had done with the sea', and that he 'had to be a writer': 'And almost without laying down the pen I wrote a preface, trying to express the spirit in which I was entering on the task of my new life.'[1] The preface may be seen, accordingly, as an attempt to chart, in aesthetic terms, the course he wished to follow in his life as a writer – just as the novel itself constitutes a philosophical clearing of the ground for his subsequent work – and the manner in which he resolved to make his 'appeal' is therefore of considerable interest.

Conrad's sense of reality, of the world outside him which he has to render, is strikingly akin to that of Virginia Woolf. For him too, in 'the remorseless rush of time', all is flux, but whereas she believes that the artist can ultimately hope to do no more than seize the moment and strike it into the stability of his art, he insists that 'to snatch . . . a passing phase of life' is 'only the beginning of the task' (p. x). The novelist, he declares, like 'all the other innumerable temperaments whose subtle and resistless power endows passing events with their true meaning' (p. ix), must be concerned with truth. The use of the word 'endows' in this context is somewhat confusing, since it implies that the artist has to create his own truth, that it is his business to add this on, as it were, to the flux that surrounds him, but the rest of the preface indicates that this is not what Conrad intends. Art, he starts by saying, 'may be defined as a single-minded attempt to render the highest kind of justice to the visible universe, by bringing to light the truth, manifold and one, underlying its every aspect' (p. vii); and he maintains that the artist has to hold up the 'fragment' that is 'rescued' from the rush of time, and 'through its movement, its form, and its colour, reveal the substance of its truth – disclose its inspiring secret' (p. x). These passages make it clear that the truth is in

fact to be found in the flux, and that the artist's task is to reveal and disclose what is hidden, to bring to light what is dark and obscure. The
artist's distinctive concern, therefore, must be to pierce through the surface
of things to their underlying reality, and art is implicitly defined as a
revelation of depths. It is characteristic of Conrad – and the enduring
'terms of his appeal' – that he should have conceived of the necessary
movement to the depths as a descent into himself: 'confronted by the . . .
enigmatical spectacle the artist descends within himself, and in that lonely
region of stress and strife, if he be deserving and fortunate, he finds the
terms of his appeal' (pp. vii–viii).

An obvious problem for a novelist concerned with shadowy depths is
how to render them clearly for the reader. Conrad's solution was to make
him responsive, first of all, to surfaces. Maintaining that 'all art . . .
appeals primarily to the senses' (p. ix), he described his task – in a pronouncement that is quoted nearly as often as that which proclaims his
belief in fidelity – as being 'by the power of the written word to make
you hear, to make you feel . . . before all, to make you *see*. That – and no
more, and it is everything' (p. x). It is this basic tenet, this determination
to immerse the reader in sense impressions, that accounts for the proliferation of images in Conrad and for the extraordinary density of the
texture of his work at its best, though it is responsible as well for the
overripe lushness of his prose at its worst. It is also the means by which
he leads the reader beyond the surface. To make the reader really see is
to give him not only those things which he may be expected to demand –
'encouragement, consolation, fear, charm' – but also perhaps 'that
glimpse of truth' for which he has 'forgotten to ask' (p. x). It is the surface
itself, in other words, that is made to manifest or body forth the truth
of the depths; and Conrad's preface to *The Nigger of the 'Narcissus'*, in
advance of the theory enunciated by James Joyce's Stephen Hero, may
be said to define an art of epiphany.[2] Nor is it only in set pieces of description that Conrad is able to achieve such happy effects. It is one of his
distinguishing features as a novelist that he is able to conceive a whole
action – the voyage of the *Narcissus*, for instance – in terms which make
it a large epiphany. And in work after work, as we shall see, the art of
epiphany is used to concentrate and focus wide areas of meaning – as in
the attack on the boat in 'Heart of Darkness'; the *Patna*'s striking of a
submerged wreck in *Lord Jim*; the progress of the lighter in the dark gulf
in *Nostromo*; the blowing up of Stevie in *The Secret Agent*; Leggatt's
throttling of the sailor in 'The Secret Sharer'; and (perhaps the purest
example) Razumov's vision of Russia under snow in *Under Western Eyes*.

It follows, furthermore, that, since all art is primarily an appeal to the
senses, the novelist cannot hope to 'persuade' his readers of the truth he
wishes to reveal to them; the more so 'because temperament, whether

individual or collective', the temperament to which he must make his appeal, 'is not amenable to persuasion' (p. ix). This view would seem to constitute an implicit rejection of nineteenth-century authorial omniscience with its concomitant persuasive commentary, and to affirm a need in the novel for 'showing' rather than 'telling'. The statement may be regarded, therefore, as heralding Conrad's concern with point of view in the novel, and particularly his subsequent experiments with dramatized narrators, such as Marlow, whose very commentary, though designed to be persuasive in the extreme, is personal and fallible, part of the 'impression' they make on us, and so conceived of as a showing.

It must be said, however, that Conrad's first major attempt at a modified omniscience through the employment of an anonymous and unspecified member of the crew as the nominal narrator in *The Nigger of the 'Narcissus'* is not impressive. It is not merely that Conrad, with blandly crude innocence, allows his narrator, as has been pointed out, to describe scenes at which he is not present and of which he could not have heard, or to communicate the thoughts of others to which he has no access. Despite attempts that have been made to justify the point of view adopted,[3] I think we cannot but conclude that it is faulty since it is inconsistent not only in the formal mechanics of narration, as indicated above, but also in its own terms, in disconcerting shifts in the angle of vision which worryingly draw attention to themselves and so disrupt the flow of the narrative – as the following two examples must suffice to indicate.

After the mustering and James Wait's dramatic arrival, the crew go back to their quarters in the forecastle. The narrator's vivid, first-hand report of interchanges among members of the crew gives way, when he focuses for a moment on Singleton, to this:

> Yet he was only a child of time, a lonely relic of a devoured and forgotten generation. . . . The men who could understand his silence were gone – those men who knew how to exist beyond the pale of life and within sight of eternity. . . . They were the everlasting children of the mysterious sea. Their successors are the grown-up children of a discontented earth. They are less naughty, but less innocent; less profane, but perhaps also less believing; and if they have learned how to speak they have also learned how to whine. But the others were strong and mute; they were effaced, bowed and enduring, like stone caryatids that hold up in the night the lighted halls of a resplendent and glorious edifice. They are gone now – and it does not matter. . . . (pp. 24–5)

It is not the self-conscious, literary quality of this passage that is the trouble, for we could easily accept the narrator's style as a matter of convention, but our sense of being spirited out of the forecastle and placed in limbo. Not even the bridge, given the kind of man Captain Allistoun is shown to be, could take the weight of this, though it would have been a better locus for the elevation of the sentiments than the forecastle. The narrator, at all events, who is clearly neither one of the men who are gone nor one of their successors, simply fades at points like this into the novelist – and what we have here is good, old-fashioned authorial commentary.

Nor are the shifts in point of view confined to those parts of the narrative which tempt to commentary; they occur just as disconcertingly in passages of straightforward description. This is how the attempt to rescue Jimmy is initially presented:

> The five men, poised and gazing over the edge of the poop, looked for the best way to get forward. They seemed to hesitate. The others, twisting in their lashings, turning painfully, stared with open lips. Captain Allistoun saw nothing; he seemed with his eyes to hold the ship up in a superhuman concentration of effort. The wind screamed loud in sunshine; columns of spray rose straight up; and in the glitter of rainbows bursting over the trembling hull the men went over cautiously, disappearing from sight with deliberate movements. (pp. 64–5)

The eye that witnesses this scene would seem to be located in a region that is removed from the immediate turmoil of the action. It is an eye that not only follows the five men as they cautiously make their way forward but also takes in the other members of the crew whom they have left behind and the distinctive figure of the captain; though a false move on the part of any of the five rescuers, who have untied themselves, could result in their being swept overboard, as nearly happens to one of them in a scene immediately preceding this passage, the eye that watches them go over the poop has leisure to notice 'the glitter of rainbows'. The five men continue to be viewed from the outside and referred to in the third person for a number of pages; then there is an uncomfortable jolt when there is a sudden switch to the first person (p. 66) – and we discover that the narrator is one of the rescuers. But Conrad too, it must be assumed, made his discoveries in the writing of *The Nigger*, and it is with the aplomb of finished accomplishment that Marlow makes his appearance as narrator in 'Heart of Darkness' or the novelist handles shifts in point of view in *Lord Jim*.

II

Conrad's aim of making the reader see is perhaps nowhere more triumphantly realized in the whole body of his work than in the storm scenes of *The Nigger of the 'Narcissus'*, in which 'the visible universe' is evoked with a battering immediacy of impact. But we can only apprehend the underlying truth of what is enacted in the storm scenes when we respond to the symbolic dimensions of Conrad's setting, which is, simply and directly enough, a ship at sea. Just how we should view the sea is suggested in most concentrated fashion in a somewhat elliptical and much discussed passage that follows the *Narcissus*'s weathering of the storm:

> On men reprieved by its disdainful mercy, the immortal sea confers in its justice the full privilege of desired unrest. Through the perfect wisdom of its grace they are not permitted to meditate at ease upon the complicated and acrid savour of existence. They must without pause justify their life to the eternal pity that commands toil to be hard and unceasing, from sunrise to sunset, from sunset to sunrise; till the weary succession of nights and days tainted by the obstinate clamour of sages, demanding bliss and an empty heaven, is redeemed at last by the vast silence of pain and labour, by the dumb fear and the dumb courage of men obscure, forgetful, and enduring. (p. 90)

If the narrator of the tale surreptitiously assumes an authorial omniscience, the sea here is depicted as having boldly usurped a divine omnipotence: 'immortal', and endowed with both 'perfect wisdom' and 'eternal pity', it 'reprieves' in its 'mercy', confers privileges in its 'justice', and balances its 'commands' with dispensations of 'grace'. But that this should not for a moment be seen as something like a Wordsworthian manifestation of God in nature is at once indicated by the ironic qualification of the divine attributes: the sea's mercy is 'disdainful'; in its justice it confers 'unrest' (the life that is desired by the reprieved men); and in its pity it ensures that toil 'be hard and unceasing'. Indeed the passage insists it would be the height of folly to seek for manifestations of the divine in nature since 'heaven' is 'empty', and the 'sages' who have obstinately demanded 'bliss' despite the fact of that emptiness have only succeeded in 'tainting' life, which is 'redeemed' not by their 'clamour' but by the 'vast silence' of dogged suffering and work. It is a metaphysical emptiness that is the basis of Conrad's fictional concern with a full possession of self, for in such a universe that is the only thing that one can rely on – as it is the first condition of the good service which is toil, and so of redemption. By the same token the metaphysical emptiness that is asserted in *The Nigger of the 'Narcissus'* is also, ultimately, the basis of the individual nullity and the moral nihilism pervading whole societies that preoccupy Conrad in the period from *Nostromo* to *Under Western Eyes*.

In the passage under consideration Conrad deliberately exploits traditional associations of the divine in order to present the sea as an epitome of the controlling force in the universe. Just what sort of force that is is unequivocally averred in a passage in which Singleton awakes to the true nature of 'the immortal sea':

> He looked upon the immortal sea with the awakened and groping perception of its heartless might; he saw it unchanged, black and foaming under the eternal scrutiny of the stars; he heard its impatient voice calling for him out of a pitiless vastness full of unrest, of turmoil, and of terror. He looked afar upon it, and he saw an immensity tormented and blind, moaning and furious, that claimed all the days of his tenacious life, and, when life was over, would claim the worn-out body of its slave. . . . (p. 99)

It is a principle of seething and restless energy that Singleton confronts, quite without feeling, and terrifying in its furious blindness. Its unfeeling remoteness from man is stressed in an earlier view of the sea's 'unconcerned immensity' (p. 16), as is its wild blindness in a reference to the world's becoming 'a raging, blind darkness that howled, flinging at the lonely ship salt sprays and sleet' (p. 55). It is most significantly characterized, however, in a repeated image: the ship is said to be 'tossed about, shaken furiously, like a toy in the hand of a lunatic' (p. 53); and then almost at once again a 'big, foaming sea' that makes for the ship, 'roaring wildly', is described as looking 'in its rush' as 'mischievous and discomposing as a madman with an axe' (p. 57). If Conrad were solely concerned with making us see, he might well have rejected these images, particularly the second of the two, because they are visually, in the diminution of scale that they enforce, quite subversive of the immensity they are meant, presumably, to evoke. But they do relate the sea in its fury to the empty heaven that looks down upon it, and strikingly succeed in suggesting that the sea represents a force that is a denial of all idea of beneficent order – or, as Royal Roussel puts it in a reference to the second image, 'how some chaotic and irrational principle remains behind the order of the surface'.[4]

The force that Conrad evokes with sustained vigour in his description of the storm is equivalent to that which he described in a letter to Cunninghame Graham of 20 December 1897. The letter was written, that is, in the same month as the last instalment of The Nigger of the 'Narcissus' appeared in the New Review; and, as Cecil Scrimgeour has remarked, it provides a gloss on the novel:[5]

> There is a – let us say – a machine. It evolved itself (I am severely scientific) out of a chaos of scraps of iron and behold! – it knits. I am horrified at the horrible work and stand appalled. I feel it ought to embroider – but it goes on knitting. . . . And the most withering thought is that the infamous thing has made itself; made itself without thought, without conscience, without foresight, without eyes,

without heart. It is a tragic accident – and it has happened. You can't interfere with it. The last drop of bitterness is in the suspicion that you can't even smash it. In virtue of that truth one and immortal which lurks in the force that made it spring into existence it is what it is – and it is indestructible!

It knits us in – and it knits us out. It has knitted time, space, pain, death, corruption, despair and all the illusions – and nothing matters. I'll admit however that to look at the remorseless process is sometimes amusing.[6]

The metaphor of the knitting machine, which has no thought, conscience, foresight, eyes or heart, also firmly places Conrad in his times, evoking, as a number of critics have pointed out, the contemporary notion of the universe as a soullessly indifferent mechanism.[7] It aligns him particularly with Hardy, whose 'unmaliced, unimpassioned, Nescient Will' may be thought of as an alternative version of the knitting machine; and whose image of Tess Durbeyfield's standing on a 'hemmed expanse of verdant flatness, like a fly on a billiard-table of indefinite length, and of no more consequence to the surroundings than that fly' concretizes Conrad's sense of 'the utter insignificance of the individual in the scheme of the universe'.[8]

The ship that makes its way through the sea in the universe of the knitting machine is itself heavily freighted:

The passage had begun, and the ship, a fragment detached from the earth, went on lonely and swift like a small planet. . . . She had her own future; she was alive with the lives of those beings who trod her decks; like that earth which had given her up to the sea, she had an intolerable load of regrets and hopes. On her lived timid truth and audacious lies; and, like the earth, she was unconscious, fair to see – and condemned by men to an ignoble fate. The august loneliness of her path lent dignity to the sordid inspiration of her pilgrimage. She drove foaming to the southward, as if guided by the courage of a high endeavour. . . . (pp. 29–30)

The quoted passage a little over-emphatically insists that the 'fragment detached from the earth' and loaded with all earth's burdens is no mere ship but a little world of man, and indeed Captain Allistoun is almost at once called 'the ruler of that minute world' (p. 31). It is a world, like man's earth and like the 'small planet' to which it is also compared, that is clearly meant to be seen as subject to the laws of the mechanical universe, to 'the remorseless process' of knitting. Marlow remarks in 'Youth' that there are some 'voyages that seem ordered for the illustration of life, that might stand for a symbol of existence' (pp. 3–4); it is apparent that this voyage – the 'pilgrimage' – enacts the journey of life (from a departure to a landfall[9]) in a godless universe. Though it is no part of my intention to pursue the quasi-religious implications of Conrad's position of non-belief, it is characteristic of him that he should conceive of such a voyage as a pilgrimage. Indeed, as I shall have occasion to point out in relation to *Lord Jim*, he might be said – despite both the knitting machine and his Catholic background – to superimpose on a theology a psychology which is Calvinistic in tendency. And his large concern with the question of possession and dispossession, though expressed in terms which turn the devil (whenever he appears) into a psychological metaphor, would certainly seem to stem from traditional religious belief.

Given a godless universe, Conrad is invoking more than the time-honoured notion of the mortal journey when he uses the word 'pilgrimage'; the word suddenly comes to life in his transvaluation of the figure, and we realize that it is the journey itself, simple dogged living, that sanctifies. The making of a living, which is 'the sordid inspiration' of the pilgrimage, is thus balanced by the redemptive act of living. And that act of living is not only 'lent dignity' by 'the august loneliness' of the ship's path; the 'conditions of complete isolation from all land entanglements' enable Conrad to make the problem he wishes to explore 'stand out with a particular force and colouring'.[10] But this freedom from the perplexities of land also means that the nature of the pilgrimage is radically simplified: everything is reduced to the 'high endeavour' of making headway through that blind and lunatic sea.

III

In the preface to *The Nigger of the 'Narcissus'*, Conrad declares that the artist must be prepared to devote himself unswervingly 'to the perfect blending of form and substance', but his elaboration of this notion as 'an unremitting never-discouraged care for the shape and ring of sentences' (p. ix) implies that he thinks of such a blending as the wedding of style to matter. The novel itself, however, achieves the larger blending, and its substance is best approached by way of its structure. The structural principle of *The Nigger* is contrast. It is the voyage of the *Narcissus* that gives the tale shape, and that voyage is conceived in terms of radical contrast: the ship is first hit by the storm, and then, surviving it, it is becalmed; the crew at first maintain perfect discipline, but then come close to mutiny. There are other contrasts too. There is the contrast between the good health of the crew and Jimmy Wait's illness, a contrast which expands into one between life and death. There are strong colour contrasts: Jimmy is the only black man among the white crew; the contrast between light and dark that is established in the opening sentence when Mr. Baker steps 'in one stride out of his lighted cabin into the darkness of the quarter-deck' is maintained throughout. Some of the terms in the various pairs of contrasts, furthermore, are interlinked, thus binding the tale together still more firmly. Both the storm and the incipient mutiny, for instance, threaten the safety of the ship, suggesting that there is perhaps a common significance in the inner and outer weather to which the ship is exposed. When we relate this structural principle to the carefully presented setting of the novel, it would seem that its substance should be sought in contrasting or alternative attitudes to life in the kind of universe that is imaged by the ship's pilgrimage through the sea.

The specific problem which confronts man in such a universe is powerfully suggested – it is the central epiphany of the novel – by what both the storm and the calm do to the ship. The final effect of the storm is to turn the ship over on its side, with its masts 'inclined nearly to the horizon' (p. 58), and so leave it subject to drift – which is how it is left in the calm. A ship adrift in the kind of sea in which Conrad locates it in *The Nigger* is so expressive an image that it hardly calls for comment, but a simile that appeared years later in *The Shadow-Line* (published 1917) provides a perfect gloss on it: the hands of a man grasping the spokes of a ship's wheel are said to stand out 'lighted on the darkness; like a symbol of mankind's claim to the direction of its own fate' (p. 76). So long as the weather is propitious, that is, man can delude himself into believing he is effectively in control of things; what the voyage of the *Narcissus* makes clear is the extent to which he is in fact at the mercy of a blind force outside himself. And what a ship adrift epitomizes is a complete lack of purposive direction – is the inherent meaninglessness of life under an empty heaven.

An obvious objection to this account of the theme of the novel is that it ignores the dominating presence of Jimmy Wait. But if we pay attention to the way in which he is presented, we see that he too has his place in the pattern. From the moment that Jimmy boards the ship the crew become aware of his terrible, racking cough. It is in a description of the cough that Conrad reveals how his imagination has seized on the 'substance' of his tale as one and indivisible: 'Then James Wait had a fit of roaring, rattling cough, that shook him, tossed him like a hurricane, and flung him panting with staring eyes headlong on his sea-chest' (p. 24). The effect on Jimmy of his cough, the outward sign of his mortal illness, is depicted in terms that make it analogous to that of the storm on the ship; and when he becomes more and more ill, his condition, as he succumbs to utter prostration, may be thought of as being analogous to that of the ship in the calm: when a sick-bay is fitted up for him in the deck-house, his belongings are transported there, 'and then – notwithstanding his protests

34

– Jimmy himself. He said he couldn't walk. Four men carried him on a blanket' (p. 46); in the sick-bay, waiting for death, Jimmy lies 'stretched out, chin on blanket, in a kind of sly, cautious immobility' (p. 140). The effect of these analogies, which the novelist makes us *see*, is to set up a further implied analogy: Jimmy's experience being apparently parallel to that of the ship, we realize that he too is subject to drift – the drift towards death.

We become aware, moreover, that there is in the novel an insistent death imagery that is not related to Jimmy. At first it seems that it must be merely a macabre imagination that is bent on seeking intimations of mortality in the bustling forecastle: 'heads with blinking eyes' are said to stick out over the rims of the berths, 'but the bodies were lost in the gloom of those places, that resembled narrow niches for coffins in a white-washed and lighted mortuary' (p. 8). The idea is repeated when the men prepare for sleep: 'At the other end of the ship the forecastle, with only one lamp burning now, was going to sleep in a dim emptiness traversed by loud breathings, by sudden short sighs. The double row of berths yawned black, like graves tenanted by uneasy corpses' (p. 22); a little later, Singleton, standing at the door, is the only one awake in the forecastle, and he looks very old: 'old as Father Time himself, who should have come there into this place as quiet as a sepulchre to contemplate with patient eyes the short victory of sleep, the consoler' (p. 24); and when the men lie in their bed-places resting, their 'hung-up suits of oilskin' are said to swing 'out and in, lively and disquieting like reckless ghosts of decapitated seamen dancing in a tempest' (p. 54). But the imagery is also extended beyond the forecastle. During the day Captain Allistoun pervades the poop: 'At night, many times he rose out of the darkness of the companion, such as a phantom above a grave, and stood watchful and mute under the stars, his night-shirt fluttering like a flag – then, without a sound, sank down again' (p. 30). Mr. Baker, worrying about the men during the storm, crawls along the poop: 'In the dark and on all fours he resembled some carnivorous animal prowling amongst corpses' (p. 78). After robbing Jimmy, Donkin leaves the sick-bay and comes out on to the deck: 'Sleeping men, huddled under jackets, made on the lighted deck shapeless dark mounds that had the appearance of neglected graves' (p. 155).

This line of imagery makes it clear that it is not Jimmy alone who is subject to the drift towards death. The images suggest that the whole crew also carry death with them, imaging especially in sleep (the little death) that to which they too are drifting. The novel, we are accordingly made to see, is concerned with two kinds of drift – the drift of meaning-lessness, and the drift towards death. In a world without God attitudes to the two kinds of drift are related, and Conrad is concerned with contrast-ing or alternative responses to them. His large concern, in short, in the

striking phrase that he uses in the preface to *The Nigger of the 'Narcissus'*,
is with 'the hazardous enterprise of living' (p. vii).

IV

The hazards of a life at sea are magnificently communicated in the long
description of the storm and of the toppling of the *Narcissus* on to its side:

> She gave another lurch to leeward; the lower deadeyes dipped
> heavily; the men's feet flew from under them, and they hung kicking
> above the slanting poop. They could see the ship putting her side in
> the water, and shouted all together: – 'She's going!' Forward the
> forecastle doors flew open, and the watch below were seen leaping
> out one after another, throwing their arms up; and, falling on hands
> and knees, scrambled aft on all fours along the high side of the deck,
> sloping more than the roof of a house. . . . Men were slipping down
> while trying to dig their fingers into the planks; others, jammed in
> corners, rolled enormous eyes. They all yelled unceasingly: 'The
> masts! Cut! Cut! . . .' A black squall howled low over the ship. . . .
> Captain Allistoun struggled, managed to stand up with his face near
> the deck, upon which men swung on the ends of ropes, like nest
> robbers upon a cliff. One of his feet was on somebody's chest; his face
> was purple; his lips moved. He yelled also; he yelled, bending down:
> –'No! No!' Mr. Baker, one leg over the binnacle-stand, roared out: –
> 'Did you say no? Not cut?' He shook his head madly. 'No! No!' . . .
> Voices took up the shout – 'No! No!' Then all became still. They
> waited for the ship to turn over altogether, and shake them out into
> the sea; and upon the terrific noise of wind and sea not a murmur of
> remonstrance came out from those men, who each would have given
> ever so many years of life to see 'them damned sticks go overboard!'
> They all believed it their only chance; but a little hard-faced man
> shook his grey head and shouted 'No!' without giving them as much
> as a glance. They were silent, and gasped. . . . Singleton had stuck to
> the wheel. His hair flew out in the wind; the gale seemed to take its
> life-long adversary by the beard and shake his old head. He wouldn't
> let go, and, with his knees forced between the spokes, flew up and
> down like a man on a bough. As Death appeared unready, they began
> to look about. Donkin, caught by one foot in a loop of some rope,
> hung, head down, below us, and yelled, with his face to the deck: –
> 'Cut! Cut!' Two men lowered themselves cautiously to him; others
> hauled on the rope. They caught him up, shoved him into a safer
> place, held him. He shouted curses at the master, shook his fist at him
> with horrible blasphemies, called upon us in filthy words to 'Cut!

Don't mind that murdering fool! Cut, some of you!' One of his rescuers struck him a back-handed blow over the mouth; his head banged on the deck, and he became suddenly very quiet, with a white face, breathing hard, and with a few drops of blood trickling from his cut lip. . . . (pp. 58–60)

As the ship rolls over on to its side with its deck 'sloping more than the roof of a house' and the men's feet fly from under them, what is immediately dramatized is the necessity of taking a stand in a world that has suddenly gone awry. In view of the conflict that develops, the fact that Captain Allistoun struggles and 'manages to stand up' is expressively contrasted with Donkin's hanging 'head down . . . with his face to the deck'. The specific issue on which it is at once necessary to take a stand is whether the masts should be cut or not, and Conrad could not have found a better one for his purposes – though it arises with complete naturalness in the action. The narrator subtly indicates what is involved in the choice between cutting and not cutting in a simile that he uses just before the demand to cut is first voiced: in a description (omitted from the cited passage) of how the crew's belongings are washed out of the forecastle, reference is made to their chests, which, 'waterlogged and with a heavy list', pitch heavily 'like dismasted hulks' before they sink (p. 58). To cut the masts which seem to be pulling the ship under may hold out hope of righting it, in other words, but would turn it into a hulk, condemned at the very least – for the fate of the chests is ominous – to unending drift. Once again *The Shadow-Line* provides us with a commentary on what remains powerfully implicit in *The Nigger*: the captain-narrator in that work recounts how he has 'a morbid vision' of his ship as 'a floating grave': 'Who hasn't heard of ships found drifting, haphazard, with their crews all dead?' (p. 92); and in his diary he remarks how 'ships have been dismasted in squalls simply because they weren't handled quick enough', and adds: 'It's like being bound hand and foot preparatory to having one's throat cut' (pp. 106–7). In 'Falk' a dismasted ship is referred to as a 'dead and drifting carcase' (p. 229).

Since dismasting threatens disaster, the almost general demand to cut the masts is shown to be the result of a panic-stricken fear of death. The crew, losing their heads, blindly cling only to immediate life. Their '[rolling] enormous eyes' as they yell for the masts to be cut is one outward sign of their panic – they are not much more restrained than Donkin, who lets go altogether with his 'horrible blasphemies' and incitement to mutiny – and indeed a rolling of the eyes in Conrad, as we shall see, repeatedly signifies panic. On the *Narcissus* panic is vividly depicted as a falling to pieces, an almost visible loss of self. The steward, for instance, is 'paralysed with fright', and when he is made fast and falls doubled over the rope that is holding him, he resembles 'a bundle of wet rags' (p. 60). Jimmy, who is trapped in his sick-bay when the ship turns on its side, is the representative instance in this respect. When he realizes members of the crew are trying to get to him, he keeps up 'a distracting row', screaming 'like a tortured woman', and banging with his hands and feet (p. 67). With 'the last remnant of wits' scared out of him (p. 68), he presses his head to the hole that Archie finally succeeds in making in the bulkhead with a crowbar, 'trying madly to get out through that opening one inch wide and three inches long' (p. 69) – as if he has in fact disintegrated. When the hole is enlarged sufficiently for him to get his head and shoulders out, he sticks halfway and, 'with rolling eyes', begins to foam at the mouth (p. 70). Rescued at last, it seems as if there is nothing left of him: he appears to have had 'all the stiffening knocked out of him'; he is 'only a cold black skin loosely stuffed with soft cotton wool'; and while his head rolls about, his arms and legs swing 'jointless and pliable' (p. 71).

The overwhelming panic that seizes the crew of the *Narcissus* when it seems the masts are going to pull the ship under manifests itself, in analogous terms to the way in which Jimmy lets go, as a desire to cut loose. What this in turn involves is a despairing acceptance of drift. For Conrad, indeed, the idea of drift seems early on to have been associated with despair, with a resigned hopelessness, as is indicated in a letter by the connections he made in a very different sphere. Writing to Spiridion Kliszczewski on 19 December 1885 in the wake of the results of the elections in England and in the conviction that there was now no barrier left 'to the pressure of infernal doctrines born in continental back-slums', of social-democratic ideas, that is, which were likely to destroy all that was 'respectable, venerable and holy', Conrad said:

> You wish to apply remedies to quell the dangerous symptoms: you evidently hope yet.
> I do so no longer. Truthfully, I have ceased to hope a long time ago. We must drift![11]

The full implications of an acceptance of drift were not worked out, interestingly enough, in any of Conrad's tales of life at sea but, nearly twenty years after he had completed *The Nigger*, in his portrayal of Axel Heyst in *Victory*. At the age of eighteen, Heyst lives for three years with his father, a disillusioned thinker, who is 'angry with all the world' and no longer deems mankind worthy of the 'moral and intellectual liberty' he claims they have a right to:

> Three years of such companionship at that plastic and impression-able age were bound to leave in the boy a profound mistrust of life. The young man learned to reflect, which is a destructive process, a reckoning of the cost. It is not the clear-sighted who lead the world.

38

Great achievements are accomplished in a blessed, warm mental fog, which the pitiless cold blasts of the father's analysis had blown away from the son.

'I'll drift,' Heyst had said to himself deliberately.

He did not mean intellectually or sentimentally or morally. He meant to drift altogether and literally, body and soul, like a detached leaf drifting in the wind-currents under the immovable trees of a forest glade; to drift without ever catching on to anything.

'This shall be my defence against life,' he had said to himself with a sort of inward consciousness that for the son of his father there was no other worthy alternative. (pp. 91–2)

Heyst's intention to drift clearly springs from his father's disillusionment with life and conviction of the unworthiness of mankind. The son's 'mistrust of life' is so radical as to amount to a loss of belief in everything, and so to an acceptance of general meaninglessness. But his determination to drift, 'like a detached leaf', if it reflects his desire to move through life without forming any attachments or hazarding a purposive action, suggests, in the image he fixes on, the extent to which this means he is ready to cut himself off from that which could sustain him. The 'pitiless cold blasts of the father's analysis' may have dispersed the son's mental fogs, but we see too that they have detached the leaf from the tree; and though Heyst believes that to drift will be his 'defence against life', it is precisely the detached leaf that is at the mercy of every wind. It is also a leaf which, sooner or later, cannot but dry up, and Heyst's decision condemns him to an ultimate impotence. It is an impotence which vitiates his relationship with Lena, morally if not sexually, for even when she is dying he cannot bring himself to tell her he loves her, 'his fastidious soul . . . even at that moment [keeping] the true cry of love from his lips in its infernal mistrust of all life' (p. 406). And it is an impotence which effectively prevents him from taking any action against the infamous trio who invade his island, for, faced with them, Heyst, 'the man of universal detachment', as Conrad refers to him in his Author's Note to *Victory*, 'loses his mental self-possession, that fine attitude before the universally irremediable which wears the name of stoicism' (p. x). Confronted, in the end, with the consequences of his impotence, Heyst despairingly takes his own life – and it is made clear what an acceptance of drift finally leads to.

On board the *Narcissus*, despite the general panic, there are those who do not let go in face of what seems to be the universally irremediable. If Donkin and Jimmy typify one extreme response to the situation in which they find themselves, then, among members of the crew, it is pre-eminently Singleton who exemplifies an alternative reaction. What he does, it will be recalled from the cited passage, is with admirable self-possession to '[stick] to the wheel': 'He wouldn't let go, and, with his knees forced between the spokes, flew up and down like a man on a bough.' It is, expressively, a determination to hang on that is posed against the temptation to cut loose or let go, and this is dramatized not only in the case of Singleton. The men who set out to rescue Jimmy, for instance, long 'to abandon him' and to return to the poop where they 'could wait passively for death in incomparable repose' (p. 67), but they stick at it. When they succeed in releasing him and drag him out to 'the side of the house' that is 'more smooth than glass and more slippery than ice', there is 'nothing to hang on to but a long brass hook used sometimes to keep back an open door'. Wamibo holds on to the hook, and the others, clutching Jimmy, hold on to him. Everything depends, therefore, on Wamibo's hanging on, but the men are 'not afraid of [his] letting go' since 'the brute' is 'stronger than any three men in the ship' (p. 71). Slowly they manage to make their way to safety, hanging on to Jimmy having become a personal obsession: 'We had so far saved him; and it had become a personal matter between us and the sea. We meant to stick to him' (p. 72). When Captain Allistoun discerns there is a chance to right the ship and gives the command to 'square the main yard', the men have to try to haul the yard: 'Haul men! Try to move it! Haul, and help the ship,' he says; and they haul 'and [hang] in bunches on the rope' until the yards move and come 'slowly square against the wind' (p. 86). Later, pulling on a rope to set the main topsail, the men are sent sprawling by 'a sea' that boards the quarter-deck: 'Mr. Baker, knocked down with the rest, screamed – "Don't let go that rope! Hold on to it! Hold!" And sorely bruised by the brutal fling, they held on to it, as though it had been the fortune of their life'; with the topsails and foresail set, the ship begins to make headway (p. 94).

But of course the most striking example of an inflexible will to hang on is provided by Captain Allistoun when he refuses to let the masts be cut. It is his self-possession at that crucial moment that saves the ship. And what his determination to hang on implies, despite the ship's helplessness as it drifts along, half submerged in the heavy seas, is the belief that with courage and knowledge – through a combination, that is, of personal quality and technical command of a craft – the ship can be righted, that it can bounce back, as it were, from the blows of the sea and be steered (battered but purposively afloat) to its chosen destination.

Captain Allistoun's self-possession, however, could not by itself have saved the ship. When he gives the order not to cut the masts, the yelling crew subside and quietly wait 'for the ship to turn over altogether, and shake them out into the sea', offering 'not a murmur of remonstrance', though they believe they have lost 'their only chance'. In part they respond to the note of authority which the 'little hard-faced man' sounds as he shouts 'No'; but it is also obviously their own ingrained sense of discipline and duty that makes them obey him. Once again it is Singleton who most forcefully dramatizes the issue here. In sticking to the wheel, he also sticks to his duty as he sees it; and so unbending is his sense of duty that he stays at the wheel unrelieved for more than thirty hours throughout the worst part of the storm. When he finally leaves the wheel and comes down to the forecastle, he suddenly falls, 'crashing down, stiff and headlong like an uprooted tree' (p. 97); it is his devotion to duty which has rooted him in the world, so to speak, and it is only when his duty is done that he allows himself to fall. The maintenance of discipline by everyone except Donkin when the captain gives his decisive order implies the strong cohesiveness of officers and crew as a social group; and the crew show their solidarity with the captain by quickly silencing Donkin when he tries to incite them. Subsequently repeated acts of solidarity are dramatized: at the height of the storm, when the crew are all fastened to anything that will hold them, a bearded shellback 'with prudence' works himself 'out of his coat' and throws it over the youthful Charley, who lies shivering next to him (pp. 61–2); similarly, Belfast strips to his shirt and puts his 'oilskin and jacket over [the] half-dead nayggur' he has helped to rescue (p. 79), the rescue itself being illustrative of selfless fellow-feeling; in impossible conditions the cook is inspired to make coffee for the men – 'As long as she swims I will cook!' (p. 81) – and, having lost most of their belongings in the storm, the 'men [chum] as to beds', and take turns at 'wearing boots and having the use of oilskin coats' (pp. 95–6). In 'Falk' alternatively, 'the organized life of the ship' comes to an end once 'the solidarity of the men [has] gone' (p. 231), and this breakdown culminates in the grisly killings and cannibalism that take place on the *Borgmester Dahl*.

On board the *Narcissus* it is the holding together that makes the hanging on possible, as is literally the case when the men cling to the rope in struggling to set the topsail, for instance.[12] In *The Nigger* a sense of solidarity emerges as Conrad's major social value, the equivalent, in its expression as social cohesion or integration, of the individual capacity for self-possession, and comparable in the social sphere to its importance in the personal. A 'conviction of solidarity', furthermore, Conrad maintains in the preface to this work, is what sustains the artist and what he must 'speak to':

> He speaks to our capacity for delight and wonder, to the sense of mystery surrounding our lives; to our sense of pity, and beauty, and pain; to the latent feeling of fellowship with all creation – and to the subtle but invincible conviction of solidarity that knits together the

loneliness of innumerable hearts, to the solidarity in dreams, in joy, in sorrow, in aspirations, in illusions, in hope, in fear, which binds men to each other, which binds together all humanity – the dead to the living and the living to the unborn. (p. viii)

It is the conviction of solidarity, we note, not the worship of God, that 'binds together all humanity'; and it is the 'knitting together' of innumerable hearts that is implicitly set against the remorseless working of the knitting machine. Donkin, as might be expected, 'knows nothing of courage, of endurance, and of the unexpressed faith, of the unspoken loyalty that knits together a ship's company' (p. 11), but the crew as a whole are 'knitted together . . . into a ready group by the first sharp order of an officer coming to take charge of the deck in bad weather' (p. 51).

Self-possession and solidarity, then, are revealed as prime values in the world in which Conrad places the *Narcissus*, are, indeed, literally shown to be a saving force;[13] but towards the end of the tale the novelist indicates an awareness that to demonstrate these virtues in circumstances that are not freed from 'all land entanglements' may be beyond even the most stalwart seaman:

> One by one they came up to the pay-table to get the wages of their glorious and obscure toil. They swept the money with care into broad palms, rammed it trustfully into trousers' pockets, or, turning their backs on the table, reckoned with difficulty in the hollow of their stiff hands. – 'Money right? Sign the release. There – there,' repeated the clerk, impatiently. 'How stupid those sailors are!' he thought. Singleton came up, venerable – and uncertain as to daylight; brown drops of tobacco juice hung in his white beard; his hands, that never hesitated in the great light of the open sea, could hardly find the small pile of gold in the profound darkness of the shore. 'Can't write?' said the clerk, shocked. 'Make a mark, then.' Singleton painfully sketched in a heavy cross, blotted the page. 'What a disgusting old brute,' muttered the clerk. Somebody opened the door for him, and the patriarchal seaman passed through unsteadily, without as much as a glance at any of us. (pp. 168–9)

We should not make too much, perhaps, of a scene that can hardly be said to offer a view of the complexities of life ashore, but in relation to the voyage that has preceded it, its ironies are insistent. It is Singleton, the member of the crew who has most conspicuously not blotted his page in the crisis of the storm, indeed the one who made his mark with his memorable feat of endurance at the wheel, that is the particular butt of the clerk. What is more striking, however, is the way in which the clerk's scorn seems to discompose him, though he remained unmoved, a veritable rock, throughout the trial at sea. He is 'uncertain as to daylight'; his hands hesitate and can 'hardly find the small pile of gold'; and he passes through the door 'unsteadily'. In the presence of the scornful clerk, in short, Singleton's self-possession seems to desert him. As does his sense of solidarity, for on land he acknowledges no bond with the men with whom he has braved the storm, and passes through the door 'without as much as a glance' at any of them. What the little scene effectively dramatizes, then, is the way in which the qualities and values that have been so strongly affirmed in 'the great light of the open sea' seem unaccountably to be set at naught in 'the profound darkness of the shore'. Which leads straight to Kurtz in 'Heart of Darkness'.

V

Since that part of the tale which concerns Jimmy's dying comes in the end to focus on the question of self-deception, both as regards Jimmy's in relation to the nature of his illness and the crew's in relation to the death they slowly witness, it is of some consequence to establish the extent to which the self-deceived are aware they are allowing themselves to be taken in. John Dozier Gordan, following his examination of the manuscript of the novel, is emphatic that Conrad deliberately made Jimmy unaware of his true condition:

> A change in the manuscript suggests that at first [Conrad] meant Wait to be aware of his approaching death and then made him ignorant of it. The Nigger's self-deception was substantially increased by a cut in the account of his attitude after the storm. . . . The passage implied that Wait recognized a certain truth in his vaunted relationship with death and was no longer so eager to boast of his illness. The cancellations left the confident Nigger unaware that he was dying. . . . [Conrad] decided Wait must have no idea that he was playing in earnest the part of the dying man which he had assumed for convenience.[14]

But this is simply to ignore other indications in the published text that Jimmy is not as ignorant as claimed. It is true that he starts life aboard the *Narcissus* with the apparent intention of malingering, in accordance with the occupational custom that he has established at this point in his career. Thus he almost at once begins to prepare the ground by asserting that he is dying and railing at the crew for not allowing him to sleep (p. 35); thereafter he 'parades' the idea of his death 'unceasingly' before the men, and 'on the slightest provocation' shakes before their eyes 'the bones of his bothersome and infamous skeleton' (p. 36). But well before the storm (and the cancelled passages in the manuscript) Conrad clearly

indicates Jimmy's growing realization of his condition, though the crew
remain as puzzled as ever. The change comes when on one occasion
Belfast says to him, 'We all know ye are bad – very bad,' and Jimmy
seems 'rather startled', sits up 'with incredible suddenness and ease',
and says 'gloomily': 'Ah! You think I am bad, do you? . . . Do you?'
(p. 39), thereby revealing how a sudden fear as to his condition has gripped
him. Though there is no explicit reference to the fact, and though Conrad
does not develop this idea in *The Nigger*, it is significant – in view of the
long line of characters who will subsequently exemplify an analogous
phenomenon – that Jimmy may be regarded as implicitly surrendering
himself at this point to a panicky fear of death, and being thereafter
possessed by his fear.

The apparently objective view that Belfast offers Jimmy is sufficiently
disturbing to activate forebodings that he cannot conceal, and for good
measure his body betrays him into full awareness of his position:

> He became the tormentor of all our moments; he was worse than
> a nightmare. You couldn't see that there was anything wrong with
> him: a nigger does not show. He was not very fat – certainly – but
> then he was no leaner than other niggers we had known. He coughed
> often, but the most prejudiced person could perceive that, mostly, he
> coughed when it suited his purpose. He wouldn't, or couldn't, do
> his work – and he wouldn't lie up. One day he would skip aloft with
> the best of them, and next time we would be obliged to risk our lives
> to get his limp body down. . . .
> He refused steadily all medicine; he threw sago and cornflour
> overboard till the steward got tired of bringing it to him. . . . Donkin
> abused him to his face, jeered at him while he gasped; and the same
> day Wait would lend him a warm jersey. Once Donkin reviled him for
> half an hour; reproached him with the extra work his malingering
> gave to the watch; and ended by calling him 'a black-faced swine'.
> Under the spell of our accursed perversity we were horror-struck.
> But Jimmy positively seemed to revel in that abuse. It made him look
> cheerful – and Donkin had a pair of old sea boots thrown at him.
> 'Here, you East-end trash,' boomed Wait, 'you may have that.' (pp.
> 44–5)

That 'limp body', dangerously perched aloft, is something that Jimmy
cannot fake; it is indicative, rather, of the seriousness of his condition –
and of his desperate need to attempt work for which he is no longer fit
just because he realizes the seriousness and would deny it by skipping
along 'with the best of them', only to be unpredictably let down by his
failing body. Hence his steady refusal of all medicine; and hence his
revelling in Donkin's abuse, which comes as a reassuring antidote to

Belfast's concern, a reassurance he is prepared to pay for. As Dickens has Pip reflect in *Great Expectations*, 'All other swindlers upon earth are nothing to the self-swindlers... That I should innocently take a bad half-crown of somebody else's manufacture, is reasonable enough; but that I should knowingly reckon the spurious coin of my own make, as good money!'

For the crew, as for Jimmy, self-deception takes the form of a deliberate denial of their own sense impressions, of what they feel on their pulses. The narrator, after all, is supposed to be a member of the crew, and he reports, presumably, what they all see and hear. Minutes after his dramatic boarding of the ship, Jimmy begins to cough:

> Suddenly the nigger's eyes rolled wildly, became all whites. He put his hand to his side and coughed twice, a cough metallic, hollow, and tremendously loud; it resounded like two explosions in a vault; the dome of the sky rang to it, and the iron plates of the ship's bulwarks seemed to vibrate in unison, then he marched off forward with the others. (pp. 18–19)

It is the reader alone – for the narrative is determinedly non-retrospective – who can relate that wild rolling of the eyes to a later scene and infer here Jimmy's incipient (though still unconscious) panic at what the coming coughs signify; but what the narrator registers, as the coughs resound 'like two explosions in a vault', is that Jimmy's cough is tearing him apart. And yet, in the previously cited passage, the narrator states that one cannot 'see' there is 'anything wrong' with Jimmy, and that 'the most prejudiced person' can 'perceive' that for the most part he coughs 'when it [suits] his purpose'. Similarly, even when the men who rescue Jimmy from the sick-bay cannot help noticing that he shows 'about as much life as an old bolster would do', they nevertheless hate him: 'We could not get rid of the monstrous suspicion that this astounding black-man was shamming sick, had been malingering heartlessly in the face of our toil, of our scorn, of our patience – and now was malingering in the face of our devotion – in the face of death' (pp. 72–3). The crew, it is clear, perceive only what their fear allows them to perceive, and suspect what they wish to believe. As Thomas Moser has well said, 'They see in Jimmy's impending death their own mortality, and they cannot bear the sight of it.'[15] In other words, if Jimmy 'symbolizes' anything, then despite the kind of symbol-mongering that bedevils so much Conrad criticism (and that would even make the Nigger the Devil of the *Narcissus*), he embodies nothing more esoteric than the fear of death – though we might well agree with Ian Watt that, 'more widely' than this, he also projects 'the universal human reluctance to face those most universal agents of anti-climax, the facts'.[16] Given Jimmy's drift towards death, then, the issue

THE NIGGER OF THE 'NARCISSUS'

dramatized in this section of the novel is whether the crew can bring themselves to accept it or, alternatively, whether they will continue to deny it.

The crew very nearly erupt in mutiny when the captain forbids Jimmy to leave his sick-bay. The captain and the two mates are drawn to Jimmy's cabin by the 'holy row going on in [it]' when Jimmy resists the attempt of the cook to 'save' him in the face of 'the everlasting fire' that awaits him:

'Keep him away from me,' said James Wait at last in his fine baritone voice, and leaning with all his weight on Belfast's neck. 'I've been better this last week . . . I am well . . . I was going back to duty . . . to-morrow – now if you like – Captain.' Belfast hitched his shoulders to keep him upright.

'No,' said the master, looking at him, fixedly.

Under Jimmy's armpit Belfast's red face moved uneasily. A row of eyes gleaming stared on the edge of light. They pushed one another with elbows, turned their heads, whispered. Wait let his chin fall on his breast and, with lowered eyelids, looked round in a suspicious manner.

'Why not?' cried a voice from the shadows, 'the man's all right, sir.'

'I am all right,' said Wait, with eagerness. 'Been sick . . . better . . . turn-to now.' He sighed. – 'Howly Mother!' exclaimed Belfast with a heave of the shoulders, 'stand up, Jimmy.' – 'Keep away from me then,' said Wait, giving Belfast a petulant push, and reeling fetched against the doorpost. His cheekbones glistened as though they had been varnished. He snatched off his night-cap, wiped his perspiring face with it, flung it on the deck. 'I am coming out,' he declared without stirring.

'No. You don't,' said the master, curtly. Bare feet shuffled, disapproving voices murmured all round; he went on as if he had not heard: – 'You have been skulking nearly all the passage and now you want to come out. You think you are near enough to the pay-table now. Smell the shore, hey?'

'I've been sick . . . now – better,' mumbled Wait, glaring in the light. – 'You have been shamming sick,' retorted Captain Allistoun with severity. 'Why . . .' he hesitated for less than half a second. 'Why, anybody can see that. There's nothing the matter with you, but you choose to lie-up to please yourself – and now you shall lie-up to please me. Mr. Baker, my orders are that this man is not to be allowed on deck to the end of the passage.' (pp. 119–20)

Following this, the agitation of the men increases, culminating in a declaration that 'the port watch will refuse duty' – and, after Donkin's hissing that they should 'go for' the officers in the dark, in his narrowly missing the captain with an iron belaying-pin that he throws at him (pp. 120–4). This, then, is the second time that the safety of the *Narcissus* is threatened, and – as before – what needs to be established is the significance of the captain's stand.

The captain's motive in issuing his order is clear enough. Having watched Jimmy 'with a quiet and penetrating gaze' (p. 119), and seeing what should be apparent to everyone as Jimmy leans 'with all his weight' on Belfast and then 'reels' when Belfast calls on him to 'stand up', that Jimmy is so ill he is incapable of standing unaided, he is actuated by a feeling of profound pity for him. Understanding what the extremity of Jimmy's wish to deny the death that is claiming him is forcing him to, the captain deliberately plays up to his self-deception in order to protect him from himself. The question is whether his pity must be seen as corrupting. Both Albert Guerard and Ian Watt have no doubt that it is: '. . . even the captain is finally corrupted by pity,' says Guerard. 'He pretends to share in Wait's self-deception . . . And this moment of pity causes the incipient mutiny';[17] and Watt writes: 'That it is the most total act of sympathy for Wait which precipitates the mutiny . . . dramatizes one of the general themes in *The Nigger of the "Narcissus"* . . . : pity, emotional identification with others, as an active danger to society.'[18]

Some support for these views would seem to be provided by a striking insight of the narrator (who once again fades into the novelist):

> The latent egoism of tenderness to suffering appeared in the developing anxiety not to see [Jimmy] die. . . . He was demoralising. Through him we were becoming highly humanised, tender, complex, excessively decadent: we understood the subtlety of his fear, sympathised with all his repulsions, shrinkings, evasions, delusions – as though we had been over-civilised, and rotten, and without any knowledge of the meaning of life. (pp. 138–9)

It must be insisted, however, that it is the crew, not the captain, who demonstrate 'the latent egoism of tenderness to suffering' in their attitude to Jimmy;[19] and that it is their self-centred and deluded pity, not the captain's, which is demoralizing and corrupting. His pity, on the contrary, is disinterested and clear-eyed; and, squarely facing the fact of Jimmy's approaching death and his harrowing fear of it, he gives expression to the kind of fellow-feeling (or 'emotional identification with others') that Conrad surely believes is necessary in any society and not 'an active danger' to it. The captain, as he spontaneously takes pity on Jimmy, demonstrates the kind of human solidarity that has previously been established as a saving grace, not an over-civilized decadence.

What is it, then, that goes wrong? Why does the captain's 'moment of pity [cause] the incipient mutiny'? It is first of all a question whether it is actually the captain's pity that causes the mutiny. What the quoted scene in fact dramatizes is that it is the woeful inability of the crew to comprehend what lies behind the captain's ruling that is the immediate cause of the trouble. And they cannot begin to understand what actuates the captain because of their own imperative need to believe 'the man's all right', because their own fear of death effectively prevents them from seeing what the captain sees. It is in these circumstances that the crew lose their heads and seem ready to refuse duty. What a refusal of duty implies has earlier been intimated:

> 'That's the blooming way to do 'em!' [Donkin] yelped, with forced heartiness. Jimmy said: – 'Don't be a dam' fool,' in a pleasant voice. Knowles, rubbing his shoulder against the doorpost, remarked shrewdly: – 'We can't all go an' be took sick – it would be mutiny.' – 'Mutiny – gawn!' jeered Donkin, 'there's no bloomin' law against bein' sick.' – 'There's six weeks' hard for refoosing dooty,' argued Knowles. . . .
> Knowles, with surprising mental agility, shifted his ground. 'If we all went sick what would become of the ship? eh?' He posed the problem and grinned all round. – 'Let 'er go to 'ell,' sneered Donkin. 'Damn 'er. She ain't yourn.' – 'What? Just let her drift?' insisted Knowles in a tone of unbelief. – 'Aye! Drift, an' be blowed,' affirmed Donkin with fine recklessness. (pp. 107–8)

As in the storm, in other words – and the way in which Conrad subtly makes the episode of the mutiny parallel to that of the storm is one of the exceptionally fine things in a fine novel – the crew's fear of death makes them emotionally ready to opt for drift.

How, then, can we explain the fact that, whereas during the storm the men are able to overcome their fear, maintain discipline, and obey their captain, they seem to be capable of none of these as they seethe in the darkness outside Jimmy's cabin? The conclusion seems inescapable that it is their captain who saves them in the first instance, and fails them in some way in the second. But not because of his pity for Jimmy.

The immediate cause of the captain's lapse is his failure to take sufficiently into account the reaction of the crew to his order. When, despite the obvious evidence of Jimmy's condition, Belfast's face – under Jimmy's very armpit – moves 'uneasily' in response to the captain's prohibition, when the crew begin to stare and whisper, when 'a voice from the shadows' directly challenges his ruling and insists that Jimmy is all right, even when 'disapproving voices' begin to murmur 'all round' and it is clear beyond a doubt that his ruling has been completely misinterpreted, he simply goes on 'as if he [has] not heard'. His decision to do so is the more foolhardy since he later admits to Mr. Baker, who remarks that the crew have been 'simmering for the last month', that he has 'noticed' this (p. 121). Thus, though he remains 'composed in the tumult' (p. 121), he actually loses control of the situation when he could have prevented it from deteriorating by reversing his order. It is his duty as captain to put the safety of his ship first, certainly before the ease of any individual; and when it begins to become apparent that the growing unrest of the crew may constitute a threat to the ship, it is his duty to sacrifice Jimmy.

To the extent, therefore, that the captain fails to gauge the temper of the crew, and fails to foresee the possible consequences of his own persistence, he loses command – as he seems ruefully to realize immediately afterwards:

> 'Did you think I had gone wrong there, Mr. Baker?' He tapped his forehead, laughed short. 'When I saw him standing there, three parts dead and so scared – black amongst that gaping lot – no grit to face what's coming to us all – the notion came to me all at once, before I could think. Sorry for him – like you would be for a sick brute. If ever creature was in a mortal funk to die! . . . I thought I would let him go out in his own way. Kind of impulse. It never came into my head, those fools. . . . H'm! Stand to it now – of course.' He stuck the belaying-pin in his pocket, seemed ashamed of himself, then sharply: – 'If you see Podmore at his tricks again tell him I will have him put under the pump. Had to do it once before. The fellow breaks out like that now and then. Good cook tho'.' (pp. 126–7)

It is tempting to fix on the captain's outrunning 'impulse' of pity, on his sudden letting go 'before [he] could think', as the crux of the matter – and so to rejoin Guerard and Watt; but, though the reference is ambiguous, I do not think it is of his pity that he seems 'ashamed'. That, in the circumstances, is its own validation; and since it is a humane response to a situation which he has sized up with precision, it is also measured and argues no loss of control. It seems to me he is ashamed, rather, that 'it never came into [his] head' the crew could react so foolishly. Ironically, for the cook has his own very different view of the events that lead to the crisis, Podmore's verdict on the captain's behaviour would seem to be the correct one: 'Judgment capsized all in a minute' (p. 144).

What is it, we ask ourselves, that upsets the captain's judgement? Why does he insist on his prohibition in spite of the obvious unrest of the crew, especially since he is said to be 'one of those commanders who speak little, seem to hear nothing, look at no one – and know everything, hear every whisper, see every fleeting shadow of their ship's life' (p. 125)? Conrad does not give us much help here, but it would seem that the captain fails through an excess of the virtue that saves the ship during the storm, that, having taken a stand, he is temperamentally incapable of relinquishing it. Indeed it is earlier suggested that a concomitant of his habitual composure is a lack of flexibility, an angular stiffness of being: as the officers approach Jimmy's cabin at the start of the scene, the captain stands 'revealed' between the two mates, 'in shabby clothes, stiff and angular, like a small carved figure, and with a thin, composed face' (p. 118). We may guess, moreover, that there is also an element of self-importance and self-assertion in his insistence on Jimmy's staying in his cabin, for this is certainly revealed in his later announcement to the mates that he is going to let Jimmy 'die in peace': 'I am master here after all' (p. 127). On the same occasion his already quoted determination to 'stand to it now – of course' suggests, in its automatic assumption, the kind of inflexibility that would account for his sticking to his ruling at the time. Though it is a hanging on that saves the ship during the storm, we are made to see that it nearly leads to disaster when the crew's disaffection in regard to Jimmy manifests itself. What Conrad seems fitfully to grasp, for this is no more than implied at this stage, is that the paradoxical condition of full self-possession may, where necessary, be a readiness to let go, even if this involves a loss of face. But that is something he is not yet ready to acknowledge – and consequently this section of the novel is blurred, for the point is never actually made, and what is finally emphasized is the need to hang on unremittingly: 'Keep them on the move to-night, gentlemen,' the captain says to the mates; 'just to let them feel we've got hold all the time – quietly, you know' (p. 126). Sticking to his decision, it is with perfect aplomb that he handles the men the next morning and, in squashing Donkin, puts an end to the affair.

There remains the consummation of Jimmy's death – and of the voyage of the *Narcissus*. Conrad had his reservations about the conclusion of his tale: 'I think however that artistically the end of the book is somewhat lame. I mean after the death [of Jimmy]. All that rigmarole about the burial and the ship's coming home seems to run away into a rat's tail – thin at the end. Well! It's too late now to bite my thumbs and tear my hair.'[20] It is true enough that the end of the book cannot match the episodes of the storm and the mutiny, but the 'rigmarole' does resolve the issues raised by Jimmy's illness. To the crew, of course, Jimmy's death comes 'as a tremendous surprise', but it breaks the 'bond of a sentimental lie'; and 'like a community of banded criminals disintegrated by a touch of grace', they are 'profoundly scandalised with each other' (pp. 155–6). Grace, in the Conradian universe, would thus seem to lie (among other things) in the acceptance of death; and when that is finally symbolized by Belfast's pushing Jimmy's unmoving body into the sea, a breeze suddenly springs up and (to echoes of *The Ancient Mariner*) the ship is released from its becalming (pp. 160–1).[21]

CHAPTER THREE

'Heart of Darkness'

I

IN 'Heart of Darkness', as in *The Nigger of the 'Narcissus'*, the narrative is shaped by the contours of a voyage. It is a voyage which is also referred to as a 'pilgrimage', but the distance Conrad has travelled since the earlier work is suggested by the transformation of this image:

> We called at some more places with farcical names, where the merry dance of death and trade goes on in a still and earthy atmosphere as of an overheated catacomb; all along the formless coast bordered by dangerous surf, as if Nature herself had tried to ward off intruders; in and out of rivers, streams of death in life, whose banks were rotting into mud, whose waters, thickened into slime, invaded the contorted mangroves, that seemed to writhe at us in the extremity of an impotent despair. Nowhere did we stop long enough to get a particularized impression, but the general sense of vague and oppressive wonder grew upon me. It was like a weary pilgrimage amongst hints for nightmares. (p. 62)

The journey, on this occasion, is not a vigorous assertion of life and of the doggedness which may inform and sanctify it; it is, rather, an impingement on death, a movement in 'the merry dance of death and trade' – in which it is the Company traders who call the tune and are throughout venomously distinguished as the 'pilgrims' – a movement along 'streams of death in life'. It is a journey which consequently implies a state of devitalization, being associated with a weary, despairing impotence (though it is also linked with the kind of slimy rottenness that – like Nile mud – may presage fertility). The pilgrimage, in short, does not image a journey by day to a final dark destination, as in *The Nigger*, but a progress in darkness.

In such a progress it is an ability to penetrate, rather than a capacity to steer, that is of primary importance. The journey up the mighty river is, first of all, a movement into darkest Africa, to 'the farthest point of navigation' where Kurtz has his station (p. 51); and Marlow recounts how he and the pilgrims 'penetrated deeper and deeper into the heart of darkness' (p. 95). But since Marlow says that 'the essentials of [the Kurtz] affair

51

lay deep under the surface' (p. 100), the movement to him may also be seen as a penetration into the depths. An expedition into the jungle, at any rate, is seen in such terms: 'In a few days the Eldorado Expedition went into the patient wilderness, that closed upon it as the sea closes over a diver' (p. 92); and progress up the river is viewed analogously as a journey back to a substratum of history: 'Going up that river was like travelling back to the earliest beginnings of the world, when vegetation rioted on the earth and the big trees were kings' (pp. 92–3). The penetration, if we link these images to Marlow's weary pilgrimage, would appear to be into the kind of depths that are hinted at in nightmares.

As Marlow struggles to get to the bottom of things, to the underlying truth of the affair, the aesthetic which Conrad enunciated in the preface to *The Nigger of the 'Narcissus'* becomes the ethic of 'Heart of Darkness'. Indeed the difficulties of pushing up the river and down into the unconscious are in part rendered in terms of sight, that artistic imperative of the preface. Just before Kurtz's station is reached, the steamboat is enveloped in 'a white fog, very warm and clammy, and more blinding than the night', with the result that the travellers' eyes are 'of no more use' to them than if they 'had been buried miles deep in a heap of cotton wool' (pp. 101, 107); at the climax of his encounter with Kurtz, Marlow has 'to go through the ordeal of looking into' Kurtz's soul, and he comes to realize that he has been confronted with 'an impenetrable darkness' (pp. 145, 149). But Marlow gets to the station, and looks into himself as well as into Kurtz. Penetration, in the end, is defined as insight.

To take this view of Marlow's journey is to see him, as a number of critics have insisted in spite of his opening disclaimer, as the central figure in his tale.[1] 'I don't want to bother you much,' he tells his listeners at the start of his story, 'with what happened to me personally' (p. 51), thereby introducing himself, as it were, as an observer-narrator in the tradition of Nelly Dean in *Wuthering Heights*; and indeed there are so many anticipatory references to the extraordinary Mr. Kurtz that there is a ready assumption that Marlow's tale, like Nelly's, is to focus on someone larger than life. But Marlow's affinities, *qua* narrator, are rather with the unnamed narrator in Henry James's *The Sacred Fount*; and it is only when we place Marlow as a protagonist-narrator that we can begin to relate the narrative method to the outward shape of the tale.

Marlow begins by asserting that England, when the Romans first came to it, was also 'one of the dark places of the earth' (pp. 48–9), and he asks his listeners to imagine what it must have been like for 'a decent young citizen in a toga' to find himself there:

'Land in a swamp, march through the woods, and in some inland post feel the savagery, the utter savagery, had closed round him, –

all that mysterious life of the wilderness that stirs in the forest, in the jungles, in the hearts of wild men. There's no initiation either into such mysteries. He has to live in the midst of the incomprehensible, which is also detestable. And it has a fascination, too, that goes to work upon him. The fascination of the abomination – you know, imagine the growing regrets, the longing to escape, the powerless disgust, the surrender, the hate.'

He paused.

'Mind,' he began again, lifting one arm from the elbow, the palm of the hand outwards, so that, with his legs folded before him, he had the pose of a Buddha preaching in European clothes and without a lotus-flower – 'Mind, none of us would feel exactly like this. What saves us is efficiency – the devotion to efficiency. But these chaps were not much account, really. . . .' (p. 50)

In the light of what is to follow, there seems to be an obvious explanation of Marlow's choice of this opening for his tale. Granted the analogy between the decent young citizen and Kurtz, and between the Roman's surrender to savagery in ancient Britain and Kurtz's in darkest Africa, Marlow would seem to be judiciously preparing his audience for the less easily assimilable collapse. And in positing the continuous 'fascination of the abomination', he would seem to be quietly enlarging the perspective of his latter-day story of degeneration by insisting that civilized man is constantly threatened by the savage. But Conrad here also makes his narrator reveal more than he realizes. It is clear why civilized life is always menaced by the savage: it is because 'all that mysterious life of the wilderness that stirs in the forest, in the jungles', stirs also 'in the hearts' of men. Marlow, however, says that it stirs 'in the hearts of wild men', making the reservation despite the fact that, before he is through, he will have occasion to relate how he himself once 'confounded the beat' of a savage drum 'with the beating of [his] heart' (p. 142). Our suspicion that Marlow is defensively resisting the application to himself of his own generalizations is strengthened by the final qualification he makes. We could more readily accept his asseveration of superiority over the lesser breed of Roman chaps, and hence of the exemption of the privileged group (and, by extension, of the English) from the general fate,[2] were it not for the asserted ground of salvation. 'Efficiency – the devotion to efficiency', Marlow of all people should know, did not save Kurtz, who certainly started his career in Africa as a most efficient servant of the Company, being repeatedly referred to as 'a first-class agent', 'the best agent' it has (pp. 69, 75), even if his methods are later said to have 'ruined the district' in the end (p. 131). Marlow, in short, is at this point implicitly dissociating himself and his listeners from Kurtz (as well as from the Roman), as if they were different in kind from him, though before the conclusion of his narrative he will even come to accept a kinship with black savages. It is strongly suggested, therefore, that, though Marlow's narrative is retrospective, it being one of the functions of the frame narrative to create this dimension, he does not recount his experiences in the light of a gained knowledge, as Dickens's Pip does, for instance, in *Great Expectations*.[3] On the contrary, his striking 'the pose of a Buddha preaching in European clothes' exemplifies an inappropriateness that rubs off on to his conclusions. Since he does not fully understand the meaning of his experience when he begins the narrative, the tale itself becomes not only a reliving of that experience but a progressive attempt to penetrate its significance.

Some support for this view of Marlow as a narrator is provided by his own sense of the difficulties he labours under in telling his story, his conviction that 'it is impossible to convey the life-sensation of any given epoch of one's existence'. He has just told his listeners that he 'went for [Kurtz] near enough to a lie':

'I became in an instant as much of a pretence as the rest of the bewitched pilgrims. This simply because I had a notion it somehow would be of help to that Kurtz whom at the time I did not see – you understand. He was just a word for me. I did not see the man in the name any more than you do. Do you see him? Do you see the story? Do you see anything? It seems to me I am trying to tell you a dream . . .'

He paused again as if reflecting, then added –

'Of course in this you fellows see more than I could then. You see me, whom you know. . . .'

It had become so pitch dark that we listeners could hardly see one another. For a long time already he, sitting apart, had been no more to us than a voice. There was not a word from anybody. The others might have been asleep, but I was awake. I listened, I listened on the watch for the sentence, for the word, that would give me the clue to the faint uneasiness inspired by this narrative that seemed to shape itself without human lips in the heavy night-air of the river. (pp. 82–3)

Alerted by Marlow's questioning of his listeners as to what they see, we see what Conrad has quietly arranged for us to notice – that Marlow tells his story in the dark, and should consequently be seen not so much as an unreliable narrator as one in search of illumination. And the knowledge that is light, he intimates, reveals what cannot otherwise be seen, for he blandly says to his listeners, 'You see me, whom you know,' though the frame-narrator hastens to point out it is 'so pitch dark' they can 'hardly see one another'. Sight, that is to say, is insight. But at the same time

Marlow seems to insist that illumination is first of all a matter of seeing, and so he asks his listeners whether they 'see the story'; likewise the frame-narrator, who is the most responsive to him, listens 'on the watch' for a clue to the uneasiness inspired by Marlow's narrative. His narrative, as he strives to penetrate to its dark heart, should be viewed, that is, as an attempt at a progressive clarification of obscurities.

One of the marked effects of Marlow's penetration is to subvert the traditional valuation of light and dark given us by the frame-narrator as he sets the scene for Marlow's tale:

> Afterwards there was silence on board the yacht. For some reason or other we did not begin that game of dominoes. We felt meditative, and fit for nothing but placid staring. The day was ending in a serenity of still and exquisite brilliance. The water shone pacifically; the sky, without a speck, was a benign immensity of unstained light; the very mist on the Essex marshes was like a gauzy and radiant fabric, hung from the wooded rises inland, and draping the low shores in diaphanous folds. Only the gloom to the west, brooding over the upper reaches, became more sombre every minute, as if angered by the approach of the sun.
>
> And at last, in its curved and imperceptible fall, the sun sank low, and from glowing white changed to a dull red without rays and without heat, as if about to go out suddenly, stricken to death by the touch of that gloom brooding over a crowd of men. (p. 46)

For the frame-narrator the light is associated with all that is calm, for it shines with a pacific and serene stillness, and clear – even pure, for its radiance is 'without a speck' and 'unstained'. It is also associated with the good, for it is 'benign', and, in its 'exquisite brilliance', with the beautiful. The dark or gloom, on the other hand, brooding sombrely, 'as if angered by the approach of the sun', is seen as a menace to the light, lying in sullen and insidious ambush for it; and indeed as the sun sets, it is as if its light is suddenly quenched by the darkness, 'stricken to death' by its destructive touch. The frame-narrator would thus seem to be unwittingly providing a neatly symbolic set for Marlow's decent young Roman citizen, who succumbs to the powers of darkness – which is what Marlow begins with. But before he completes his narrative, his presentation of the pilgrims of light and of his cannibal crew, not to mention Kurtz's savage woman, will compel us to a recognition of very different attributes of the light and the dark. Indeed, if the sun is put to death by the darkness as Marlow begins his tale, sitting in the dark, that implies it will rise reborn on the morrow – that light may come out of darkness.

II

As Marlow penetrates deeper and deeper into the dark continent, he encounters three major forms or manifestations of darkness. The first, not unexpectedly, is that located in the jungle:

The reaches opened before us and closed behind, as if the forest had stepped leisurely across the water to bar the way for our return. We penetrated deeper and deeper into the heart of darkness. It was very quiet there. At night sometimes the roll of drums behind the curtain of trees would run up the river and remain sustained faintly, as if hovering in the air high over our heads, till the first break of day. Whether it meant war, peace, or prayer we could not tell. . . . We were wanderers on a prehistoric earth, on an earth that wore the aspect of an unknown planet. We could have fancied ourselves the first of men taking possession of an accursed inheritance, to be subdued at the cost of profound anguish and of excessive toil. But suddenly, as we struggled round a bend, there would be a glimpse of rush walls, of peaked grass-roofs, a burst of yells, a whirl of black limbs, a mass of hands clapping, of feet stamping, of bodies swaying, of eyes rolling, under the droop of heavy and motionless foliage. The steamer toiled along slowly on the edge of a black and incomprehensible frenzy. The prehistoric man was cursing us, praying to us, welcoming us – who could tell? We were cut off from the comprehension of our surroundings; we glided past like phantoms, wondering and secretly appalled, as sane men would be before an enthusiastic outbreak in a madhouse. We could not understand because we were too far and could not remember, because we were travelling in the night of first ages, of those ages that are gone, leaving hardly a sign – and no memories. (pp. 95–6)

The kind of darkness encountered here is defined by its metaphorical analogue, 'the night of first ages' in which the travellers find themselves. It is a darkness of savagery, a modern manifestation of 'the utter savagery' which Marlow earlier imagined his young Roman must have met in ancient Britain and now thinks of as having rampaged on a 'prehistoric earth'. What characterizes the savagery, as the black people yell and clap and stamp and sway in a 'frenzy', is its wild physical abandon, its lack of restraint. Indeed the way in which these people roll their eyes relates their letting go to the analogous phenomenon of physical panic so vividly evoked in *The Nigger of the 'Narcissus'*. Here their abandon appears to be so radical as to suggest derangement, of a kind that may be compared to an 'outbreak in a madhouse'.[4] Though the movement from the lunatic seas of *The Nigger* to the savages of Africa represents a shift from the cosmic to the human plane, it is much the same problem that man has to contend with, a similar 'inheritance' that has to be 'subdued'. Here, however, an added dimension is implied. The suggestion that the spectacle which meets the travellers' eyes is alien and incomprehensible, as though they were 'the first of men' wandering on 'an unknown planet', evokes not only the infancy of the race – 'those ages that are gone, leaving hardly a sign – and no memories' – but also, when related to Marlow's earlier sense of a descent into nightmare, the infancy of the individual psyche with its buried strata. We are not surprised that the civilized travellers, who cannot 'understand' what they see because they are 'too far' and '[cannot] remember', should be 'secretly appalled' at the riotous show that confronts them.

The kind of abandon that evokes 'the night of first ages' is related through another image of night to a further aspect of the darkness of the jungle. In recording a sense of having 'turned to the wilderness', Marlow feels as if he has been 'buried in a vast grave full of unspeakable secrets': 'I felt an intolerable weight oppressing my breast, the smell of the damp earth, the unseen presence of victorious corruption, the darkness of an impenetrable night' (p. 138). Corruption, the corruption of flesh, which is the dark savour of the wilderness here, is associated elsewhere both with the mystery of the jungle and with cannibals who spring from it: Marlow, registering his gratitude to his cannibal crew for not eating each other before his face, is reminded that 'they had brought along a provision of hippo-meat which went rotten, and made the mystery of the wilderness stink in [his] nostrils' (p. 94). It is, furthermore, in response to a look of a cannibal that Marlow experiences his darkest moment:

> We were on deck at the time, and the headman of my wood-cutters, lounging near by, turned upon [the Russian] his heavy and glittering eyes. I looked around, and I don't know why, but I assure you that never, never before, did this land, this river, this jungle, the very arch of this blazing sky, appear to me so hopeless and so dark, so impenetrable to human thought, so pitiless to human weakness. (p. 127)

Though Marlow says he does not know why this is such an oppressive moment for him, we may guess he senses the headman is looking at the Russian as if he would like to make a meal of him. In the end it is cannibalism that is seen as the epitome of savage abandon, the heart of darkness that can cast even a 'blazing sky' into shadow. We begin to understand the force of Marlow's early reference to a Roman's being likely to find 'precious little to eat fit for a civilized man' in ancient Britain (p. 49); and of his insistence that what 'moors' a civilized man, 'like a hulk with two anchors', is his having not only 'two good addresses' but also 'a butcher round one corner, a policeman round another' (p. 114).

In 'Heart of Darkness', therefore, the notion of abandon is given a different dimension from that in *Almayer's Folly* and *An Outcast of the Islands* where it is related directly to sexual passion, but the moral position in regard to it seems at first to be much the same as that taken in the earlier works: it is a lack of restraint, a letting go, that is – pejoratively – the mark of the savage, of the uncivilized, and that in itself constitutes a danger. This is a view that emerges explicitly in Marlow's estimate that the 'savages' who have attacked the steamboat are filled with 'unrestrained grief', and that the travellers' 'danger, if any', lies in their 'proximity to a great human passion let loose' (p. 107). It is a view that is implicit in his early responses to what he encounters in white as well as black Africa, informing his attitude to his predecessor's death, for instance. Fresleven, he discovers, was killed 'in a scuffle with the natives' as a result of 'a misunderstanding about some hens', but he may be said to have succumbed not only to the spear that goes 'quite easy' between his shoulder-blades, for – though 'the gentlest, quietest creature that ever walked on two legs' – he had gone ashore and 'started to hammer the chief of the village with a stick' (pp. 53–4). Similarly, one of the outward signs of 'the great demoralization of the land' (p. 68) is the way in which the white traders, seemingly subduing themselves to what they work in, have allowed things to fall apart: at the Company's station Marlow sees 'an undersized railway-truck lying . . . on its back with its wheels in the air', one of which is off; comes upon 'more pieces of decaying machinery'; discovers that 'a lot of imported drainage-pipes for the settlement' have been 'tumbled' into a ravine in 'a wanton smash-up'; and, when he later needs rivets desperately, thinks of the 'cases of them' that he saw 'down at the coast – cases – piled up – burst – split! You kicked a loose rivet at every second step in that station yard on the hillside' (pp. 63–4, 65–6, 83).

But the simple formula or equation of the Malayan novels breaks down when it comes to Kurtz's black woman. A 'wild and gorgeous apparition of a woman', moving to the 'slight jingle and flash of barbarous ornaments', she is unquestionably a savage and recognizably kin to the people whose affinity was said to be with the inhabitants of a madhouse. She, however, walks 'with measured steps':

> She was savage and superb, wild-eyed and magnificent; there was something ominous and stately in her deliberate progress. And in the hush that had fallen suddenly upon the whole sorrowful land, the immense wilderness, the colossal body of the fecund and mysterious life seemed to look at her, pensive, as though it had been looking at the image of its own tenebrous and passionate soul. (pp. 135–6)

The darkness of the jungle is here given its most striking embodiment, and what is manifested in the flesh is the tenebrous soul of the night of first ages. Like a bird at rest that is instinct with flight, what the woman images in her wild-eyed, passionate ominousness and in her stately and deliberate progress is a capacity for both abandon and restraint. It is a capacity that is subversive of any easy categorizing, and accordingly she is seen as both 'savage and superb', both 'wild-eyed and magnificent'. Hers is the powerful containment of a force that has been consummated in release. She compels the beholder to a recognition that the dark savagery of the jungle may have as a concomitant of its frenzy a fine fecundity, an abundant vitality or power for 'mysterious life'. It is a power that is directly imaged in the jungle, a similar reconciliation of opposites being evoked in its embodiment of stationary exuberance, soundless riot, and arrested motion: 'The great wall of vegetation, an exuberant and entangled mass of trunks, branches, leaves, boughs, festoons, motionless in the moonlight, was like a rioting invasion of soundless life, a rolling wave of plants, piled up, crested, ready to topple over the creek, to sweep every little man of us out of his little existence' (p. 86).

*   *   *

The second form of darkness Marlow encounters is easily penetrable, and from the outset he sees through the rhetoric of the frame-narrator, who presents it not as a darkness but as a light. The frame-narrator believes 'nothing is easier' for a man who has 'followed the sea' than 'to evoke the great spirit of the past upon the lower reaches of the Thames':

> Hunters for gold or pursuers of fame, they all had gone out on that stream, bearing the sword, and often the torch, messengers of the might within the land, bearers of a spark from the sacred fire. What greatness had not floated on the ebb of that river into the mystery of an unknown earth! . . . The dreams of men, the seed of common-wealths, the germs of empires. (p. 47)

For the frame-narrator the personal motives of the 'hunters for gold' or the 'pursuers of fame' count for little beside the facts of their achievement, the establishment of commonwealths and empires. And he thinks of them as conquerors in a double sense, men who have not only conquered territory with their swords but darkness with their torches, the darkness of 'an unknown earth' that is like the night of first ages. For the frame-narrator, in short, colonizers are civilizers, the bearers of a light that is kindled by 'a spark from the sacred fire'. It is in such terms, indeed, that Kurtz initially conceived his venture into Africa. 'Each station,' he is reported to have said, 'should be like a beacon on the road towards better things, a centre for trade of course, but also for humanizing, improving, instructing' (p. 91).

Marlow, however, is more down to earth. When his aunt, who has procured him his position with the Company, insists on regarding him as 'an emissary of light', he ventures to hint to her that the Company is 'run for profit' (p. 59); and, in talking of the Romans in Britain, he makes clear what is involved in the conquest of a land by the sword:

> They were no colonists; their administration was merely a squeeze, and nothing more, I suspect. They were conquerors, and for that you want only brute force – nothing to boast of, when you have it, since your strength is just an accident arising from the weakness of others. They grabbed what they could get for the sake of what was to be got. It was just robbery with violence, aggravated murder on a great scale, and men going at it blind – as is very proper for those who tackle a darkness. The conquest of the earth, which mostly means the taking it away from those who have a different complexion or slightly flatter noses than ourselves, is not a pretty thing when you look into it too much. What redeems it is the idea only. An idea at the back of it; not a sentimental pretence but an idea; and an unselfish belief in the idea – something you can set up, and bow down before, and offer a sacrifice to. . . . (pp. 50–1)

Making a characteristic effort to 'look into' the meaning of 'the conquest of the earth', what Marlow sees is that the conquerors bring with them their own darkness when they invade the dark lands, the darkness of blindness, of 'men going at it blind'. His view links up with the ironically subversive implications of a painting by Kurtz which he sees at the Central Station, Kurtz having painted it about a year earlier while waiting to go to the Inner Station:

> Then I noticed a small sketch in oils, on a panel, representing a woman, draped and blindfolded, carrying a lighted torch. The background was sombre – almost black. The movement of the woman was stately, and the effect of the torch-light on the face was sinister. (p. 79)

The overt intention of the painter would seem to be clear. Kurtz, who is described to Marlow on the same occasion as 'an emissary of pity, and science, and progress, and devil knows what else' (p. 79), would appear to be expressing his belief that the civilizer may move with stately confidence into the darkness, may indeed go into it blindfolded, because he can rely blindly on the force of his own civilized values, on the lighted torch he carries with him.[5] But 'the effect of the torch-light' on the face of the woman is 'sinister', because what it ominously illuminates is an unheeding blindness. If the painting symbolizes Kurtz's own confident aspirations as he prepared to go into the heart of darkness, it also reveals that the woman cannot but be blind to the darkness into which she is moving – and to herself; a further and unwitting significance which Kurtz himself exemplifies in due course.

That Marlow should look with a jaundiced eye on the torch the lady carries is implicit in his account of the Roman conquerors of Britain. The torch, we see, is simply a blind to the 'squeezing' and the 'grabbing', and the civilizers no better than racialist plunderers out to dispossess those who have 'a different complexion or slightly flatter noses' than their own.[6] The blind, in other words, is the 'sentimental pretence' that has to be distinguished from the 'idea' which may 'redeem' such conquest. Marlow does not specify the nature of the redemptive idea, though it is presumably the kind of genuine belief that initially prompted Kurtz to wish to set up his beacons. But in positing the worship of such an idea – 'something you can set up, and bow down before, and offer a sacrifice to' – Marlow in effect aligns the civilizer with the savage idolater while differentiating him from the devotee of Mammon, and suggests that at the heart of even an unstained light there is a darkness. Kurtz, at any rate, ends by 'getting *himself* adored' (p. 129); and Marlow perceives – in 'the blinding sun-shine' of Africa – that the pilgrims have their being in an ultimate darkness of damnation:

> I've seen the devil of violence, and the devil of greed, and the devil of hot desire; but, by all the stars! these were strong, lusty, red-eyed devils, that swayed and drove men – men, I tell you. But as I stood on this hillside, I foresaw that in the blinding sunshine of that land I would become acquainted with a flabby, pretending, weak-eyed devil of a rapacious and pitiless folly. How insidious he could be, too, I was only to find out several months later and a thousand miles farther. (p. 65)

*   *   *

The third form of darkness is only lightly adumbrated, but our perception of it is crucial, I shall argue, to our understanding of the most puzzling and disputed feature of the tale, Marlow's lie to the Intended. Indeed a number of the images through which this form of darkness is projected are concentrated in a passage which describes Marlow's thoughts as he waits for admission to the Intended's house:

> I thought [Kurtz's] memory was like the other memories of the dead that accumulate in every man's life – a vague impress on the

61

brain of shadows that had fallen on it in their swift and final passage; but before the high and ponderous door, between the tall houses of a street as still and decorous as a well-kept alley in a cemetery, I had a vision of him on the stretcher, opening his mouth voraciously, as if to devour all the earth with all its mankind. He lived then before me; he lived as much as he had ever lived – a shadow insatiable of splendid appearances, of frightful realities; a shadow darker than the shadow of the night, and draped nobly in the folds of a gorgeous eloquence. . . . (p. 155)

This darkness is the darkness of shadow, 'the shadow of the night', but the image of shadow is diversified, as its use in this passage indicates. It suggests, first, semblance as opposed to substance, and hence insubstantial being. It is in this sense, I take it, that the memories of the dead are no more than shadowy impressions on the brain; and it is in this sense that the Africans 'lying confusedly in the greenish gloom' of the grove of death are described as 'black shadows of disease and starvation' (p. 66). Those black shadows naturally evoke the darkness of death, the shades, into which they are about to disappear; and the image is used in a way which incorporates not only notions of death but of ghosts and phantoms which are readily suggested by it. In the grove of death one of the black shadows stares at nothing while 'his brother phantom [rests] its forehead, as if overcome with a great weariness' (p. 67). Kurtz, sitting up 'lank' on his stretcher and extending a 'thin arm', is referred to not only as a 'shadow' which looks 'satiated and calm' but as an 'atrocious phantom', an 'apparition', and 'an animated image of death' (pp. 133–5). This is the 'vision of him on the stretcher' that Marlow has in the street that calls to mind 'a well-kept alley in a cemetery'; and this is the 'shadow insatiable of splendid appearances, of frightful realities' that lives before him as he goes into the house. These, then, are the main related dimensions of the darkness of shadow; but the quoted passage extends them in a further and important respect, for the insatiable shadow is also said to be 'a shadow darker than the shadow of the night, and draped nobly in the folds of a gorgeous eloquence'. The image links up here with the darkness of damnation into which Kurtz falls, but it also takes on the meaning of an intense and hidden darkness, for the shadow is both darker than the night and concealed by the drapery of eloquence. The darkness of shadow may accordingly also be seen as the darkness of a powerful but hidden reality, and this is a darkness that is spectrally apparent in the jungle as well: 'Beyond the fence the forest stood up spectrally in the moonlight, and through the dim stir, through the faint sounds of that lamentable courtyard, the silence of the land went home to one's very heart – its mystery, its greatness, the amazing reality of its concealed life' (p. 80).

III

It is his attitude to the various forms of darkness he has encountered in Africa that Marlow tries to clarify and define as he relives the experience in the telling of the tale. About the flabby devil disguised as a bearer of light he is scathingly clear from the start; it is the apparently 'incomprehensible frenzy' of the people who seem to have sprung from 'the night of first ages' that challenges him to an accounting:

> The earth seemed unearthly. We are accustomed to look upon the shackled form of a conquered monster, but there – there you could look at a thing monstrous and free. It was unearthly, and the men were – No, they were not inhuman. Well, you know, that was the worst of it – this suspicion of their not being inhuman. It would come slowly to one. They howled and leaped, and spun, and made horrid faces; but what thrilled you was just the thought of their humanity – like yours – the thought of your remote kinship with this wild and passionate uproar. Ugly. Yes, it was ugly enough; but if you were man enough you would admit to yourself that there was in you just the faintest trace of a response to the terrible frankness of that noise, a dim suspicion of there being a meaning in it which you – you so remote from the night of first ages – could comprehend. And why not? The mind of man is capable of anything – because everything is in it, all the past as well as all the future. What was there after all? Joy, fear, sorrow, devotion, valour, rage – who can tell? – but truth – truth stripped of its cloak of time. Let the fool gape and shudder – the man knows, and can look on without a wink. But he must at least be as much of a man as these on the shore. He must meet that truth with his own true stuff – with his own inborn strength. Principles won't do. Acquisitions, clothes, pretty rags – rags that would fly off at the first good shake. No; you want a deliberate belief. An appeal to me in this fiendish row – is there? Very well; I hear; I admit, but I have a voice, too, and for good or evil mine is the speech that cannot be silenced. Of course, a fool, what with sheer fright and fine sentiments, is always safe. Who's that grunting? You wonder I didn't go ashore for a howl and a dance? Well, no – I didn't. Fine sentiments, you say? Fine sentiments, be hanged! I had no time. I had to mess about with white-lead and strips of woollen blanket helping to put bandages on those leaky steam-pipes – I tell you. I had to watch the steering, and circumvent those snags, and get the tin-pot along by hook or by crook. There was surface-truth enough in these things to save a wiser man. . . . (pp. 96–7)

The spectacle of the frenzied savages arouses in Marlow none of the ambivalence that he later feels towards Kurtz's black woman; it unmitigatedly evokes the 'monstrous'. It is significant, however, that the horror of the experience seems to be related not so much to the qualities of the monster as to the fact of its being 'free', for Marlow admits – almost with non-chalance – to being 'accustomed to look upon the shackled form of a conquered monster'. It is, therefore, the notion of release, the evident abandon, that is appalling, the more so since Marlow, recognizing that it is a touch of the monster that makes the whole world kin, however 'remotely', feels, however 'faintly', a capacity for such abandon in himself. The mind of man, as he says, is 'capable of anything' and contains 'every-thing'. Having admitted so much, Marlow takes a further leap and suggests that in civilized man the monster is not as firmly restrained as he would like to believe; it is merely hidden, rather than shackled, concealed by the 'cloak of time' he has thrown over it during the course of his long trek from the night of first ages. Marlow maintains, indeed, that it behoves a man who has the courage of his manhood to refuse a flabby blindness and to look underneath the cloak, being prepared to see unabashedly what is there. Seeing, Marlow implies once again, is knowing: the man, as opposed to the gaping and shuddering fool, 'knows, and can look on without a wink'.

What in effect shackles the monster that stirs under the cloak is, first of all, the existence of curbs devised by civilized man, the kind of curb that is embodied in the person of the policeman and the butcher. But Marlow is implicitly concerned here with a capacity for restraint in the absence – in a dark land – of what he elsewhere calls 'external checks' (p. 74). It was a devotion to the job in hand, he avers, that prevented him from going ashore 'for a howl and a dance', and he has previously affirmed the salutary effects of work. It was work that enabled him to 'keep [his] hold on the redeeming facts of life' at the Central Station (p. 75); it is work, he believes, that gives a man 'the chance to find [himself]' (p. 85). But in relation to the monster, he nevertheless implicitly concedes, work is no more than an expedient, for what protected him was the fact of his having had 'no time'. Since work, moreover, offers only a 'surface-truth', it is not proof against the thrust of a monstrous truth from the depths – as Kurtz exemplifies. Nor, Marlow contends, are principles. Since they are 'acquired', they too, like work, are seen as external and so of the surface, the 'pretty rags' being merely a more insubstantial version of the cloak of time. Something more solid than rags is required to with-stand the thrust of a force that, we assume, is as imperative as hunger: 'No fear can stand up to hunger, no patience can wear it out, disgust simply does not exist where hunger is; and as to superstition, beliefs, and what you may call principles, they are less than chaff in a breeze' (p. 105).

Freed, then, from all external restraint, and deprived of external support, what does civilized man have to fall back on in contending with the monster? It is at this point, it seems to me, that both Conrad and his narrator may be accused of the mistiness which E. M. Forster believes characterizes Conrad's thought as a whole.[7] Asserting that 'principles won't do', Marlow says that what is needed is 'a deliberate belief', though it is not clear, in this context, what the precise difference between a principle and a belief is; and indeed beliefs are scattered like chaff along with principles where hunger is concerned. Alternatively, and more promisingly, civilized man must summon up the strength to oppose his 'voice' to the 'fiendish row' outside him, an opposition that presumably expresses itself in the sound of silence, an attempt to demonstrate control in the face of its abandon. The resolution for such control stems from a man's 'own true stuff', from his 'own inborn strength', stems, in short, from an innate capacity to hold himself together, from an innate self-possession. The idea is still a little misty, substituting, Forster might have said, a mystery for a muddle, but it points to the clearer psychic geography of *Lord Jim*.

As Marlow faces the yelling and stamping throng on the shore and finds a voice to oppose to theirs, his implicit assumption seems to be that it is the civilized man who has the inborn strength to restrain himself, the savage who manifestly lacks it. But his experience soon teaches him this is an untenable position. Not only does he have to account, by the time he reaches the Inner Station, for the fact of Kurtz; almost at once he becomes an observer of the impressive behaviour of his cannibal crew. The cannibals, as the journey progresses, are left with only 'a few lumps of some stuff like half-cooked dough' to eat, and they eat such small quantities of this that 'it [seems] done more for the looks of the thing than for any serious purpose of sustenance'. In the circumstances Marlow cannot help wondering why 'in the name of all the gnawing devils of hunger' they do not 'go for' the white men, whom they outnumber 'thirty to five'. He is forced to conclude that 'something restraining, one of those human secrets that baffle probability' has come into play; and that, though the cannibals have 'no earthly reason for any kind of scruple', and one might 'just as soon have expected restraint from a hyena prowling amongst the corpses of a battlefield' as from them, they do in fact exercise control even when 'brought to the test of an inexorable physical necessity'. And 'it takes a man', Marlow reflects (bringing the wheel full circle), 'all his inborn strength to fight hunger properly' (pp. 104–5). The cannibal crew thus posit a capacity for the ultimate abandon of utter savagery at the same time as they exemplify the innate restraint that Marlow considers the only effective safeguard of civilized behaviour. As with Kurtz's savage woman, we are confronted with a human mystery that, so to speak, transcends black and white categories.

The case of Kurtz himself offers a phenomenon of a directly opposite kind. Marlow tells his listeners that he is 'trying to account to [himself] for – for – Mr. Kurtz – for the shade of Mr. Kurtz' (p. 117), for the sort of darkness he epitomizes, that is, as well as for his ghost, but he is not notably successful in his efforts. He sees clearly enough, however, what happens to him, even if he cannot satisfactorily explain why it does:

> The wilderness had patted him on the head, and, behold, it was like a ball – an ivory ball; it had caressed him, and – lo! – he had withered; it had taken him, loved him, embraced him, got into his veins, consumed his flesh, and sealed his soul to its own by the inconceivable ceremonies of some devilish initiation. . . . He had taken a high seat amongst the devils of the land – I mean literally. You can't understand. How could you? – with solid pavement under your feet, surrounded by kind neighbours ready to cheer you or to fall on you, stepping delicately between the butcher and the policeman, in the holy terror of scandal and gallows and lunatic asylums – how can you imagine what particular region of the first ages a man's untrammelled feet may take him into by the way of solitude – utter solitude without a policeman – by the way of silence – utter silence, where no warning voice of a kind neighbour can be heard whispering of public opinion? These little things make all the great difference. When they are gone you must fall back upon your own innate strength, upon your own capacity for faithfulness. Of course you may be too much of a fool to go wrong – too dull even to know you are being assaulted by the powers of darkness. I take it, no fool ever made a bargain for his soul with the devil: the fool is too much of a fool, or the devil too much of a devil – I don't know which. . . . (pp. 115–17)

It is significant that the assault on Kurtz by 'the powers of darkness' is presented both in sexual and cannibalistic terms: the wilderness pats and caresses him; it takes, loves, and embraces him, getting into his veins and consuming his flesh. The evocation of the sexual suggests that Kurtz, in his wilderness, undergoes an experience that is analogous to that of Willems with Aïssa in the Malayan jungle. Letting go, giving in to an absolute abandon, he loses all self-possession – and, like Willems, is consequently open to a counter-possession. It is not by chance that there are so many references to devils in the quoted passage, for Kurtz is presented as a man possessed, though we may choose to regard him as being possessed rather by the non-theological monster that Marlow observed on the shore. Indeed the 'particular region of the first ages' that Kurtz's 'untrammelled feet' have taken him into is precisely 'the night of first ages' in which Marlow thinks of the savages as existing. And the kind of abandon he exemplifies, as Marlow's further reference (in the context of the cannibalistic assault) to 'the butcher and the policeman' indicates – he also refers, immediately afterwards, to the earth's being a place where, among other things, we must 'breathe dead hippo, so to speak, and not be contaminated' (p. 117) – is in effect the same as that of the savages; for, if Conrad in part complies with Henry James's preference for avoiding 'weak specifications', not much is left to the imagination: Marlow says that Kurtz presided 'at certain midnight dances ending with unspeakable rites, which – as far as I reluctantly gathered from what I heard at various times – were offered up to him – do you understand? – to Mr. Kurtz himself' (p. 118).[8] But where a liberated and cavorting monster may ultimately lead civilized man is even more graphically pointed by the note Kurtz scrawls at the end of his report (itself 'a beautiful piece of writing') for the International Society for the Suppression of Savage Customs: Marlow says 'it was very simple, and at the end of that moving appeal to every altruistic sentiment it blazed at you, luminous and terrifying, like a flash of lightning in a serene sky: "Exterminate all the brutes!" ' (p. 118).[9] This, then, is the light that comes out of Kurtz's darkness, casting a prescient shadow on the proponents of final solutions of our own times. It illuminates too a long line of characters in the works which follow 'Heart of Darkness': having let go to a degree that he has no self left to hold on to, reduced to his own nullity, Kurtz is but the first exemplar in Conrad of the moral nihilism which is the concomitant of such disintegration.

But how is it, we wonder, that a man who was so full of a genuine and energetic idealism should have been reduced to such a nullity? Marlow's answer is in line with the sort of understanding he has arrived at, but it does not take us very far. Deprived of all outer restraints, a man, when he is 'assaulted by the powers of darkness', must fall back upon his 'own innate strength'; Kurtz succumbs to the assault because he has nothing to fall back on, because he is 'hollow at the core' (p. 131). The image of hollowness may aptly evoke Kurtz's nullity (and has the incidental virtue of having been useful to T. S. Eliot), but it does not illuminate what has happened to him. Presented as the explanation of Kurtz's disintegration, moreover, it implies that he falls apart because he is empty, though there is no necessary connection between the two conditions. That disintegration is not a necessary consequence of hollowness is borne out by other hollow men in 'Heart of Darkness'. Marlow decides that the manager of the Central Station, for instance, is 'great'; 'He was great by this little thing that it was impossible to tell what could control such a man. He never gave that secret away. Perhaps there was nothing within him. Such a suspicion made one pause – for out there there were no external checks' (p. 74). Though turned by the darkness in which he moves into as blind a pilgrim and flabby a devil as one could wish, the empty manager nevertheless does not disintegrate. Nor does the man whom Marlow calls the brickmaker, that 'papier-mâché Mephistopheles', who is certainly hollow: '. . . it seemed to me,' says Marlow, 'that if I tried I could poke my forefinger through him, and would find nothing inside but a little loose dirt, maybe' (p. 81). In 'Heart of Darkness', in short, Conrad has not yet discovered a psychology which can encompass all his intuitions – though, with the notions of innate strength and inner hollowness, he is on the way to the more profound and comprehensive insights of *Lord Jim*.

IV

Marlow's own direct experience of the darkness quietly dramatizes previously established significances. As the steamboat approaches Kurtz's station, he is looking down at the sounding-pole when he is amazed to see the poleman suddenly fall flat on the deck and the fireman duck his head:

> I was amazed. Then I had to look at the river mighty quick, because there was a snag in the fairway. Sticks, little sticks, were flying about – thick: they were whizzing before my nose, dropping below me, striking behind me against my pilot-house. All this time the river, the shore, the woods, were very quiet – perfectly quiet. I could only hear the heavy splashing thump of the stern-wheel and the patter of these things. We cleared the snag clumsily. Arrows, by Jove! We were being shot at! I stepped in quickly to close the shutter on the land-side. That fool-helmsman, his hands on the spokes, was lifting his knees high, stamping his feet, champing his mouth, like a reined-in horse. Confound him! And we were staggering within ten feet of the bank. I had to lean right out to swing the heavy shutter, and I saw a face amongst the leaves on the level with my own, looking at me very fierce and steady; and then suddenly, as though a veil had been removed from my eyes, I made out, deep in the tangled gloom, naked breasts, arms, legs, glaring eyes, – the bush was swarming with human limbs in movement, glistening, of bronze colour. The twigs shook, swayed, and rustled, the arrows flew out of them, and then the shutter came to. 'Steer her straight,' I said to the helmsman. He held his head rigid, face forward; but his eyes rolled, he kept on lifting and setting down his feet gently, his mouth foamed a little. 'Keep quiet!' I said in a fury. I might just as well have ordered a tree not to sway in the wind. I darted out. Below me there was a great scuffle of feet on the iron deck; confused exclamations; a voice screamed, 'Can you turn back?' I caught sight of a V-shaped ripple on the water ahead. What? Another snag! A fusillade burst out under my feet. The pilgrims had opened with their Winchesters, and were simply squirting lead into that bush. A deuce of a lot of smoke came

up and drove slowly forward. I swore at it. Now I couldn't see the
ripple or the snag either. . . . (pp. 109–10)

The unexpected attack on the boat is a further instance of Conrad's use of
sudden epiphany. The attack is the equivalent, we realize, of that 'assault
by the powers of darkness' to which Kurtz is exposed, as are all those
who venture into dark lands, and responses to it are neatly discriminated.
There is, first, the reaction of the black helmsman. As he rolls his eyes and
foams at the mouth, we recognize the telltale physical signs of panic, the
signs being identical to those displayed by another black sailor on the
Narcissus. His panic, as he stamps his feet and champs his mouth, 'like
a reined-in horse', is portrayed as a desire to break loose, to cut free, again
recalling sailors on the *Narcissus*. When he finally lets go and allows himself to be swept by his passion of fear, like a tree swaying in the wind, he
loses control, abandons the wheel, opens the shutter Marlow has closed,
and begins to 'let off that Martini-Henry' (p. 111), a series of actions which
in the end cost him his life. His death is the occasion of one of the most
significant moments in Conrad's development to this point, Marlow
saying of him: 'Poor fool! If he had only left that shutter alone. He had
no restraint, no restraint – just like Kurtz – a tree swayed by the wind'
(p. 119). If it is the lack of restraint of the two men, their common
abandon, that suggests the comparison between them, the letting go of
the helmsman is primarily physical, while that of Kurtz is primarily
spiritual. Conrad, in other words, has begun for the first time to bring
together and relate in a common loss of self-possession the apparently
diverse phenomena of abandon, panic and nullity.

The pilgrims respond to the assault characteristically. They open up
with their Winchesters, and 'simply [squirt] lead into that bush', but the
smoke from their rifles prevents Marlow from seeing as he tries to keep
a look-out for the snag. The result of their efforts, we might say, is
obfuscation. They are also quite futile, Marlow noting from the way the
tops of the bushes rustle, that almost all their shots have gone too high:
'You can't hit anything unless you take aim and fire from the shoulder;
but these chaps fired from the hip with their eyes shut' (p. 121). In short,
they simply go at it blind.

With an instinctive certainty of response, Marlow exemplifies the
Conradian ideal throughout the attack. What he does, first of all, is to
continue to devote himself to the job in hand, to the everyday business of
piloting his craft through the river, on the watch for snags. There is
enough surface-truth in this to occupy him fully and leave him no time to
distinguish the nature of the 'little sticks' that are flying about. When it
at length penetrates his consciousness that the sticks are arrows and that
they are 'being shot at', he confronts the truth that is hidden in the dark

depths, as it were, looking 'deep' into 'the tangled gloom' of the jungle and, 'as though a veil [has] been removed from [his] eyes', steadily making out the assaulting force. Thereafter, admirably keeping his head and acting with complete self-possession, Marlow takes over the wheel that has been abandoned by the helmsman, straightens the boat, riskily crowds it into the bank despite the proximity of the attackers because the water is deeper there and he is determined to avoid the snag, and finally saves the day and puts the savages to flight by repeatedly jerking out 'screech after screech' on the boat's steam whistle (pp. 111–12). It is with due satisfaction that he registers later that 'the retreat . . . was caused by the screeching of the steam whistle' (p. 121).

Marlow pits himself against the powers of darkness for the second time when he decides to go after Kurtz, whom he discovers has left his cabin on the steamboat and headed for the midnight fires of his adorers, even though he is close to death and has to crawl 'on all-fours' to do so. He cuts Kurtz off when they are 'within thirty yards from the nearest fire':

If he makes a row we are lost, I thought to myself. This clearly was not a case for fisticuffs, even apart from the very natural aversion I had to beat that Shadow – this wandering and tormented thing. 'You will be lost,' I said – 'utterly lost.' One gets sometimes such a flash of inspiration, you know. I did say the right thing, though indeed he could not have been more irretrievably lost than he was at this very moment, when the foundations of our intimacy were being laid – to endure – to endure – even to the end – even beyond.

'I had immense plans,' he muttered irresolutely. . . . I had to deal with a being to whom I could not appeal in the name of anything high or low. I had, even like the niggers, to invoke him – himself – his own exalted and incredible degradation. There was nothing either above or below him, and I knew it. He had kicked himself loose of the earth. . . . If anybody had ever struggled with a soul, I am the man. And I wasn't arguing with a lunatic either. Believe me or not, his intelligence was perfectly clear . . . But his soul was mad. Being alone in the wilderness, it had looked within itself, and, by heavens! I tell you, it had gone mad. I had – for my sins, I suppose – to go through the ordeal of looking into it myself. No eloquence could have been so withering to one's belief in mankind as his final burst of sincerity. He struggled with himself, too. I saw it, – I heard it. I saw the inconceivable mystery of a soul that knew no restraint, no faith, and no fear, yet struggling blindly with itself. I kept my head pretty well; but when I had him at last stretched on the couch, I wiped my forehead, while my legs shook under me as though I had carried half a ton on my back down that hill. And yet I had only supported him, his bony arm clasped round my neck – and he was not much heavier than a child. (pp. 143–5)

Once again Marlow keeps his head 'pretty well', as he remarks. If under attack on the steamboat he does the right thing, now, confronting the insidious pull of the wilderness, he finds the resources to 'say the right thing'. It is not only a 'flash of inspiration' but compassion too that moves him to use the future tense and tell Kurtz he 'will be lost' when he knows that he is already 'irretrievably lost', that he has so completely broken all restraining and guiding stays as to have 'kicked himself loose of the earth'. In using the future tense, Marlow not only invokes Kurtz's present 'incredible degradation', the degradation of a man who has been 'crawling on all-fours' in the dark to savage and unspeakable rites at which he will be 'exalted', but the resplendent man he was who strode foursquare into the jungle, bearing a flaming torch. It is this figure that is momentarily recovered from the encompassing darkness and begins to talk of the 'immense plans' he once had. And if Kurtz indulges in a final and withering 'burst of sincerity', he is nevertheless led by Marlow to 'struggle blindly' with himself, a struggle that results, before his death, in his seeing at last the full horror of his descent into darkness.

The episode also helps us to clarify the important question of Marlow's relationship to Kurtz. It is on this occasion, Marlow says, that 'the foundations' of his 'intimacy' with Kurtz were laid, and he adds – with the kind of quavering portentousness that is an occasional defect of the style – that the intimacy was 'to endure – to endure – even to the end – even beyond'. Just previously, moreover, he recounts how he did not betray Kurtz when he discovered his cabin was empty: 'it was ordered I should never betray him – it was written I should be loyal to the nightmare of my choice' (p. 141). These statements would seem to lend support to Albert J. Guerard's view that what 'Heart of Darkness' fundamentally explores is 'the night journey into the unconscious, and confrontation of an entity within the self', Marlow experiencing such a confrontation through an 'alliance' with Kurtz that is an 'identification of "selves"', and Kurtz serving as Marlow's 'double' and 'secret sharer'.[10] I have indicated in what ways I think Marlow does confront an entity within the self, but it seems to me that Florence H. Ridley is surely right when she contends, in opposition to Guerard, that 'Kurtz is Marlow's opposite rather than his double'.[11] If the issue of self-possession is central, as I believe, this would certainly seem to be the case; and what the quoted episode directly dramatizes is not Marlow's identification with Kurtz, as he propels himself into the dark jungle, but his 'struggle' with his soul and his own determined opposition to the pull of the wilderness. What Marlow offers Kurtz in the face of the pilgrims' distrust and hatred of him is not the complicity of a secret sharer but merely 'support' – as is also dramatized when he leads Kurtz back to the boat with 'his bony arm clasped round [his] neck'.

Marlow's 'identification' with Kurtz is no more than a matter of his defiant acceptance of the pilgrims' view that they are in the same camp, a view advanced early on by the brickmaker: 'You are of the new gang – the gang of virtue,' he says to Marlow at the Central Station. 'The same people who sent [Kurtz] specially also recommended you. Oh, don't say no. I've my own eyes to trust' (p. 79). And once Marlow finds himself 'lumped along with Kurtz', the basis of his previously cited 'loyalty' to him is a preference that is rooted in a revulsion from the pilgrims: 'It seemed to me I had never breathed an atmosphere so vile [i.e. in the company of the manager exulting over Kurtz's "unsound" methods and the necessity of pointing this out "in the proper quarter"], and I turned mentally to Kurtz for relief – positively for relief. . . . Ah! but it was something to have at least a choice of nightmares' (p. 138). This is the 'unforeseen partnership' Marlow accepts, the 'choice of nightmares forced upon [him] in the tenebrous land invaded by [those] mean and greedy phantoms' (p. 147). And he '[remains] loyal to Kurtz to the last' because of his dying words, which he regards as 'an affirmation, a moral victory' (p. 151).

The final test of his loyalty comes in the closing moments of his meeting with Kurtz's Intended:

'Forgive me. I – I – have mourned so long in silence – in silence. . . . You were with him – to the last? I think of his loneliness. Nobody near to understand him as I would have understood. Perhaps no one to hear. . . .'

'To the very end,' I said, shakily. 'I heard his very last words. . . .' I stopped in a fright.

'Repeat them,' she murmured in a heart-broken tone. 'I want – I want – something – something – to – to live with.'

I was on the point of crying at her, 'Don't you hear them?' The dusk was repeating them in a persistent whisper all around us, in a whisper that seemed to swell menacingly like the first whisper of a rising wind. 'The horror! the horror!'

'His last word – to live with,' she insisted. 'Don't you understand I loved him– I loved him – I loved him!'

I pulled myself together and spoke slowly.

'The last word he pronounced was – your name.'

I heard a slight sigh and then my heart stood still, stopped dead short by an exulting and terrible cry, by the cry of inconceivable triumph and of unspeakable pain. 'I knew it – I was sure!' . . . She knew. She was sure. I heard her weeping; she had hidden her face in her hands. It seemed to me that the house would collapse before I could escape, that the heavens would fall upon my head. But nothing happened. The heavens do not fall for such a trifle. Would they have fallen, I wonder, if I had rendered Kurtz that justice which was his due? Hadn't he said he wanted only justice? But I couldn't. I could not tell her. It would have been too dark – too dark altogether. . . . (pp. 161–2)

There is clearly a striking lapse in the quality of the writing here, a descent to the level of cheap fiction, and an uncertainty of tone that is only accentuated by the proliferation of dots and dashes. The lapse would seem to be symptomatic of a larger failure of conception, for the episode is meant to be of central importance. It is not merely that it is the climax and conclusion of Marlow's narrative, and that, following it, we are left only with 'the heart of an immense darkness' to which the frame-narrator points. The episode is intended to bind the whole tale together, as Conrad declared in a letter to his publisher:

> . . . in the light of the final incident the whole story [i.e. 'The End of the Tether'] in all its descriptive detail shall fall into its place – acquire its value and its significance. This is my method based on deliberate conviction. I've never departed from it. I call your own kind self to witness and I beg to instance Karain – Lord Jim (where the method is fully developed) – the last pages of Heart of Darkness where the interview of the man and the girl locks in – as it were – the whole 30,000 words of narrative description into one suggestive view of a whole phase of life, and makes of that story something quite on another plane than an anecdote of a man who went mad in the Centre of Africa. . . .[12]

If we are to grant Conrad his intention, then what we make of Marlow's lie – the crux of 'the interview of the man and the girl' - should be related to what we make of the tale as a whole. Critical response has varied from an implicit rejection of the validity of the intention – '[Marlow] has made truth seem too important throughout the novel to persuade the reader now to accept falsehood as salvation'[13] – to the kind of reading that is manifestly rejected in the scene itself: 'There have been a number of explanations, but the one which seems to follow most plausibly from the novel as a whole is that however divorced from reality and in that sense false our ideals may be, they must be protected. . . . the lie does not seem to be an atonement [i.e. as Albert J. Guerard suggests]; it is rather the bulwark necessary to protect the saving illusion.'[14] But Marlow's own view of the 'saving illusion' does not permit such a reading. He has to contend, just before the lie, with the Intended's assertion of Kurtz's greatness:

> 'Yes, I know,' I said with something like despair in my heart, but
> bowing my head before the faith that was in her, before that great and
> saving illusion that shone with an unearthly glow in the darkness, in
> the triumphant darkness from which I could not have defended her –
> from which I could not even defend myself. (p. 159)

Marlow may bow his head before 'that great and saving illusion', but it
is clear that no bulwark can ultimately protect its temporary 'glow' from
'the triumphant darkness'. The darkness is triumphant because it cannot
be banished, and Marlow recognizes that the Intended cannot be defended
from it. His intuition is speedily borne out by her response to his lie, her
'exulting and terrible cry', which is revelatory of her own accommodation
of a dark abandon.

Marlow's motive for the lie is straightforward enough. He feels moved
to protect a woman, not an illusion; for, given the truth of Kurtz's life
and death, and his estimate of the inability of the Intended to cope with
that truth, he offers her his white lie in profound pity for her. This aspect
of the lie is emphasized in a passage that immediately precedes the quoted
scene: when the Intended murmurs her regret at not having been with
Kurtz when he died, the anger that has begun to stir in Marlow at the
thought of Kurtz's end '[subsides] before a feeling of infinite pity' (p.
161). His lie, that is to say, is analogous to that of Captain Allistoun's to
Jimmy, as he tries to give her what the captain wanted Jimmy to have –
'something to live with'.

But it is also quite different from Captain Allistoun's lie because
Marlow, unlike the captain, has an intense abhorrence of the act of lying.
He articulates this abhorrence fairly early on in the narrative when he
recounts how he in effect lied to the brickmaker at the Central Station:

> I would not have gone so far as to fight for Kurtz, but I went for
> him near enough to a lie. You know I hate, detest, and can't bear a
> lie, not because I am straighter than the rest of us, but simply because
> it appals me. There is a taint of death, a flavour of mortality in lies –
> which is exactly what I hate and detest in the world – what I want to
> forget. It makes me miserable and sick, like biting something rotten
> would do. Temperament, I suppose. Well, I went near enough to it
> by letting the young fool there believe anything he liked to imagine
> as to my influence in Europe. . . . (p. 82)

When Marlow expresses his horror of lying in such extreme terms, and
in a context which does little to explain his vehemence since no actual lie
provides the occasion for it, he must be seen as preparing his listeners for
the momentousness of his final lie, which he knows is to come. It is this

passage, and not the external authorial intention cited in Conrad's letter to Blackwood, that sets up expectations in the work itself and will not allow us merely to register Marlow's lie to the Intended as a white lie – and to leave it at that. And what Marlow's unexpected collocation of death and lying suggests is that – with a vivid memory of that rotting hippo meat, perhaps – he discerns a relation between them in the sense of a common corruption that they each evoke.

If this is so, then I think it must be said that, in the scene with the Intended, Conrad did not succeed in devising an action that can be readily related to the preparatory passage. Marlow's lie to her, strain as we may, obstinately remains an ordinary white lie, a humane expression of compassion without devious moral implications and by no stretch of the imagination can we regard it as evincing a form of corruption on his part. Consequently it is difficult for us to make any meaningful connection between the lie and death. All that we can say is that, in lying, Marlow in some obscure way dramatically accepts his own mortality because it is its flavour, though this is what he hates and detests and wants to forget, that he knowingly accepts when he permits himself to lie. But such an acceptance, unless he had other intimations, would seem to be a meagre gleaning from his rich African experience – and would hardly serve to bind together the whole tale as Conrad declared he intended. Indeed, that the woman who plays so large a part in this presumably climactic scene should be known as the Intended becomes unhappily suggestive of more than one unfulfilled aspiration.

Though we can legitimately make no more of the scene than this because Marlow makes no more of it and Conrad did not find a way of allowing him to do so, I think we may hazard a guess at what the novelist wished to achieve with the lie if we relate the scene to earlier thematic preoccupations and to the persistent pattern of imagery that runs through the tale. In accepting his mortality, what Marlow in effect accepts is an ultimate loss of self. Once again, then, at the end of an important early work, Conrad may be seen as obscurely and indeterminately approaching the paradox of the loss that is a finding; for, when Marlow, despite his abhorrence of lying, lets go sufficiently to tell the lie, he says he 'pulled [himself] together' to do so. This oblique and casual indication of an act of integration becomes significant if we relate Marlow's acceptance of his mortality to the image of the shadow, and infer that Conrad wished this acceptance to denote an acceptance of the shadow that is the inescapable accompaniment of life. For this shadow, we have seen, does not only evoke the darkness of death; it suggests, too, a hidden reality – the dark reality, we may say, that is hidden beneath the cloak of time. It would seem that it is this dimension of being that Marlow was intended symbolically to accept and incorporate in a unified self when he pulls himself together and lies. Such a reading, at any rate, would offer to lock the final scene into the rest of the narrative. It would also suggest, perhaps, that Conrad bungled the scene because he could not yet bring himself to face all its implications: his tale shows that if the monstrous darkness Marlow is to accept may generate a superb vitality, such vitality may be disconcertingly manifested – like that of Kurtz's savage woman – in a self-possession that appears to be founded on a capacity for abandon.

CHAPTER FOUR

A. *Lord Jim*

I

ON A FIRST reading, at least, *Lord Jim* generally proves to be so slippery as to elude one's grasp. This is doubtless mainly attributable to the fact that Marlow, who (after the first four chapters) tells Jim's story, seems himself unable to take hold and, at the end of his oral narrative, confesses that for him Jim appears 'to stand at the heart of a vast enigma' (p. 336), more inaccessible, we infer, than Kurtz at his heart of darkness. Critical response to the enigma has varied from an insistence that Conrad's art is subtly deployed to evoking it, and that we must recognize 'the process of interpreting' Jim's story is 'a ceaseless movement toward a light which always remains hidden';[1] to an assertion not only that 'the effect of muddlement which is so commonly found in *Lord Jim* comes, in short, from this – that Marlow is himself muddled' but also that 'in fact the confusion seems to extend to Conrad's conception of the story'.[2] In relation to both these statements it is perhaps salutary to bear in mind that Conrad himself at least thought he was doing something far more definite than either would allow one to believe. Writing to his publisher in the month that he completed the novel, he suggested that they should dispense with the word 'chapter' since the 'divisions' were 'not Chapters in the usual sense each carrying the action a step further or embodying a complete episode': 'I meant them only as pauses – rests for the reader's attention while he is following the development of *one* situation, only *one* really from beginning to end.'[3] It seems to me that the novel does in fact yield a clear and definite impression of such a central situation.

That Conrad chose to present the single situation in a complicated narrative form suggests we might do well to seek a clue to the nature of the situation in the form employed. The first striking formal feature is the sudden shift in point of view that occurs at the end of Chapter Four, the first four chapters constituting an introductory omniscient narrative, and Chapters Five to Thirty-Five being the oral narrative of Marlow, who tells his story to an unspecified group of listeners and appears – in contra-distinction to his role of protagonist-narrator in 'Heart of Darkness' – as an observer-narrator, a man who inspires 'infernal confidences' and serves as 'a receptacle of confessions' (p. 34). The two narrators are strongly contrasted in the way they approach the telling of a story. The omniscient narrator is severely factual, and seems to aim at a detailed precision of effect: for instance, we are not only told that Jim's work as a water-clerk consists in racing other water-clerks for ships about to anchor but 'in racing under sail, steam, or oars' (p. 3). Marlow, however, is inferential, and sets the tone for his narrative by affirming, 'upon circumstantial evidence', that he has 'a familiar devil' as well as 'a guardian angel' (p. 34). The omniscient narrator tells his part of the story in an orderly and logical manner, proceeding – once he has vividly evoked Jim as a water-clerk – to a chronological account of the main events in his life prior to his boarding the *Patna* as chief mate on the voyage that was to result in his becoming a water-clerk. Marlow's narrative, on the other hand, seems to negate an ordered chronology and to move in response to the wayward pull of personal association: in his opening remarks, for example, he complains about having been let in for 'the inquiry thing, the yellow-dog thing' (p. 34) – and the mystifying and chronologically misplaced reference to the dog is not clarified for close on forty pages.

The shift from the one narrator to the other in Chapter Five consequently effects a sharp change in perspective. The change, to make use of a distinction that Marlow draws in relation to the object of official inquiries, is one from a concern with 'the superficial how' of Jim's case, which the omniscient narrator seems to have in common with that of the inquiry, to an interest in 'the fundamental why' of the matter, which characterizes Marlow's approach. The distinction is even neatly dramatized. The insistent question that is posed by the omniscient narrative, once the narrator has done his job of placing Jim for us, of telling us how he came to be on the *Patna*, is why he is appearing at an inquiry – and it is precisely at this point that Marlow takes over. But in making the distinction referred to, Marlow also says that 'the play of questions' at the inquiry was 'as instructive as the tapping with a hammer on an iron box, were the object to find out what's inside' (p. 56); and the change of perspective effected by the shift in point of view may be thought of as manifesting itself in Marlow's attempt to disclose what is inside the box rather than describe its outside. With the advent of Marlow, that is to say, there is a focusing on the hidden.

From the outset of his narrative, moreover, Marlow seems to go out of his way to tantalize us with allusions to incidents which are clearly of the greatest importance in Jim's story but about which we know nothing. He refers, for instance, to a 'mysterious cable message' from Aden which sets the waterside 'cackling': 'I say mysterious, because it was so in a sense though it contained a naked fact, about as naked and ugly as a fact can well be. The whole waterside talked of nothing else' (p. 35); and shortly thereafter he talks of his 'first view of Jim', saying that, 'knowing all he knew and a little more too', he felt he had 'no business to look so sound' (p. 40). The 'naked fact', of course, is the abandonment of the *Patna* by its white crew; and the 'little more' that Marlow knows when he first sees Jim is that the *Patna* has not sunk, as Jim and those other members of the crew believe, but has been rescued. Without these two vital pieces of information the reader cannot begin to comprehend what Marlow is talking about, yet though he continually alludes to these facts – I have counted nearly thirty direct and indirect references to them[4] – he contrives to withhold the actual information for some hundred pages, the fact that Jim has jumped being revealed only on p. 111, and the *Patna* rescued on p. 134, while the French lieutenant's story, which fills in the details of the rescue, is delayed to pp. 137–42. It is doubtless true that Marlow's procedure effectively engenders an air of mystery and so makes for narrative interest, but such an achievement would hardly be worth the bewilderment caused the reader. Marlow's narrative seems designed, rather, to draw our attention repeatedly to the existence of hidden fact.

Further support for such a view is provided by the complicated narrative technique employed in the final chapters of the novel (Chapters Thirty-Six to Forty-Five). At the beginning of Chapter Thirty-Six the omniscient narrator returns to describe how, more than two years after the completion of Marlow's oral narrative, one of his listeners (who is referred to as 'the privileged man') receives from him an 'explanatory letter' and a written account of the end of Jim's story. This means, therefore, that throughout his long oral narrative Marlow does not know what has finally happened to Jim, that the end of Jim's story is hidden even from the narrator himself. And since the privileged man reads Marlow's letter before he turns to his written narrative, we learn that 'an awful thing has happened' (p. 340) – the opening words of an unfinished letter by Jim which Marlow encloses with his own – before we know what it is; and also that another letter, which Marlow likewise encloses, has – ominously – been 'found carefully preserved in [Jim's] writing-case' (p. 341). Marlow's earlier penchant for allusion to hidden fact, moreover, is strikingly duplicated in his letter. 'It all begins,' he writes, 'with a remarkable exploit of a man called Brown, who stole with complete success a Spanish schooner out of a small bay near Zamboanga,' but he in fact begins by reporting Brown's exultation at having 'paid out the stuck-up beggar after all' (p. 344). Thereafter in the course of his letter Marlow makes some five further more or less obscure references to the disaster that has overtaken Jim without our knowing what has actually happened to him;[5] and, since his written narrative is strictly chronological, we do not learn about the nature of the disaster until its conclusion.

Given his evident careful concern in *Lord Jim* with the hidden, and given too Marlow's sense of attracting to himself as a confessor men 'with hidden plague spots' (p. 34), Conrad, though putting a brave face on it, must have been mortified that Edward Garnett discerned such a spot in the novel itself:

> Yes! you've put your finger on the plague spot. The division of the book into two parts which is the basis of your criticism demonstrates to me once more your amazing insight; and your analysis of the effect of the book puts into words precisely and suggestively the dumb thoughts of every reader – and my own.[6]

But Garnett does not seem, in this respect, to have been as good a critic as Conrad believed him to be, for though the book does undoubtedly fall into two parts – the *Patna* and Patusan episodes – it does not fall apart. Instead of probing for a hidden weakness, therefore, we might do well to look for a hidden connection between the two parts – to accept, I shall argue later, that the structure, far from being disintegrative, enforces the fact of such connection.

A far from hidden connection between the two parts is that Jim's trials aboard the *Patna* and in Patusan constitute two tests of his quality. It may be said that Captain Allistoun and his men are tested by events aboard the *Narcissus*, and Marlow and Kurtz by exposure to the wilderness, but it is in *Lord Jim* that the idea of the test is explicitly formulated for the first time, thereafter becoming a repeatedly crucial element in most of the actions Conrad devises. At the beginning of Chapter Two the omniscient narrator points out that Jim, up to the time of his first appointment as chief mate, has never been tested:

> He was gentlemanly, steady, tractable, with a thorough knowledge of his duties; and in time, when yet very young, he became chief mate of a fine ship, without ever having been tested by those events of the sea that show in the light of day the inner worth of a man, the edge of his temper, and the fibre of his stuff; that reveal the quality of his resistance and the secret truth of his pretences, not only to others but also to himself. (p. 10)

The test, we see, has the same function in the action as Marlow's obscure allusiveness in the narrative, namely, to draw our attention to the existence of what is hidden. The test suddenly exposes to 'the light of day' what is normally concealed in the darkness, showing a man's 'inner worth', baring 'the fibre of his stuff', and revealing 'the secret truth' of his pretences. The phrases used here bring to mind those that appear in 'Heart of Darkness', where, it will be recalled, a man was said to be able, ultimately, to meet the darkness only with 'his own true stuff – with his own inborn strength', and thus suggest the continuity of Conrad's concerns. It is in *Lord Jim*, indeed, that he penetrates most profoundly into the nature of the strength – or weakness – that may be revealed by the test.

The essence of the test is that it is always unexpected, with the result that the man who fails to meet it has a defensive sense of having been 'taken unawares'. Jim has such a sense the first time he is tested on the training-ship, feeling 'angry with the brutal tumult of earth and sky for taking him unawares and checking unfairly a generous readiness for narrow escapes' (p. 9). The kind of 'readiness' required, consequently, is more than a disposition for adventure, as Jim, after the disgrace of the *Patna*, is led to see: 'It is all in being ready,' he tells Marlow. 'I wasn't; not – not then' (p. 81). In the Conradian universe, we begin to perceive, it is readiness, not ripeness, that is all:

> A marvellous stillness pervaded the world, and the stars, together with the serenity of their rays, seemed to shed upon the earth the assurance of everlasting security. The young moon recurved, and shining low in the west, was like a slender shaving thrown up from a bar of gold, and the Arabian Sea, smooth and cool to the eye like a sheet of ice, extended its perfect level to the perfect circle of a dark horizon. The propeller turned without a check, as though its beat had been part of the scheme of a safe universe . . .
>
> Jim on the bridge was penetrated by the great certitude of unbounded safety and peace that could be read on the silent aspect of nature like the certitude of fostering love upon the placid tenderness of a mother's face. . . . (p. 17)

It is folly to read 'unbounded safety and peace' into the silence of nature when that silence betokens, not the 'placid tenderness' of a mother – or Father – but an emptiness. John Dozier Gordan reports that, round about this point in the manuscript, Conrad deleted the following sentence: 'Watchfulness even seemed unnecessary in such an empty universe.'[7] The universe, that is, is like that of the *Narcissus*, and indeed the *Patna* is also seen as a planet and a world: it is said to move like 'a crowded planet speeding through the dark spaces of ether behind the swarm of suns, in the appalling and calm solitudes awaiting the breath of future creations' (p. 22); and 'when your ship fails you,' we are told, 'your whole world seems to fail you; the world that [has] made you, restrained you, taken care of you. It is as if the souls of men floating on an abyss and in touch with immensity had been set free for any excess of heroism, absurdity, or abomination' (p. 121). The last sentence even suggests that the failure of a ship leads to the kind of freedom from customary restraints that Kurtz encountered in Africa – and thus that the world of the *Patna* is yet another projection of that depicted in 'Heart of Darkness' as well. We may even note that the metaphorical pilgrims and pilgrimages of the earlier works are recalled in the actual pilgrims who board the *Patna* on a real pilgrimage. At all events, the fact of the sudden tests to which men are exposed in such a world makes it abundantly clear that, no matter how smoothly the propeller turns, there is no such thing as 'a safe universe'. What the story of the *Patna* dramatizes, rather, is that an empty world is filled with the sort of 'floating derelict' (p. 159) that the ship, quite out of the blue, runs into[8] – or, if one so wishes to designate them, with 'the dark powers' (p. 409); in short, it suggests that 'the scheme' of the Conradian universe is one of hidden wrecks. Indeed, the *Patna*'s striking of the derelict is yet another epiphany – the central epiphany, perhaps, in Conrad's *œuvre*, for it evokes a view of the nature of things that recurs again and again.

One further element adds to the emphasis on the hidden that is suggested in so many ways in the novel. After his disgrace on the *Patna*, Jim is 'under a cloud', and that is how Conrad (in the Author's Note) says he saw Jim's prototype 'one sunny morning' in an 'Eastern roadstead' (p. ix). But the phrase, as Marlow is quick to point out, also implies that Jim is hidden by his cloud: 'There is much truth – after all – in the common expression "under a cloud". It is impossible to see him clearly – especially as it is through the eyes of others that we take our last look at him' (p. 339). Sometimes Jim seems to reveal himself – 'The muscles round his lips contracted into an unconscious grimace that tore through the mask of his usual expression – something violent, short-lived and illuminating like a twist of lightning that admits the eye for an instant into the secret convolutions of a cloud' (pp. 118–19) – but generally Marlow (in a related line of imagery) is afforded no more than a 'glimpse through a rent in the mist in which he [moves] and [has] his being' (p. 128). Throughout the novel Marlow recurs to the idea of his being able to see Jim only through cloud or mist or fog, and it is in this spirit that he concludes his written narrative: 'And that's the end. He passes away under a cloud, inscrutable at heart . . . ' (p. 416).

The hidden fact which Conrad proves to be specifically concerned with in *Lord Jim* is adverted to right at the start of Marlow's oral narrative. Marlow describes how, on arrival of the *Patna* crew, curiosity makes him watch what will be the effect on Jim of 'a full information':

> I waited to see him overwhelmed, confounded, pierced through and through, squirming like an impaled beetle – and I was half afraid to see it too – if you understand what I mean. Nothing more awful than to watch a man who has been found out, not in a crime but in a more than criminal weakness. The commonest sort of fortitude prevents us from becoming criminals in a legal sense; it is from weakness

unknown, but perhaps suspected, as in some parts of the world you suspect a deadly snake in every bush – from weakness that may lie hidden, watched or unwatched, prayed against or manfully scorned, repressed or maybe ignored more than half a lifetime, not one of us is safe. We are snared into doing things for which we get called names, and things for which we get hanged, and yet the spirit may well survive – survive the condemnations, survive the halter, by Jove! And there are things – they look small enough sometimes too – by which some of us are totally and completely undone. I watched the youngster there. I liked his appearance; I knew his appearance; he came from the right place; he was one of us. He stood there for all the parentage of his kind, for men and women by no means clever or amusing, but whose very existence is based upon honest faith, and upon the instinct of courage. I don't mean military courage, or civil courage, or any special kind of courage. I mean just that inborn ability to look temptations straight in the face – a readiness unintellectual enough, goodness knows, but without pose – a power of resistance, don't you see, ungracious if you like, but priceless – an unthinking and blessed stiffness before the outward and inward terrors, before the might of nature, and the seductive corruption of men – backed by a faith invulnerable to the strength of facts, to the contagion of example, to the solicitation of ideas. Hang ideas! They are tramps, vagabonds, knocking at the back-door of your mind, each taking a little of your substance, each carrying away some crumb of that belief in a few simple notions you must cling to if you want to live decently and would like to die easy! (pp. 42–3)

Immediately afterwards Marlow disarmingly adds that 'this has nothing to do with Jim, directly' (p. 43), but actually it enables us to open the box and see what is inside, providing us with a basis for understanding not only Jim's conduct aboard the *Patna* but all his failures. It is true, however, that Marlow generalizes widely from Jim's case, and, playing the human naturalist to Stein with his beetles and butterflies, attempts here to impale no less a specimen than *homo sapiens*. What he attempts to isolate are the forces that serve to undermine or sustain civilized living, the kind of behaviour that enables one 'to live decently' and 'to die easy'. Such a life is 'backed' by a special kind of 'faith', which appears to be equivalent to the 'belief' in the 'few simple notions' to which a decent man must adhere. The notions referred to are presumably coextensive with the 'few very simple ideas . . . notably . . . the idea of Fidelity' that Conrad affirmed the world to rest on in the previously cited passage from the Familiar Preface to *A Personal Record*;[9] but they are also implicitly defined here by what the 'faith' is said to be 'invulnerable' to. It is invulnerable, we realize, precisely to those things which undermine Jim on the *Patna*: the 'strength of facts' represented by the bulging bulkhead, the 'contagion of example' embodied in the cowardly and unprincipled crew, and the 'solicitation of ideas' manifested in his own assessment of unavoidable disaster. And the faith that Jim betrays in succumbing to the varied assault on it is something larger than a conception of duty, of a necessary fidelity; it is a belief in that which makes civilized life possible, in human solidarity, that is, for – as Marlow says later – 'we exist only in so far as we hang together' (p. 223). The faith, that is to say, would seem to be similar to that which helped to save the *Narcissus* when it was battered by the storm; but to be effective, Marlow insists, the faith in something outside the self must also be allied to a power that comes from within the self, to 'the instinct of courage', which he defines as the 'inborn ability to look temptations straight in the face' – the ability, that is, in which Kurtz was so strikingly deficient. In *Lord Jim*, therefore, Conrad may be seen as pursuing a line that leads straight from *The Nigger of the 'Narcissus'* and 'Heart of Darkness', exploring further the failure of the faith which is so dramatically vindicated in *The Nigger* but shown in the subsequent tale to be liable to collapse in the absence of the policeman and the butcher.

If these are the things, then, that sustain civilized life, Marlow seems at first to suggest it is threatened by crime, by 'things for which we get called names, and things for which we get hanged', the more especially since he later maintains that 'the real significance of crime is in its being a breach of faith with the community of mankind' (p. 157). But he actually makes it clear that crime is not really a serious threat both because most people are not criminals, the 'commonest sort of fortitude' preventing us 'from becoming criminals in a legal sense'; and because, even among criminals, 'the spirit may well survive – survive the condemnations, survive the halter, by Jove!' It is not altogether clear what he means by 'the spirit', but since legal crime is contrasted with the 'things' by which 'some of us are totally and completely undone', which make us go to pieces, that is, the spirit that may survive even the halter may be thought of not simply as the soul but as the kind of self-possession that is manifested as human dignity. The threat to civilized life resides in a man's denial of his humanity, and though this may not be technically criminal, it stems from 'a more than criminal weakness'. That Marlow expects to see Jim squirm 'like an impaled beetle' suggests how reductive of human dignity such weakness is, for it is of this weakness that he self-evidently stands condemned.[10]

But it is also from such weakness, the kind of 'unknown' weakness that 'may lie hidden' for 'more than half a lifetime' that 'not one of us is safe'. The weakness, we must therefore conclude, is both innate and universal; and it is with a bold stroke that Conrad in effect asserts that the liability to be despicably less than human is part of the human condition. For Conrad, indeed, such innate weakness may be seen as constituting a non-believer's version of original sin; and it says something for the power of the religion he had abandoned that the manifestation of the weakness should be associated with the presence of 'a deadly snake'.

Given this innate, hidden weakness, a faith in the few simple notions is not sufficient to ensure civilized conduct, as Kurtz has earlier exemplified, though I hope to show the clarification of the nature of such weakness provided in *Lord Jim* – it is the theme of the novel – offers a far more satisfactory explanation of Kurtz's failure than the idea of his inner hollowness. What is required is that the inner weakness be offset by an inner strength, which can then effectively be allied to the faith; and this strength is also innate, for it is an 'inborn ability', though this is more vividly redefined as 'an unthinking and blessed stiffness before the outward and inward terrors'. Of the sexual implications of this formulation I shall have more to say later. Suffice it to note now that the stiffness is 'unthinking', a manifestation of a readiness that is 'unintellectual'. Conrad is quite Lawrencean in his sense of the way in which 'ideas' can consume one from within, for ideas are 'tramps, vagabonds, knocking at the back-door of your mind, each taking a little of your substance' – till one is consumed entirely, we may reflect, bearing in mind the fate of Kurtz, that man of ideas. Many years later, in the Author's Note to *Victory* written in 1920, Conrad even declared he felt 'compelled to say' that 'the habit of profound reflection' is 'the most pernicious of all the habits formed by the civilized man' (pp. x–xi); and indeed *Victory* may be seen as a study of a reflective man's loss of the capacity for action – or, as Lawrence might have put it, of the pernicious effects of the detached mental consciousness.

Though all men are subject to the innate weakness, it is only a privileged few – the elect, we may say – who are possessed of the countervailing innate strength. Yet, paradoxically, it is in only a comparatively few men, like Jim, that the hidden weakness is exposed. Why this should be so is suggested by Marlow's description of the life lived by Jim's family, those 'placid, colourless forms of men and women', who are said to have peopled a 'quiet corner of the world as free of danger or strife as a tomb' and to have breathed 'equably the air of undisturbed rectitude': 'It seems amazing that he should belong to it, he to whom so many things "had come". Nothing ever came to them; they would never be taken unawares, and never be called upon to grapple with fate' (p. 342). Never to be taken unawares is never to be tested, never to have one's hidden weakness suddenly revealed, and one can be protected against oneself, we see, not only by an innate strength but by an undemanding life. Yet such a life, it is intimated, is no better than death, for in its freedom from danger and strife it offers the quiet security of a tomb. The question is complicated however, by the view that the mere desire for a safe life exacerbates the weakness, like the scratching of a sore: the men, like Jim, who are 'attuned to the eternal peace of Eastern sky and sea', and so choose to remain in the East as 'officers of country ships' rather than face the difficulties and hazards of 'the home service', are said to reveal 'in their actions, in their looks, in their persons . . . the soft spot, the place of decay, the determination to lounge safely through existence' (p. 13). The mere fact, therefore, that Jim accepts a position on the *Patna* is a sign of his innate, inner weakness, here notably imaged as a 'soft spot', the 'place of decay' where the rot sets in, the point at which the snake's poison is spread throughout the system. Yet it is because Jim does not look like a man who would want to lounge through existence, because he looks rather, Marlow notes, like 'one of us', like a man, that is, whom one would expect to have both the necessary inner strength and outer faith to enable him to withstand stress, that Marlow becomes more and more interested in him. For Marlow 'the obscure truth' involved in his case seems to be 'momentous enough to affect mankind's conception of itself' (p. 93).

It certainly proves to be enough to affect Captain Brierly's conception of himself. Outwardly Brierly seems to be a refutation of Marlow's notion of the universality of the soft spot, for he appears to be solid and hard all through: 'The sting of life could do no more to his complacent soul than the scratch of a pin to the smooth face of a rock,' and his 'self-satisfaction' presents 'to the world a surface as hard as granite'. He is also said to be a man who has 'never in his life made a mistake, never had an accident, never a mishap, never a check in his steady rise', and he seems to be 'one of those lucky fellows who know nothing of indecision, much less of self-mistrust' (pp. 57–8). Yet he commits suicide shortly after serving as one of the nautical assessors at the *Patna* inquiry, doing so in a way that is anticipatory of Decoud's end in *Nostromo*, for it is assumed he put 'four iron belaying-pins' in his pockets 'to help him down' when he jumps overboard. His mate views his having recourse to the belaying-pins as 'the only sign of fluster he gave in his whole life', an indication that perhaps 'his confidence in himself was just shook a bit at the last' (pp. 61–2); but it is of course the jump itself, which has connections with that of Jim as well as with the death of Decoud, that betrays more than a sign of fluster, for it enacts the ultimate consequence of a complete loss of self-possession – the desire for, and the acceptance of a total loss of self that is suicide. Marlow makes it clear, too, why Brierly suddenly takes his own life:

'You may depend on it, Captain Jones,' said I, 'it wasn't anything that would have disturbed much either of us two,' I said; and then, as if a light had been flashed into the muddle of his brain, poor old Jones found a last word of amazing profundity. He blew his nose, nodding at me dolefully: 'Ay, ay! neither you nor I, sir, had ever thought so much of ourselves.' (p. 65)

What the story of Jim's defection does to Brierly is to force him, for the first time in his life, to recognize the existence of a soft spot in himself; and since his life has hitherto been a superb negation of even the possibility of such weakness – Marlow says earlier that his 'belief in his own splendour . . . almost cheated his life of its legitimate terrors' (p. 64) – the recognition, when it comes, is sufficiently shattering to make him go to pieces. Since the soft spot, the point at which the self may give, is both innate and universal, true self-possession, it is clear, must be based on an acknowledgement of its existence, for this is a prerequisite for coming to terms with it. This is something that Jim is never able to do; and if we are to see Conrad as in fact exploring a single situation in the novel (as he claimed in the letter to Blackwood), it is the repeated, if varied, manifestation of such a spot in Jim.

II

Jim's failure on the *Patna* is prefigured by his behaviour on the training-ship when a coaster crashes into a schooner, and one of the ship's instructors leads some boys to the rescue:

> On the lower deck in the babel of two hundred voices he would forget himself, and beforehand live in his mind the sea-life of light literature. He saw himself saving people from sinking ships, cutting away masts in a hurricane, swimming through a surf with a line; or as a lonely castaway, barefooted and half naked, walking on uncovered reefs in search of shellfish to stave off starvation. He confronted savages on tropical shores, quelled mutinies on the high seas, and in a small boat upon the ocean kept up the hearts of despairing men – always an example of devotion to duty, and as unflinching as a hero in a book.
>
> 'Something's up. Come along.'
>
> He leaped to his feet. The boys were streaming up the ladders. Above could be heard a great scurrying about and shouting, and when he got through the hatchway he stood still – as if confounded.
>
> It was the dusk of a winter's day. The gale had freshened since noon, stopping the traffic on the river and now blew with the strength of a hurricane in fitful bursts that boomed like salvoes of great guns firing over the ocean. The rain slanted in sheets that flicked and subsided, and between whiles Jim had threatening glimpses of the

tumbling tide . . . There was a fierce purpose in the gale, a furious earnestness in the screech of the wind, in the brutal tumult of earth and sky, that seemed directed at him, and made him hold his breath in awe. He stood still. It seemed to him he was whirled around.

He was jostled. 'Man the cutter!' Boys rushed past him. . . . 'Lower away!' He saw the boat, manned, drop swiftly below the rail, and rushed after her. He heard a splash. 'Let go; clear the falls!' He leaned over. The river alongside seethed in frothy streaks. . . .

Jim felt his shoulder gripped firmly. 'Too late, youngster.' The captain of the ship laid a restraining hand on that boy, who seemed on the point of leaping overboard, and Jim looked up with the pain of conscious defeat in his eyes. The captain smiled sympathetically. 'Better luck next time. This will teach you to be smart.' (pp. 6–8)

Jim, we see, from the outset of his career would seem to be a natural candidate for Marlow's élite not only by virtue of his background and training but also the aspirations revealed in his daydreams, which clearly fit him to be 'one of us'. Apart from the sequence in which he figures as 'a lonely castaway', his fantasies all project an heroic readiness to risk his life for others, and in them he is consequently an example not only of 'devotion to duty' but also of the kind of belief in human solidarity that urges him beyond the ordinary call of duty. And since he is quite 'unflinching' in the way in which he meets the dangers to which his dream expose him, he seems also to be possessed of the blessed inner stiffness which is the guarantor of the heroic. But at the same time his daydreams are, ominously, a sign of his tendency to let go, for they are like a waking sleep when he should be braced to his duty: later, when he is chief mate on the *Patna*, we are told that 'the line dividing his meditation from a surreptitious doze on his feet' is 'thinner than a thread in a spider's web' (p. 25). On the lower deck of the training-ship, as he lives adventures 'in his mind', he becomes detached not only from his surroundings but also, as it were, from himself; he 'forgets himself', giving himself up to his dreams and losing himself in them. When the sudden, testing call to action comes, therefore, it takes him unawares, and he responds to it when he comes on deck – by standing still. Remaining still, 'as if confounded', Jim seems to be overwhelmed by a sudden paralysis of the will; and though, with the gale booming 'like salvoes of great guns firing over the ocean', there is sufficient external cause for confusion, the inhibition which makes him 'hold his breath in awe' and mysteriously disables him, appears to come from within. But it is not simply a straightforward question of fear, though fear certainly plays a part, for, when it is all over, we are told 'not a particle of fear' is 'left' in him (p. 8). Since Jim subsequently and repeatedly shows he is not a coward, the source of his failure has to be sought elsewhere. The training-ship episode suggests he is disabled, rather, by the very liveliness of his imagination. His imagination unduly intensifies the danger for him, since, when he comes down to earth after the captain has gripped his shoulder and spoken to him, 'the tumult and the menace of wind and sea' appear 'very contemptible' to him, 'increasing the regret of his awe at their inefficient menace' (p. 8); and it also makes him believe he is particularly threatened, for he feels at first that 'the brutal tumult of earth and sky' is 'directed at him'. Imagination, the omniscient narrator remarks, is 'the enemy of men' – and 'the father of all terrors' (p. 11). But the possession of an overactive imagination is not Jim's hidden weakness, though it is an important factor in revealing it, as is made clear on the *Patna*. The nature of his weakness is intimated, rather, by what he does when he breaks out of his immobility. He 'rushes after' the boat only when the need for action is over, when the boat is already manned and away; and this is followed by an evident readiness for despairing action, since he seems 'on the point of leaping overboard' when the captain lays a restraining hand on him.

In a world of submerged wrecks, Jim's failure on the training-ship, which is of no great consequence in itself, becomes momentous because it presages an inability to meet a sudden test. And though his thoughts continue to be 'full of valorous deeds', and his dreams to constitute for him 'the best parts of life, its secret truth, its hidden reality' (p. 20), the hidden reality is that which he carries within him and foredooms him. After his disgrace on the *Patna* he longs to begin 'with a clean slate', but that makes Marlow 'sad': 'A clean slate, did he say? As if the initial word of each our destiny were not graven in imperishable characters upon the face of a rock' (pp. 185–6). Jim, that is to say, seems predestined – for Conrad is a very Calvinist of non-belief – to fail, to go from the training-ship to the *Patna*, and from it to Patusan.

The passage in which Marlow tries to understand what happened to Jim on the *Patna* is long, but it is of central importance and must be quoted in full:

> You must remember he believed, as any other man would have done in his place, that the ship would go down at any moment; the bulging, rust-eaten plates that kept back the ocean, fatally must give way, all at once like an undermined dam, and let in a sudden and overwhelming flood. He stood still looking at these recumbent bodies, a doomed man aware of his fate, surveying the silent company of the dead. They *were* dead! Nothing could save them! There were boats enough for half of them perhaps, but there was no time. No time! No time! It did not seem worth while to open his lips, to stir hand or foot. Before he could shout three words, or make three steps, he would be floundering in a sea whitened awfully by the desperate

struggles of human beings, clamorous with the distress of cries for help. There was no help. He imagined what would happen perfectly; he went through it all motionless by the hatchway with the lamp in his hand – he went through it to the very last harrowing detail. I think he went through it again while he was telling me these things he could not tell the court.

'I saw as clearly as I see you now that there was nothing I could do. It seemed to take all life out of my limbs. I thought I might just as well stand where I was and wait. I did not think I had many seconds . . .' Suddenly the steam ceased blowing off. The noise, he remarked, had been distracting, but the silence at once became intolerably oppressive.

'I thought I would choke before I got drowned,' he said.

He protested he did not think of saving himself. The only distinct thought formed, vanishing, and reforming in his brain, was: eight hundred people and seven boats; eight hundred people and seven boats.

'Somebody was speaking aloud inside my head,' he said a little wildly. 'Eight hundred people and seven boats – and no time! Just think of it.' He leaned towards me across the little table, and I tried to avoid his stare. 'Do you think I was afraid of death?' he asked in a voice very fierce and low. He brought down his open hand with a bang that made the coffee-cups dance. 'I am ready to swear I was not – I was not . . . . By God – no!' He hitched himself upright and crossed his arms; his chin fell on his breast. . . .

'Some of the crew were sleeping on the number one hatch within reach of my arm,' began Jim again.

You must know they kept Kalashee watch in that ship, all hands sleeping though the night, and only the reliefs of quartermasters and look-out men being called. He was tempted to grip and shake the shoulder of the nearest lascar, but he didn't. Something held his arms down along his sides. He was not afraid – oh no! only he just couldn't – that's all. He was not afraid of death perhaps, but I'll tell you what, he was afraid of the emergency. His confounded imagination had evoked for him all the horrors of panic, the trampling rush, the pitiful screams, boats swamped – all the appalling incidents of a disaster at sea he had ever heard of. He might have been resigned to die but I suspect he wanted to die without added terrors, quietly, in a sort of peaceful trance. A certain readiness to perish is not so very rare, but it is seldom that you meet men whose souls, steeled in the impenetrable armour of resolution, are ready to fight a losing battle to the last, the desire of peace waxes stronger as hope declines, till at last it conquers the very desire of life. Which of us here has not observed this, or maybe experienced something of that feeling in his own person

– this extreme weariness of emotions, the vanity of effort, the yearning for rest? Those striving with unreasonable forces know it well, – the shipwrecked castaways in boats, wanderers lost in a desert, men battling against the unthinking might of nature, or the stupid brutality of crowds. (pp. 86–8)

The immediate link between Jim's response to the emergency on the training-ship and that on the *Patna* is that he is again subject to something like sudden physical paralysis: he 'stands still' looking at the recumbent bodies; he does not think it worth while 'to stir hand or foot'; he goes through it all 'motionless by the hatchway'; he thinks he may just as well 'stand' where he is 'and wait'; his arms seem to be 'held down along his sides'. In the description that follows the quoted passage, there is a repeated insistence on this fact, Jim's actions – until he jumps – falling into a recurrent pattern of sporadic movement and renewed paralysis: he stands 'stock-still by the hatch' for some two minutes until he decides to try to free the life-boats, finds the other white men getting one of the boats off the chocks, is attacked by the chief engineer who mistakes him for a 'nigger', and responds by lifting him up as though he were a child and flinging him away (pp. 89–91); when he is told that the white men have decided to 'clear out', he neither moves nor speaks, seems turned 'into cold stone from the soles of his feet to the nape of his neck', and together with the two Malays at the wheel remains looking on 'in complete immobility' (pp. 91–7), but when the first engineer begs him to come and help free the boat and catches hold of him, he hits him, and then suddenly goes to work trying to cut the life-boats clear, 'slashing as though he had seen nothing, had heard nothing, had known of no one on board' (pp. 99–103); when the men succeed in getting their boat clear, he moves away as far as he can 'get from them – the whole breadth of the ship', and his feet remain 'glued to that remote spot', while he lets 'a tumult of events and sensations' beat around him 'like the sea upon a rock' (pp. 104–8) – until he suddenly moves to make his jump (pp. 109–11).

It would seem likely that the various instances of Jim's immobility are a product of the same fundamental cause, and it is this that is strikingly clarified in the quoted passage. We note, first, that a concomitant of Jim's involuntary paralysis is his sense of the loss of all volition, of the power to determine his own actions: 'something', he says, holds his arms to his sides; and even when he can eventually bring himself to admit to Marlow that he jumped, he clearly feels he was impelled to do so by some force outside himself: 'I told you I jumped; but I tell you they [i.e. the white crew] were too much for any man. It was their doing as plainly as if they had reached up with a boat-hook and pulled me over' (p. 123). At the same time he also experiences a sense of dissociation, of alienation from himself, as if it were not he that is involved in the emergency: 'Somebody was speaking aloud inside my head,' he says 'a little wildly', and he views his jump in analogous terms: ' "I had jumped . . . " He checked himself, averted his gaze. . . . "It seems," he added' (p. 111). Jim's loss of volition and sense of alienation from self dramatize the fact that, at the crucial moment, he is not himself, and this is symbolized by his being taken for the donkey-man (who acted as third engineer) by the men in the life-boat: 'They were abusing me – ' he tells Marlow, 'abusing me . . . by the name of George' (p. 116). At the crucial moment, in short, Jim loses that full possession of himself which is the condition of good service, it being not so much the jump as his initial response to the emergency that manifests this. And he enacts one of the consequences of a loss of self-possession while he relives the experience in talking to Marlow about it:

> He was not speaking to me, he was only speaking before me, in a dispute with an invisible personality, an antagonistic and inseparable partner of his existence – another possessor of his soul. These were issues beyond the competency of a court of inquiry: it was a subtle and momentous quarrel as to the true essence of life, and did not want a judge. He wanted an ally, a helper, an accomplice. I felt the risk I ran of being circumvented, blinded, decoyed, bullied, perhaps, into taking a definite part in a dispute impossible of decision if one had to be fair to all the phantoms in possession – to the reputable that had its claims and to the disreputable that had its exigencies. (p. 93)

It is an iron law in Conrad, as we have already seen in the cases of Willems and Kurtz, that when one loses one's self-possession, one lays oneself open to being possessed. Though I should in general like to keep to the terms of Conrad's art and not attempt to use those which may be drawn from established schools of psychology, the description of the 'possessor of [Jim's] soul' is highly suggestive. Marlow's reference to the 'phantoms in possession' recalls the shadow imagery in 'Heart of Darkness'; and the 'antagonistic and inseparable partner' of Jim's existence that is said to have taken possession of his soul when he lost it may be viewed as strikingly similar in nature to the Jungian shadow. It, of course, is precisely not 'one of us', and functions to subvert the values to which Jim consciously adheres.[11]

The French lieutenant takes a commonsense view of Jim's jump, seeing it as a straightforward manifestation of 'abominable funk' and panic: there is 'a point', he tells Marlow, even 'for the best of us', when 'you let go everything' (p. 146). Though such a view is adequate to the case of the other men who abandon the *Patna*, for we are told that it is a 'turmoil of terror' that has 'scattered their self-control like chaff before the wind' (p. 104) (the simile recalling what happens to principles in 'Heart of Darkness'), it misses the mark with Jim. Jim himself insists that he was not afraid, and the imagery he uses in his account of his response to the captain's attack on him at the life-boats would seem to indicate that it is not fear that is his soft spot: ' "The skipper . . . came at me head down, growling like a wild beast. I flinched no more than a stone. I was as solid standing there as this," he tapped lightly with his knuckles the wall beside his chair' (p. 91). His loss of self-possession is attributable, rather, to the way in which his imagination works. It does not function here to magnify the danger, as it did on the training-ship, for if he believes the ship is about to sink, so would 'any other man . . . in his place'. Nor does it focus the danger on himself, for he protests, and should be believed, that he 'did not think of saving himself'. But it is his imagination which jumps, so to speak, for, confronted with 'the bulging, rust-eaten plates', it transforms a possibility into accomplished fact: Jim not only sees himself as 'a doomed man' but concludes that the pilgrims '[are] dead' and that 'nothing [can] save them'; imagining 'what would happen perfectly', he is certain 'there [is] no help'. His response is strongly contrasted to that of the two Malays who remain throughout at the wheel partly because no order has been given to leave it, but also because they do not 'think' about the situation or try to imagine what may happen (pp. 97–8).

A passage in *Nostromo* serves as a useful gloss on how Jim's imagination paralyses him: it is 'the crushing, paralysing sense of human littleness', we are told there, 'which is what really defeats a man struggling with natural forces . . .' (p. 433); and it is Jim's overwhelming sense of hopelessness that incapacitates him: 'He told me,' says Marlow, 'that his first impulse was to shout and straight away make all those people leap out of sleep into terror; but such an overwhelming sense of his helplessness came over him that he was not able to produce a sound' (p. 85). And afterwards he feels he has been 'tricked into that sort of high-minded resignation which prevented him lifting as much as his little finger' (p. 95). But perhaps the most suggestive comment is that made by Marlow with reference to the hazards of a life at sea, among which he numbers the sort of derelict into which the *Patna* smashes:

> Such wandering corpses are common enough in the North Atlantic, which is haunted by all the terrors of the sea, – fogs, icebergs, dead ships bent upon mischief, and long sinister gales that fasten upon one like a vampire till all the strength and the spirit and even hope are gone, and one feels like the empty shell of a man. (p. 159)

Marlow, we see, turns a gale into a vampire that sucks a man's hope from him, but clearly it is a man's own despair that drains him of hope and leaves him an 'empty shell'. The empty shell once again recalls Kurtz, who is 'hollow at the core', and suggests that it is also hope that he lets go of in his abandon, that his failure is also attributable to the surrender of despair.

This, at all events, is what happens to Jim – his own sense of his paralysis makes that clear: 'I saw,' he says, '. . . that there was nothing I could do. It seemed to take all life out of my limbs.' If it is his hopelessness that paralyses Jim, this is felt as devitalizing, as draining him of life, because it is expressive of his giving up the ghost. As Marlow says, 'the desire of peace waxes stronger as hope declines, till at last it conquers the very desire of life'; and 'the yearning for rest' manifests itself in a letting go that marks the abandonment of struggle. The innate, universal weakness, in short, the soft spot that reveals itself under the pressure of stress, is a despairing desire for death – a desire for rest or inertia.[12] Or it may be regarded as a faintheartedness, of a kind that is dramatized at the end of *The Shadow-Line* as the potential death we all carry with us: the sick Ransome, who has heroically risked himself on the voyage, confesses after it that he is 'in a blue funk' about his heart, and the captain listens to him 'going up the companion stairs cautiously, step by step, in mortal fear of starting into sudden anger our common enemy it was his hard fate to carry consciously within his faithful breast' (p. 133).

Given the inevitable manifestations of Jim's soft spot in the circumstances in which he finds himself aboard the *Patna* – and, given the universality of this weakness, there is no one who could say for certain that he would have responded differently – there is only one thing that could have saved Jim, and this he lamentably lacks: the possession of a soul, 'steeled in the impenetrable armour of resolution', that would have made him 'ready to fight a losing battle to the last'. The steeled soul which would never let go, never give way in despair, is the polar opposite, of course, of the soft spot – and it is also the equivalent of the 'blessed stiffness before the outward and inward terrors' that was previously referred to. If the prevalence of the soft spot is Conrad's version of original sin, then the possession of a steeled soul is his sign of grace, an outward mark of this condition being – as in the system to which it offers a parallel – the refusal of despair. It is, moreover, only the elect who are favoured with such souls, for it is only 'seldom' that one may meet men who have them.[13]

Jim's previously referred to bursts of activity and freezings into immobility may be regarded as a reflection of the tension between opposed desires for life and death, and the temporary dominance of one or the other. His jump, viewed both *sub specie aeternitatis* and through his own retrospective (and defiantly puzzled) gaze, offers a nice instance of the opposition. Jim thinks of his jump as a culminating act of despair – we may choose to regard it, in this respect, as equivalent to his apparent readiness to throw himself overboard on the training-ship – and consciously he certainly has no intention of saving himself, as the following exchange with Marlow indicates:

'Suppose I had not – I mean to say, suppose I had stuck to the ship? Well. How much longer? Say a minute – half a minute. Come. In thirty seconds, as it seemed certain then, I would have been overboard; and do you think I would not have laid hold of the first thing that came in my way – oar, life-buoy, grating – anything? Wouldn't you?'
'And be saved,' I interjected.
'I would have meant to be,' he retorted. 'And that's more than I meant when I' . . . he shivered as if about to swallow some nauseous drug . . . 'jumped,' he pronounced with a convulsive effort . . . (p. 130)

But in fact, of course, Jim jumps not into the sea but into the life-boat, the inglorious victim of his own imperative need to live.[14] As Marlow says, he knows no more 'of the cause' that tears him 'out of his immobility' than 'the uprooted tree knows of the wind that [lays] it low' (p. 109). The tree image not only recalls Singleton in The Nigger of the 'Narcissus', who collapses 'like an uprooted tree' only when he has done his duty, and whose sticking to the wheel accordingly offers an instructive contrast with Jim's jump; but also the black helmsman in 'Heart of Darkness', whose fear sweeps him like a tree swaying in the wind and propels him to death. The comparison, in Jim's case, effectively extends the ambiguities in which his jump is enveloped: he is swept by a force he is unable to deny, a force that blindly asserts the primacy of the individual life; but the uprooted tree is laid low by the wind that sweeps it, and Jim jumps to the kind of saving that is its own destruction.

III

Stein, who arranges for Jim to go to Patusan, forms an obvious bridge between the two parts of the book, between the Patna and Patusan episodes. He is important structurally, therefore, but he does not seem to me to be of much consequence thematically, though a great deal of critical energy and ingenuity has been invested in interpreting his oracular utterance about the destructive element:

'We want in so many different ways to be,' he began again. 'This magnificent butterfly finds a little heap of dirt and sits still on it; but man he will never on his heap of mud keep still. He want to be so, and again he want to be so. . . .' He moved his hand up, then down. . . . 'He wants to be a saint, and he wants to be a devil – and every time he shuts his eyes he sees himself as a very fine fellow – so fine as he can never be. . . . In a dream. . . .' . . .

'And because you not always can keep your eyes shut there comes the real trouble – the heart pain – the world pain. I tell you, my friend, it is not good for you to find you cannot make your dream come true, for the reason that you not strong enough are, or not clever enough. *Ja!* . . . And all the time you are such a fine fellow, too! *Wie? Was? Gott in Himmel!* How can that be? Ha! ha! ha!'

The shadow prowling amongst the graves of butterflies laughed boisterously.

'Yes! Very funny this terrible thing is. A man that is born falls into a dream like a man who falls into the sea. If he tries to climb out into the air as inexperienced people endeavour to do, he drowns – *nicht wahr?* . . . No! I tell you! The way is to the destructive element submit yourself, and with the exertions of your hands and feet in the water make the deep, deep sea keep you up. So if you ask me – how to be?'

His voice leaped up extraordinarily strong, as though away there in the dusk he had been inspired by some whisper of knowledge. 'I will tell you! For that, too, there is only one way.' (pp. 213–14)

The passage about a man's falling into a dream is usually referred to in isolation, but I think we can better understand what Stein is talking about if we relate it to its context of the butterfly sitting still on its heap of dirt. The 'magnificent butterfly' exemplifies an acceptance of gross materiality that man – so Stein asserts – is incapable of achieving, for he 'will never on his heap of mud keep still', but tries to move away from it, whether upwards or downwards (as Stein moves his hands). Man tries, in short, to transcend his condition by aiming to be what he is not, a saint or a devil. Such an aspiration is, for Stein, the mark of the romantic – after hearing Marlow's account of Jim, he declares that 'he is romantic' (p. 212) – though the term 'romantic' seems virtually to be synonymous with 'human', for it is 'man' who denies the base reality of mud and tries to live according to his dream-image of himself as saint or devil. But, it should be noted, the maintenance of the dream-image, according to which man can see himself 'as a very fine fellow' (or, presumably, as suitably satanic), is dependent on his keeping his eyes shut. It is when man's eyes are opened to the discrepancy between his dream and the reality that he suffers; and, since such an awakening or awareness would appear to be an inevitable development for all men, it is the cause of *Weltschmerz*.

It is this view of the human condition, I take it, that is reflected in

Stein's elaborate sea metaphor. The fall 'into the sea', to which a fall 'into a dream' is compared, is what happens to every man, for it is the fall of 'a man that is born', and so may be thought of as equivalent to man's movement from his heap of mud. The fall into the sea, that is, is romantic man's inevitable movement from *terra firma* into the fluidity of his dream-image.[15] But once one has fallen into the sea, Stein insists, one's best bet is to stay there, for if one succumbs to a panic-stricken effort 'to climb out' of the water, one is more than likely to drown – just as, he implies, a romantic man's attempt to bring himself forcibly back to earth would be to court disaster. But if staying in the sea means submitting to 'the destructive element', it is by way of swimming in it, by making it keep one up through one's own 'exertions'; similarly, the only option open to romantic man is to try to gain support for his dream-image by playing the dream for all it is worth.

Read in this way, the passage has a clear application to Jim: what Stein does in making it possible for Jim to go to the remote and dangerous Patusan is give him an opportunity to live up to his dream-image of himself as a hero. If this is so, however, I think it should be said that Stein's sea is productive of a number of red herrings. Though placed for maximum emphasis at the centre of the novel, and delivered with apparent profundity, Stein's pronouncement should not be given undue weight, for it suggests a misleading view of Jim's case: Jim's trouble, we should be sufficiently aware by the time Marlow goes to see Stein, is not so much a lack of opportunity to lead an heroic life and so live up to his own dream-image as the hidden weakness which will ineluctably subvert any such attempt. Moreover, Stein must be thought of not so much as giving Jim a chance as sending him to his doom, for – if Stein's unmediated transition from one metaphor to another may be taken as a sanction for mixing them – it is precisely a man's submission to the destructive element that leads to the opening of his eyes, 'because you not always can keep your eyes shut', and so to 'real trouble'. Which is what happens to Jim in Patusan. But since Stein would seem to believe this is anyway bound to happen to every man, he may more charitably be viewed as presenting Jim with a better option than any apparently available to him at the time. And Stein's conception of the heap of mud on which man refuses to remain, if not that of the destructive element, does help – as we shall see – to clarify what happens to Jim when he encounters Brown in Patusan.

It would seem that Conrad imagined Patusan as another heart of darkness. Marlow tells us that Jim, at the end of his visit to him, accompanied him on the first stage of his journey back to 'the world he had renounced, and the way at times seemed to lead through the very heart of untouched wilderness' (p. 331). Patusan is situated 'three hundred miles beyond the end of telegraph cables and mail-boat lines' (p. 282); and it is cut off from the world by 'thirty miles of forest': 'The stream of civilisation, as if divided on a headland a hundred miles north of Patusan, branches east and south-east, leaving its plains and valleys, its old trees and its old mankind, neglected and isolated, such as an insignificant and crumbling islet between the two branches of a mighty, devouring stream' (p. 226). But this section of the novel sometimes gives the impression of being an uninspired repetition of 'Heart of Darkness' rather than an imaginative recreation of some of its materials. There are echoes not only of the characteristic imagery of the earlier work but of its ironies as well: Marlow says, for instance, that there are few places 'in the Archipelago' Stein has not seen 'in the original dusk of their being, before light (and even electric light) had been carried into them for the sake of better morality and – and – well – the greater profit, too' (p. 219), his evident embarrassment at coming out with the reference to profit stemming, perhaps, from his consciousness of repeating himself.

The repetition of the setting also suggests, however, that Jim, who ventures alone into the darkness, has affinities with Kurtz. It is here that there are indications of Conrad's attempting a reworking of the earlier situation, for Jim is also Kurtz's antithesis and succeeds precisely where Kurtz fails, though Conrad does not seem to be able to bring to the description of such success the imaginative vigour that informed his account of the failure.[16] Unlike Kurtz, Jim succeeds in establishing a 'social fabric of orderly, peaceful life, when every man [is] sure of tomorrow' (p. 373). Unlike Kurtz, that is, Jim is a match for the darkness, the very phrase with which Marlow registers his survival recalling Kurtz's capitulation to it: 'And the shadows were very real around us, but Jim by my side looked very stalwart, as though nothing – not even the occult power of moonlight – could rob him of his reality in my eyes. Perhaps, indeed, nothing could touch him since he had survived the assault of the dark powers' (p. 246). And unlike Kurtz, Jim, though similarly a representative of a race that has 'emerged from the gloom' and consequently regarded as a god-like figure by the benighted, successfully resists the temptations of his elevation: 'And there I was with him,' says Marlow, 'high in the sunshine on the top of that historic hill of his. He dominated the forest, the secular gloom, the old mankind. He was like a figure set up on a pedestal, to represent in his persistent youth the power, and perhaps the virtues, of races that never grow old, that have emerged from the gloom' (p. 265). In part Jim is able to succeed where Kurtz fails because, while Kurtz lets go, he manages to hang on – 'Peaceful here, eh?' he asks Marlow, and adds: 'Look at these houses; there's not one where I am not trusted. Jove! I told you I would hang on' (p. 246) – and indeed Marlow reflects that he has never seen Jim 'look so grave, so self-possessed, in an impenetrable, impressive way' (p. 229). But his success is also due to the fact that the challenges he is called on to face in Patusan are not of a kind to bring out or expose his hidden weakness – not until Brown appears on the scene, that is to say. Brown at once seems to see through Jim. 'I could see directly I set my eyes on him what sort of a fool he was,' he tells Marlow. 'He a man! Hell! He was a hollow sham' (p. 344). The image Brown uses is an unilluminating throwback to the less profound psychology of 'Heart of Darkness', but it decisively indicates the extent to which Conrad's treatment of Jim is a further exploration of the same subject. Keeping to the terms established in *Lord Jim*, we may perhaps say that the moment Brown meets Jim he sniffs the smell of decay that emanates from his soft spot.

That the story of Brown's encounter with Jim is told in Marlow's final written narrative means that this section of the novel is isolated from the main narrative in much the same way as the opening omniscient narrative which tells the story of the *Patna*'s collision with the submerged wreck. The structural device effectively highlights the Patna and Brown episodes, and also juxtaposes them. And indeed, when Brown and Jim first meet, Brown time and again inadvertently forces Jim to recall the *Patna* and the personal disgrace which he has come to believe he has at last lived down in his success in Patusan:

'Who are you?' asked Jim at last, speaking in his usual voice. 'My name's Brown,' answered the other, loudly; 'Captain Brown. What's yours?' and Jim after a little pause went on quietly, as if he had not heard: 'What made you come here?' 'You want to know,' said Brown, bitterly. 'It's easy to tell. Hunger. And what made you?'

'The fellow started at this,' said Brown, relating to me the opening of this strange conversation between those two men, separated only by the muddy bed of a creek, but standing on the opposite poles of that conception of life which includes all mankind. . . .

'All we wanted from him was to come on in the devil's name and have it out. "God d-n it," said I, while he stood there as still as a wooden post, "you don't want to come out here every day with your glasses to count how many of us are left on our feet. Come. Either bring your infernal crowd along or let us go out and starve in the open sea, by God! . . .

"What do you know more of me than I know of you? I came here for food. D'ye hear? – food to fill our bellies. And what did *you* come for? What did you ask for when you came here? We didn't ask you for anything but to give us a fight or a clear road to go back whence we came. . . ." "I would fight with you now," says he, pulling at his little moustache. "And I would let you shoot me, and welcome," I said. "This is as good a jumping-off place for me as another. I am sick

99

of my infernal luck. But it would be too easy. There are my men in the same boat – and, by God, I am not the sort to jump out of trouble and leave them in a d-d lurch," I said. . . .' (pp. 380–83)

. . . When he asked Jim, with a sort of brusque despairing frankness, whether he himself – straight now – didn't understand that when 'it came to saving one's life in the dark, one didn't care who else went – three, thirty, three hundred people' – it was as if a demon had been whispering advice in his ear. 'I made him wince,' boasted Brown to me. 'He very soon left off coming the righteous over me. He just stood there with nothing to say, and looking as black as thunder – not at me – on the ground.' He asked Jim whether he had nothing fishy in his life to remember that he was so damnedly hard upon a man trying to get out of a deadly hole by the first means that came to hand – and so on, and so on. And there ran through the rough talk a vein of subtle reference to their common blood, an assumption of common experience; a sickening suggestion of common guilt, of secret knowledge that was like a bond of their minds and of their hearts. (pp. 386–7)

What Brown's incursion into Patusan does is to force Jim from his pedestal and bring him down to the muddy creek at which they meet. Brown brings Jim down to earth, that is, down to Stein's 'heap of mud', from which he has tried to ascend as hero-god to the people of Patusan. The enforced descent has a number of consequences. First, the jolt ensures that Jim can no longer keep his eyes shut and so maintain himself in his dream. The overt indication that Jim's eyes have at last been opened is his failure to meet Brown's eyes when he, with demonic inspiration, talks of what is likely to happen when it comes 'to saving one's life in the dark': Brown notes how he 'winces' and stands 'with nothing to say . . . looking as black as thunder – not at me – on the ground'. That the cap fits is suggested by Jim's readiness to wear it. Jim, in other words, who strenuously resisted such a view of his conduct in the long talks he has with Marlow during the inquiry and after, who insisted that he had not tried to save himself, here seems tacitly to admit that that is what his behaviour on the *Patna* amounts to after all. The totally unexpected irruption of the past is too forcible to be withstood; and indeed its sudden springing to life when he had thought it decently buried seems to fill Jim with the same kind of paralysing and devitalizing despair to which he succumbed on the *Patna*: when Brown asks him what made him come to Patusan, and so first recalls the *Patna*, Jim stands 'as still as a wooden post'.

Second, Jim's descent to earth deprives him of the afflatus to deal effectively with Brown. When he puts his opening question to him, it is, he would appear to believe, from an impregnable position of moral superiority that he will be able to treat with the renegade. Accordingly, when Brown asks him his name, he does not even bother to reply, indicating the extent to which he disdains to be held accountable by such a man, even in as little as a name. But under Brown's remorseless probing, his position collapses, and he soon leaves off 'coming the righteous' over him, as Brown says. Jim's failure with Brown is often ascribed to a paralysing identification with him,[17] but it seems to me that Brown's insinuation of their 'common guilt' and of there being 'a bond' between them forces Jim not so much to an identification as to a recognition that the disreputable outlaw is in fact a better man than he morally, for he roundly asserts he would not do what Jim has done: he would not 'jump out of trouble' and leave his men in the lurch. Jim is morally disarmed by the consciousness of his own muddy past, and his consequent feeling of defencelessness proves inhibiting, since though he knows well enough what he should do – he demands that Brown and his men should surrender their arms if he decides to let them go unmolested – he does not have the strength to insist on this when Brown refuses, saying, 'as if speaking to himself, "I don't know whether I have the power" ' (p. 388). It is the moral, not the physical, force that he lacks, even though Brown misinterprets his words; and his giving way on this point marks the beginning of the rot. Jim now, ironically, puts his trust in a man who is manifestly not 'one of us', and Brown conforms to type in his treacherous attack on Dain and his men. It is when Jim is sure he is well and honourably rid of Brown that the news is brought him, suddenly confronting him with disaster – like the submerged derelict into which the *Patna* runs, and with an impact as devastating, for it shatters his position in Patusan, just as a man's world seems to fail him, we were told, when his ship fails. Though the *Patna* and the Brown episodes are so dissimilar, they may nevertheless be seen as analogues; and the connection between the two parts of the novel (for Jim's encounter with Brown is the crux of the Patusan section) is revealed in their linked enclosure in a universe of hidden wrecks – and in their common disclosure of Jim's soft spot.

It takes some time for Jim to grasp the full implications of the news that Tamb' Itam brings:

> Then Jim understood. He had retreated from one world, for a small matter of an impulsive jump, and now the other, the work of his own hands, had fallen in ruins upon his head. It was not safe for his servant to go out amongst his own people! I believe that in that very moment he had decided to defy the disaster in the only way it occurred to him such a disaster could be defied; but all I know is that, without a word, he came out of his room and sat before the long table, at the head of which he was accustomed to regulate the affairs

of his world, proclaiming daily the truth that surely lived in his heart. The dark powers should not rob him twice of his peace. He sat like a stone figure. Tamb' Itam, deferential, hinted at preparations for defence. The girl he loved came in and spoke to him, but he made a sign with his hand, and she was awed by the dumb appeal for silence in it. She went out on the verandah and sat on the threshold, as if to guard him with her body from dangers outside.

What thoughts passed through his head – what memories? Who can tell? Everything was gone, and he who had been once unfaithful to his trust had lost again all men's confidence. . . . Later, towards the evening, he came to the door and called for Tamb' Itam. 'Well?' he asked. 'There is much weeping. Much anger, too,' said Tamb' Itam. Jim looked up at him. 'You know,' he murmured. 'Yes, Tuan,' said Tamb' Itam. 'Thy servant does know, and the gates are closed. We shall have to fight.' 'Fight! What for?' he asked. 'For our lives.' 'I have no life,' he said. Tamb' Itam heard a cry from the girl at the door. 'Who knows?' said Tamb' Itam. 'By audacity and cunning we may even escape. There is much fear in men's hearts, too.' He went out, thinking vaguely of boats and of open sea, leaving Jim and the girl together.

I haven't the heart to set down here such glimpses as she had given me of the hour or more she has passed in there wrestling with him for the possession of her happiness. Whether he had any hope – what he expected, what he imagined – it is impossible to say. He was inflexible, and with the growing loneliness of his obstinacy his spirit seemed to rise above the ruins of his existence. She cried 'Fight!' into his ear. She could not understand. There was nothing to fight for. He was going to prove his power in another way and conquer the fatal destiny itself. . . . (pp. 408–10)

Both Tamb' Itam and Jewel are convinced that, in the circumstances in which Jim finds himself, there are only two alternatives open to him: he must fight or try to escape; and these options, we see, duplicate the choice between hanging on and jumping that confronted him on the *Patna*. It is clear that Jim does not think of jumping this time. In 'retreat from one world', Jim has in more than one sense come to the end of the world, and there is now nowhere for him to go. But he also never considers fighting either, never entertains the possibility of refusing, as a man with a steeled soul would do, to give way, to let go in surrender, even though accepting responsibility for what has happened. Instead of making ready to fight even a losing battle to the last, he once again concludes that his position is hopeless, deciding that his world has 'fallen in ruins upon his head', and that 'everything [is] gone'. What he longs for, accordingly, is peace and cessation from struggle; and granting Jim his view of his jump from the *Patna* as a jump into death, Marlow sees an analogy between his position then and now: 'the dark powers', he imagines him thinking, 'should not rob him twice of his peace'. Once again, that is, his soft spot manifests itself in a despair that both paralyses him and drains him of the desire for life: 'I have no life,' he says, and wonders that Tamb' Itam and Jewel cannot understand that there is 'nothing to fight for'. As he sits and broods about the one course of action that he considers is left him, for he has previously declared to Doramin that he is 'ready to answer with his life for any harm that should come to [the people of Patusan] if the white men with beards were allowed to retire' (p. 392), he sits 'like a stone figure' – his posture signifying his immobilizing wish for a final fixity, his abandonment of himself to death, rather than his summoning of self for a vital affirmation of principle. It is in vain, therefore, that Jewel wrestles with him 'for the possession of her happiness'; possessed by his own despair, Jim is in no position to bestow what she craves, and is indeed readying himself to desert her, as he once deserted others who depended on him. She later tells Marlow that he was 'driven away from her by a dream', and he reflects that there seems to be 'no forgiveness for such a transgression' (p. 349).

If Jim is presented as 'inflexible', therefore, bent on 'defying the disaster' and on 'proving his power in another way' by 'conquering the fatal destiny itself', this should not be found puzzling, for his inflexibility is the unliving hardness of stone. And if, having announced that he has come 'ready and unarmed', he stands 'stiffened and with bared head' as he waits for Doramin to shoot him (pp. 415–16), it is not the blessed stiffness that he exemplifies. It is doubtless true that Jim views his unarmed readiness to accept the consequences of his mistake with Brown as heroic conduct, as a final affirmation of the code of behaviour he has previously failed to live up to, and this would account for his 'proud and unflinching glance' (p. 416) as he dies; but we must not forget that he has disarmed himself, and Marlow in the end ironically qualifies such a view by thinking of him as having gone away 'from a living woman to celebrate his pitiless wedding with a shadowy ideal of conduct' (p. 416). We remember, too, that Marlow has earlier wondered who could tell 'what flattering view' Brierly had 'induced himself to take of his own suicide' (p. 64) – and the same might appropriately be asked of Jim.[18] 'Suicide,' as Marlow remarks elsewhere, 'is very often the outcome of mere mental weariness – not an act of savage energy but the final symptom of complete collapse.'[19]

B. *'Typhoon'*

CONRAD originally conceived of 'Typhoon' as a short story to be called 'Equitable Division',[1] which suggests he initially thought of the crux of the tale as Captain MacWhirr's solution to the problem posed by the money that Jukes and his men wrest from the fighting Chinese passengers. In the finished work, however, the division of the money figures merely as a neat culmination of an action of altogether different dimensions; and the tale affords yet another instance of how Conrad was able to transform a casual anecdote recollected fortuitously into the stuff of his own pre-occupations.[2] What his imagination actually seized on was the fact of the typhoon and the ordeal of the men who have to confront it. 'Typhoon', that is to say, has its obvious place in the line of work that begins with *The Nigger of the 'Narcissus'*, and indeed its magnificently achieved storm scenes make it in that respect a fitting companion-piece to it. But its immediate affinities are with *Lord Jim*. Completed (in January 1901) some six months after *Lord Jim*, 'Typhoon' is perhaps best thought of as a reworking of Jim's story. No more than an appendix to the larger and more ambitious work, it nonetheless serves as a balance to it by offering a less starkly pessimistic view of the effects of the innate and ubiquitous 'soft spot'. It also concludes what Conrad has to say on this subject, and so brings to an end the first phase of his major work, a phase primarily concerned with the question of physical self-possession. By the time he reached this point, Conrad – who had his living to earn – found himself ruefully reflecting that he had perhaps been too exhaustive in his explora-tion of the theme that had chosen him: in the Author's Note to *Nostromo* he confessed to having been caused 'some concern' when, 'after finishing the last story of the "Typhoon" volume it seemed somehow that there was nothing more in the world to write about' (p. xv).

We are first alerted to a possible connection between 'Typhoon' and *Lord Jim* by the analogies of situation that suggest themselves. The eight hundred pilgrims who are packed into the *Patna* are matched, in 'Typhoon', by the 'two hundred Chinese coolies returning to their village homes . . . after a few years of work in various tropical colonies' (p. 6) who are stowed in the *Nan-Shan*. Just as the question that is posed for the white crew of the *Patna* when it runs into the derelict is whether the pilgrims should be left to sink with the ship, so at the height of the typhoon which strikes the *Nan-Shan* it is whether the Chinese should similarly be abandoned to their fate and left, in Captain MacWhirr's words, to batter themselves to pieces (p. 88), fighting for the money that has been thrown out of their chests in the storm. Whereas the captain of the *Patna* has no hesitation in ignoring his responsibility to the pilgrims, it is indicative of the difference in mood of 'Typhoon' that Captain MacWhirr, though he thinks of the Chinese only as 'coolies' and cannot even understand to whom Jukes is referring when he talks about their 'passengers' (p. 31), has no doubt of the necessity 'to do what's fair' (p. 82) and sends his mate to establish order among them.

Second, on the day the *Nan-Shan* runs into the typhoon, 'the morning [is] fine' and 'there [is] no wind' (p. 6). The affliction that awaits the ship – it is first pointed to by a sudden and ominous fall of the barometer – may thus be said to come on it out of the blue, to be analogous to the hidden menace that lies in the path of the *Patna*. Accordingly, the crew of the *Nan-Shan*, like that of the *Patna*, are subjected to a sudden and unexpected test.

In 'Typhoon' the significance of the Conradian test is expanded. Though Captain MacWhirr is an old and experienced sailor, he – like Jim when he joins the *Patna* – has previously never really been tested:

> The sea . . . had never put itself out to startle the silent man, who seldom looked up, and wandered innocently over the waters with the only visible purpose of getting food, raiment, and house-room for three people ashore. Dirty weather he had known, of course. . . . But he had never been given a glimpse of immeasurable strength and of immoderate wrath, the wrath that passes exhausted but never appeased – the wrath and fury of the passionate sea . . . . Captain MacWhirr had sailed over the surface of the oceans as some men go skimming over the years of existence to sink gently into a placid grave, ignorant of life to the last, without ever having been made to see all it may contain of perfidy, of violence, and of terror. There are on sea and land such men thus fortunate – or thus disdained by destiny or by the sea. (pp. 18–19)

What Conrad implies now is that the test, when it comes, does not only reveal what is normally hidden in a man, his inner strength or weakness, but also exposes hitherto unrealized dimensions of the universe in which he lives, the 'immeasurable strength and immoderate wrath' of the sea, for instance. The test may also be thought of as functioning in a way that is analogous to that art to which Conrad dedicated himself in the preface to *The Nigger of the 'Narcissus'*, for those that are subjected to it are finally 'made to see' what life contains and are 'given a glimpse' of its inmost truth. The knitting machine that knits men in and knits men out, we perceive, is not without its own artifices – and ultimately it does not 'disdain' Captain MacWhirr. The 'innocence' with which he is said to have wandered for a lifetime 'over the waters' may be a mark of the straightforward honesty of purpose he has brought to his profession, but, like that of a babe, it is also a sign of an unlived life. In life, as in art, it is the depths that count, and Captain MacWhirr's sailing 'over the surface of the oceans' has been a superficial skimming of existence, a life to all intents lived with more than one foot in the 'placid grave' that awaits those who remain 'ignorant of life to the last'. Disdained for so long, he is favoured by the typhoon that opens his eyes, experiencing a Conradian version of the fortunate fall.

In their initial untested innocence Captain MacWhirr and Jim are thus alike, but in most other important respects they are polar opposites. The captain, notably, is totally unimaginative. The sudden fall of the ship's barometer on the day of the typhoon is 'of a nature ominously prophetic', but since he is capable of responding only to achieved fact, omens are 'as nothing to him', and he is 'unable to discover the message of a prophecy till the fulfilment [has] brought it home to his very door' (p. 6). Far from filling his mind with daydreams of a reconstituted past or calamitous future, MacWhirr lives in an eternal present, for 'to his mind' the past is simply 'done with' and the future 'not there yet' (p. 9). He is also literal-minded to a degree that makes him appear positively stupid – to the end Jukes remains unshaken in his conviction that his captain is 'a stupid man' (the last words of the tale) – but though his refusal to countenance 'the use of images in speech' makes conversation with him a trial, the exchanges between him and Jukes on such subjects as the Siamese flag or the weather (pp. 10–11, 25) are marked by a welcome if unwonted humour on the part of the novelist.

It is, however, in his refusal to adopt a 'storm strategy' that Captain MacWhirr is most strikingly differentiated from Jim:

'If the weather delays me – very well. There's your log-book to talk straight about the weather. But suppose I went swinging off my course and came in two days late, and they asked me: "Where have you been all that time, Captain?" What could I say to that? "Went around to dodge the bad weather," I would say. "It must've been dam' bad," they would say. "Don't know," I would have to say; "I've dodged clear of it." See that, Jukes? I have been thinking it all out this afternoon.'

He looked up again in his unseeing, unimaginative way. No one had ever heard him say so much at one time. Jukes, with is arms open in the doorway, was like a man invited to behold a miracle. Unbounded wonder was the intellectual meaning of his eye, while incredulity was seated in his whole countenance.

'A gale is a gale, Mr. Jukes,' resumed the Captain, 'and a full-powered steamship has got to face it. There's just so much dirty weather knocking about the world, and the proper thing is to go through it with none of what old Captain Wilson of the *Melita* calls "storm strategy". . . .' (p. 34)

Captain MacWhirr's refusal 'to dodge the bad weather', we see, is the precise opposite of Jim's jump from the *Patna*: faced by an unrealized menace, he insists on carrying on as usual, whereas Jim, as it were, is swept off his feet by it. Where the captain's imaginative dealings with the future are confined to the vivid assertion that 'a gale is a gale', Jim's expansively convert a bulging bulkhead into an accomplished disaster. If *Lord Jim*, however, makes us aware of the defects of an overactive imagination, 'Typhoon' makes us realize the limitations of a lack of the same faculty, and in a context more damaging than that of a ridiculous personal stolidity: Captain MacWhirr's decision to meet the typhoon head-on must be adjudged rash to the point of irresponsibility since it nearly results in the ship's destruction. At the same time, for the novelist's presentation of MacWhirr has its niceties, the very lack of imagination which accounts for his decision not to dodge the storm is seen as the source of his self-possession: 'Having just enough imagination to carry him through each successive day, and no more, he [is] tranquilly sure of himself' (p. 4); and if his 'physiognomy', which is 'the exact counterpart of his mind', is said to be 'simply ordinary' and 'irresponsive', it is also 'unruffled' (p. 3). The captain remains sure of himself and unruffled throughout the time the *Nan-Shan* is battered by the typhoon, demonstrating the kind of 'unthinking and blessed stiffness before the outward and inward terrors' that Jim so notably lacked on the *Patna*, and showing in relation to the ship, passengers and crew under his care a sense of 'the proper thing' to do that exemplifies Marlow's concept of what it means to live up to 'a fixed standard of conduct'. In the upshot, MacWhirr's literal-mindedness, stupidity, even rashness do not appear to be an exorbitant price for the boon of such self-possession.

If the captain is regarded as the protagonist of 'Typhoon', then the tale would seem to stand in a relation of simple reversal to *Lord Jim*. This is how it is often viewed, Bernard C. Meyer, for instance, describing it as 'an antidote to the novel': 'It is as if in telling a story of quiet heroism and undeviating devotion to duty [Conrad] was seeking to cleanse his mouth of the bad taste left there by Jim's neurotic suffering and erratic behaviour.'[3] But I would argue that Conrad is as much concerned with Jukes as MacWhirr; and since Jukes is a potential Jim, a man who would indubitably have gone the way of Jim were it not for the grace of his captain, the tale is more a complement than an antidote to the novel. To assert, moreover, that 'Typhoon' is not concerned with 'a man's dark

traffic with himself'[4] or with 'the shadowy places of human nature'[5] is
to turn Jukes into a far more self-effacing character than he is shown to be.

That Jukes's story should be regarded as a re-enactment of Jim's is
suggested by the terms in which the test he is called on to face is presented.
Jukes is said to be 'as ready a man' as any other young mate, and though
'somewhat taken aback by the startling viciousness of the first squall', he
at once '[pulls] himself together' (p. 39). But then 'the real thing'
comes:

> It was something formidable and swift, like the sudden smashing
> of a vial of wrath. It seemed to explode all round the ship with an
> overpowering concussion and a rush of great waters, as if an immense
> dam had been blown up to windward. In an instant the men lost
> touch of each other. This is the disintegrating power of a great wind:
> it isolates one from one's kind. An earthquake, a landslip, an
> avalanche, overtake a man incidentally, as it were – without passion.
> A furious gale attacks him like a personal enemy, tries to grasp his
> limbs, fastens upon his mind, seeks to rout his very spirit out of him.
> Jukes was driven away from his commander. . . . (pp. 40–41)

In separating one man from another, the 'disintegrating power' of the
wind is clearly not so much that it physically isolates the individual as
that it tempts him to 'lose touch' spiritually with his kind. The additional
threat to the *Nan-Shan* that the typhoon brings with it is that the sense
of solidarity of those aboard be disintegrated – just as that of the white
crew of the *Patna* was undermined by the anticipated engulfment of the
sea. Furthermore, the typhoon 'seeks to rout [a man's] very spirit out of
him', seeks, we may say when we recall Jim's experience on the *Patna*, to
reduce a man to a condition in which he is despairingly ready to give up
the ghost. And indeed the first onslaught at once weakens Jukes's 'faith
in himself' (p. 42), suggesting that it is this faith rather than that in a
fixed standard of conduct which is the crucial issue.

As the storm increases in intensity, Jukes becomes convinced there is
'nothing to be done':

> If the steering-gear did not give way, if the immense volumes of
> water did not burst the deck in or smash one of the hatches, if the
> engines did not give up, if way could be kept on the ship against this
> terrific wind, and she did not bury herself in one of these awful seas,
> of whose white crests alone, topping high above her bows, he could
> now and then get a sickening glimpse – then there was a chance of her
> coming out of it. Something within him seemed to turn over, bringing
> uppermost the feeling that the *Nan-Shan* was lost.
> 'She's done for,' he said to himself, with a surprising mental

agitation, as though he had discovered an unexpected meaning in this thought. One of these things was bound to happen. Nothing could be prevented now, and nothing could be remedied. The men on board did not count, and the ship could not last. This weather was too impossible. (p. 45)

In his capacity for inconsolable imaginings Jukes is a very Jim, and like Jim on the *Patna*, he lives the various possibilities of disaster that seem to threaten the ship. His imagination of catastrophe is so intense that, like Jim again, he converts possibility into certainty, for he decides that one of the conceivable calamities is 'bound to happen', and so concludes hopelessly that the ship is 'done for'. His sense of hopelessness characteristically expresses itself in his succumbing to the resignation of despair, a condition which enables him to absolve himself from acting, for he also concludes that nothing can be either 'prevented' or 'remedied'. Believing similarly that no one on board 'counts', he feels absolved too from a sense of responsibility for the crew and passengers. Jukes, that is to say, would seem to be as little equal to the test that has come upon him as Jim, but unlike Jim he has Captain MacWhirr to fall back on. When he feels the captain's arm 'thrown heavily over his shoulders', he clasps him, and the two men stand 'bracing each other against the wind' (p. 45). For Jukes, at least, this is also a bracing into vital being, for when the captain removes his arm and he is left unsupported, a threatened spiritual collapse is pointed to by his readiness to let go physically: he begins to 'let himself go limp all over' and to 'sink slowly into the depths of bodily misery' (p. 48).

Jukes is in this condition when the boatswain manages to make his way to the captain and informs him that 'all them Chinamen in the fore tween-deck have fetched away':

Jukes remained indifferent, as if rendered irresponsible by the force of the hurricane, which made the very thought of action utterly vain. Besides, being very young, he had found the occupation of keeping his heart completely steeled against the worst so engrossing that he had come to feel an overpowering dislike towards any other form of activity whatever. He was not scared; he knew this because, firmly believing he would never see another sunrise, he remained calm in that belief.

These are the moments of do-nothing heroics to which even good men surrender at times. Many officers of ships can no doubt recall a case in their experience when just such a trance of confounded stoicism would come all at once over a whole ship's company. Jukes, however, had no wide experience of men or storms. He conceived himself to be calm – inexorably calm; but as a matter of fact he was daunted; not abjectly, but only so far as a decent man may, without becoming loathsome to himself.

It was rather like a forced-on numbness of spirit. The long, long stress of a gale does it; the suspense of the interminably culminating catastrophe; and there is a bodily fatigue in the mere holding on to existence within the excessive tumult; a searching and insidious fatigue that penetrates deep into a man's breast to cast down and sadden his heart, which is incorrigible, and of all the gifts of the earth – even before life itself – aspires to peace. . . .

The spell of the storm had fallen upon Jukes. He was penetrated by it, absorbed by it; he was rooted in it with a rigour of dumb attention. . . . (pp. 51–2, 53)

'Rooted' in the storm, Jukes, we realize (again recalling Jim), has fallen under a spell which immobilizes him, leaving him physically paralysed.[6] But it is a spell that is worked from within, not without, for his paralysis is the outer expression of his inner 'numbness of spirit', of the 'trance of confounded stoicism' to which he has 'surrendered'. Consequently finding 'the very thought of action utterly vain', Jukes remains irresponsibly 'indifferent' to the plight of the Chinese passengers, being spiritually ready, that is, to abandon them in their need. It is an 'insidious fatigue' that has worn down this generally responsible officer, a fatigue that stems from the effort of 'holding on' to life in the storm and so breeds an insidious desire to let go. As in *The Nigger of the 'Narcissus'*, the need to hang on is set against the desire to let go; but with the writing of *Lord Jim* behind him, Conrad knows exactly what the desire to let go portends. It is a desire for cessation of struggle, a corrupt 'craving for peace' (p. 53), a readiness to lose the self in death, for peace is put 'even before life itself'. The desire, in short, is a manifestation of man's hidden weakness, of what in *Lord Jim* is referred to as his 'soft spot', or of what in *The Shadow-Line* is symbolized as faintheartedness.

In *Lord Jim*, it will be recalled, it is suggested that, in the last resort, a man can counter the effect of his inner weakness only by the force of his own inner strength, of a blessed stiffness of being – or, to use an image in the passage quoted above, of a 'steeled heart'. In 'Typhoon' Conrad envisages a further possibility. Craving only for peace and rooted in the storm though he is, Jukes, when the captain repeatedly shouts his name, feels 'he [has] to answer that voice that [will] not be silenced'. What that invincible voice insists on is that they 'ought to see . . . what's the matter' with the Chinese (pp. 53–4), that Jukes should 'go down below – to see' (p. 59); and 'all at once' Jukes understands he will 'have to go' (p. 60). Jukes's triumphing desire to let go, in other words, is countered by something outside himself, by the compulsion of his captain's indomitable authority and steadfastness, by a voice which is backed by 'the tyranny of training and command' (p. 53). Given a MacWhirr, we see, a Jukes can be saved from himself; and with the buckling steel of his heart reinforced, Jukes goes off to do his duty.

Not that he remains untempted by another voice. When he gets to the crew who are huddled in the alleyway, he feels 'as though he could throw himself down amongst them and never move any more'; and, when he is lowered into the bunker, he has 'half a mind to scramble out again', but 'the remembrance of Captain MacWhirr's voice' makes this impossible (pp. 61–2). Finally, he decides he is going in among the Chinese 'to pick up the dollars':

> A frenzy possessed Jukes. By the time he was back amongst the men in the darkness of the alleyway, he felt ready to wring all their necks at the slightest sign of hanging back. The very thought of it exasperated him. *He* couldn't hang back. They shouldn't.
>
> The impetuosity with which he came amongst them carried them along. They had already been excited and startled at all his comings and goings – by the fierceness and rapidity of his movements; and more felt than seen in his rushes, he appeared formidable – busied with matters of life and death that brooked no delay. At his first word he heard them drop into the bunker one after another obediently, with heavy thumps.
>
> They were not clear as to what would have to be done. 'What is it? What is it?' they were asking each other. The boatswain tried to explain; the sounds of a great scuffle surprised them: and the mighty shocks, reverberating awfully in the black bunker, kept them in mind of their danger. When the boatswain threw open the door it seemed that an eddy of the hurricane, stealing through the iron sides of the ship, had set all these bodies whirling like dust: there came to them a confused uproar, a tempestuous tumult, a fierce mutter, gusts of screams dying away, and the tramping of feet mingling with the blows of the sea.
>
> For a moment they glared amazed, blocking the doorway. Jukes pushed through them brutally. He said nothing, and simply darted in. Another lot of coolies on the ladder, struggling suicidally to break through the battened hatch to a swamped deck, fell off as before, and he disappeared under them like a man overtaken by a landslide.
>
> The boatswain yelled excitedly: 'Come along. Get the mate out. He'll be trampled to death. Come on.'
>
> They charged in . . . (pp. 76–7)

As Jukes and his men face the 'whirling bodies' of the Chinese and there comes to them the 'confused uproar', the 'tempestuous tumult' of their struggle, it is clear that the human storm they are required to confront is every bit as menacing as the typhoon that is smashing at the ship. Indeed, it has earlier been said, when the boatswain pulls back the bolt of the bunker door, that it is as though he has 'opened the door to the sounds of the tempest' (p. 57); and Jukes later feels that 'in his mad struggle down there he [has] overcome the wind somehow' (p. 79). As he leads the way to the Chinese, therefore, Jukes has to cope with the possibility that his men, already beaten by the storm and now called on to expose themselves to danger of a like order, may be tempted by their craving for the immobility of peace to 'hang back'. They respond obediently to 'his first word', however, and this suggests that the newly 'formidable' Jukes, having conquered (with the help of his captain) his own insidious desire to hang back, has now developed a compelling voice of his own. And if the men do at first stand 'amazed' at the sight that meets them, they are quickly drawn into action both by the force of Jukes's example as he plunges alone into the mass of bodies and by their sense of solidarity with him. Conquering their desire to hang back, they are able to hang together.

Triumphantly returned to his captain from the foray for the dollars, Jukes finds the other storm unabated. MacWhirr, facing the possibility of his being swept overboard with a matter-of-fact acceptance, adjures Jukes not to be 'put out by anything' should he be required to take over, and to 'keep a cool head':

> For some reason Jukes experienced an access of confidence, a sensation that came from outside like a warm breath, and made him feel equal to every demand. The distant muttering of the darkness stole into his ears. He noted it unmoved, out of that sudden belief in himself, as a man safe in a shirt of mail would watch a point. (p.89)

At the start of his initiating experience, we recall, the typhoon undermined Jukes's 'faith in himself'; now his having won through to a 'belief in himself' is indicative of a newly won knowledge of self. It is in the consciousness of a self that is safely anchored in its own inner firmness that he now feels 'equal to every demand' and notes the storm 'unmoved'. Jukes, that is, as the shirt of mail simile suggests, has now developed a steeled heart.

CHAPTER FIVE

Nostromo

I

Nostromo may well have the distinction of being the novel that more than any other in English seems determined to induce its readers to lay it down in despair before they are half-way through it. This is due to the apparent incomprehensibility, on a first reading, of its narrative movement. No sooner do we imagine we have taken our bearings than shifts backwards and forwards in time and from one character to another confuse our sense of direction. Albert J. Guerard, indeed, maintains that even repeated readings of the novel fail to yield an ordered chronology:

> It has been my sad experience, each time I have tried to disentangle the time-scheme of *Nostromo*, to come up with a different result. Some of the difficulty is caused by a moment of extreme carelessness or of Faulk[n]erian perversity. For the banquet attended by Ribiera occurs eighteen months before the Sulaco riots . . . but the riots occur about six months after a 'visit' which presumably refers to the banquet . . . – unless we are to assume that the briefly flaring Monterist revolution lasted a year or more. It is as difficult to know how many hours intervened between the embarkation of General Barrios and the Sulaco riots as to know how many years went into the regeneration of the San Tomé mine. . . .[1]

I find, however, that Conrad does provide us with all the clues necessary to disentangle the chronology and so to resolve the difficulties referred to by Guerard. And when we get our bearings at last, we are surprised to find how simple the time-scheme is – for all the prodigies of complication with which Conrad has contrived to dislocate it.

In Part First (pp. 1–131) of the novel there are a considerable number of time-shifts, and these are made the more confusing in that we often do not know how far backwards or forwards in time the action has been shifted. The narrative movement is further complicated by numerous introductory and summarizing accounts of the past lives of characters. Decoud, for instance, makes his first appearance at the beginning of

Chapter Three, Part Second, as an unnamed 'young man of thirty at most' (p. 151), who is present at the harbour on the day General Barrios and his men embark for Cayta. Thereupon the rest of the chapter (pp. 151–9) is devoted to an outline of his antecedents, and it is not till the beginning of Chapter Four that there is a return to the scene at the harbour. This may not technically be a time-shift since it is experienced as a moment of narrative timelessness, a pause or marking time in the movement of the action, but it distractingly takes us into the past nonetheless.

The fictional present is initially established with the first dramatized scene in the narrative, that in the Viola household in Chapter Three, Part First. This scene takes place on the first day of the riots, and it is therefore this day that serves as the central point of reference in the time-scheme of the novel. In Chapter Five, with the description of the dinner-party held to mark 'the turning of the first sod' of the National Central Railway (p. 34), we go back eighteen months from this day; and in Chapter Six, with the scenes between Mr. and Mrs. Gould that take place in Italy on the day he receives the news of his father's death and proposes to her (pp. 61–6), we move still further back into the past. Just how much further back in time we have been taken at this point is nowhere explicitly indicated though our comprehension of the temporal range of the action is dependent on our knowing this. We do know that Gould must be twenty-four years old at this time since he says (at a later stage) that his father had not seen him 'for ten years' when he died though he wrote to him 'every month of [his] life for ten years' (p. 73); and he has been away from Costaguana for ten years when he learns of his father's death (p. 61), having gone to England for his education (and begun to receive letters from his father) at the age of of fourteen (p. 57). It is not until Chapter One, Part Third, however, that we learn Gould is thirty years old at the time of the riots (p. 317), and so can conclude that the scenes in Italy take place some six years before the initial fictional present of the narrative, and that the second time-shift takes us back about four and a half years from the time of the festive dinner. From this point we move forward to a scene between the Goulds that follows their entertainment of Holroyd in Sulaco and takes place 'just about a year' after their marriage (p. 67), but set into this scene is another between Gould and Holroyd that takes place in San Francisco about a year earlier (p. 79). We then go back to a number of scenes that are not specifically located in time but are related to the reactivation of the mine, which extends over a period of about a year (p. 106). Finally, at the end of Part First, we move forward again to a number of scenes that take place on the day of the railway dinner.

Though (to our continuous confusion on a first reading) we are thus jerked backwards and forwards in time throughout Part First, a reconstitution of the chronology of this section discloses a time-scheme which, in relation to the events mentioned, is simplicity itself. We may think of the main action as starting with Gould's determination, on the death of his father, to re-activate the mine and with his securing the support of Holroyd for this project. There follows a period of about a year during which this work is successfully undertaken, a period terminating with Holroyd's visit to Sulaco. Three and a half years later the railway is inaugurated. Eighteen months thereafter the riots break out.

The second section of the novel opens with a non-dramatized account of the history of Costaguana which continues to jerk us about in time – we are taken as far back as the days of Guzman Bento and then move forward to the outbreak of Montero's revolt some six months after the railway dinner (p. 145)[2] – but there is only one time-shift in Part Second. This occurs with the presentation of the scene at the harbour when General Barrios and his men embark for Cayta. At first there is no indication when this takes place, but some sixty pages later we discover that it is on the day before the riots begin, for there is a reception at the Gould home on the day of Barrios's departure, and that night Gould tells his wife he is bringing down a consignment of silver on the morrow (p. 208), the consignment which the rioting populace try to capture. The time-shift at this point, that is to say, is to one day prior to the initial fictional present. There follows the important scene between Decoud and Mrs. Gould on the same night, and then at last, nearly half-way through the novel, the narrative catches up with itself, as it were, when Decoud writes his letter to his sister one day after the start of the rioting: 'It was not so quiet around here yesterday,' he writes. 'We had an awful riot – a sudden outbreak of the populace, which was not suppressed till late today' (p. 224). Thereafter, allowing for the handling of separate strands in an intricately webbed action (and with one significant exception which remains to be discussed), the narrative is kept within the bounds of a regular chronology.

Why, we cannot help wondering, does the novelist go out of his way to complicate a narrative which I have tried to show is essentially simple in its temporal range? Indeed he dislocates the chronology to such effect that on occasion he succeeds even in confusing himself.[3] The dislocations of the first half of the narrative might be taken merely to reflect a temperamental obsession, for their effect, as the action seems unable to get under way, is of an elaborate holding back, a refusal to let go; but we come to realize that the form is strictly functional and serves a number of artistic ends. To begin with, an immediate result of the method is that the reader, as has been observed,[4] finds himself in a position which is analogous to that of later visitors to Sulaco who are privileged to hear Captain Mitchell's account of those days, for they, we are told, are 'stunned and as it were annihilated mentally by a sudden surfeit of sights, sounds, names, facts, and complicated information imperfectly apprehended' (pp. 486–7). Thomas Moser has suggested, in this regard, that it is one of Conrad's purposes 'so to assault the reader that he will experience some of the emotional chaos of the characters',[5] but though such emotional chaos may no doubt be assumed, *Nostromo* is not notable for its actual presentation. Carrying his confusion with him, the reader would seem to be forced, rather, to experience a sense of the general disorder that characterizes the revolutionary times Conrad is depicting. He is forced, too, to register his confusion as a mark of his own inadequacy, and is readily led to believe that the fictional world which confronts him is so vast and complex in its ramifications that he cannot possibly hope to take it all in at once. The method thus ensures that if the reader, like one of Mitchell's listeners, is stunned, it is into an acceptance of the utter solidity and reality of the imaginary state Conrad has created. Verisimilitude, we see, may thus be achieved by means of intricate artifice; though *Nostromo*, in this respect, offers an instructive contrast to *Chance*, where the verisimilitude of the tale is positively undermined by the artificiality of the method that is designed to ensure it.

A further effect of the method is most palpably manifest towards the end of the novel when we are suddenly whisked a number of years into the future by a time-shift that audaciously takes place in mid-sentence:

> The next day was quiet in the morning, except for the faint sound of firing to the northward, in the direction of Los Hatos. Captain Mitchell had listened to it from his balcony anxiously. The phrase, 'In my delicate position as the only consular agent then in the port, everything, sir, everything was a just cause for anxiety', had its place in the more or less stereotyped relation of the 'historical events' which for the next few years was at the service of distinguished strangers visiting Sulaco.... Captain Mitchell ... insisted that it was a memorable day. On that day, towards dusk, he had seen 'that poor fellow of mine – Nostromo. The sailor whom I discovered, and, I may say, made, sir. The man of the famous ride to Cayta, sir. An historical event, sir!'
>
> Regarded by the O. S. N. Company as an old and faithful servant, Captain Mitchell was allowed to attain the term of his usefulness in ease and dignity at the head of the enormously extended service. The augmentation of the establishment ... secured a greater leisure for his last years in the regenerated Sulaco, the capital of the Occidental Republic.... (pp. 473–4)

This passage, which opens Chapter Ten, Part Third, follows a chapter in which the narrative has generated a great deal of tension. With both

Pedrito Montero and Sotillo in occupation of Sulaco, the position appears to be hopeless for the supporters of Ribiera; and Dr. Monygham's proposal to Nostromo that he try to reach Barrios at Cayta seems to hold out small prospect of a turn of fortune. At the end of the chapter, moreover, it is by no means clear whether Nostromo will agree to undertake the mission. The effect of the time-shift, therefore, is one of anticlimax. The tense narrative gives way to Mitchell's 'stereotyped relation', and it is in a most undramatic and casual manner that we learn of Nostromo's success-ful ride to Cayta. Though the fact that Decoud's plan to establish an Occidental Republic has been implemented is communicated in much the same way, this is not as reductive of tension only because we have been parenthetically informed of it more than a hundred pages earlier (p. 354). Mitchell's narrative (pp. 473–89) is full of similarly brusque and perfunc-tory revelations of crucial developments in the action. To refer only to the fate of major characters, we learn that Gould, whom we have last seen fencing with Pedrito Montero over the mine, was 'led out to be shot' but was saved at the last minute by the miners who 'had marched upon the town' (p. 477); that Decoud, whom Nostromo had left safe and sound on the island, is dead (p. 478); and that Monygham, who had begun to play his 'game of betrayal' with Sotillo, had 'the rope already round his neck' when he was saved by the arrival of Barrios (p. 484).

It might be said that Captain Mitchell's narrative merely affords Conrad a ready and summary means of winding up a large and compli-cated action towards the end of an already long book, but its effect is seen to be significant when related to that of the method employed earlier. The narrative as a whole seems to be designed to thwart and frustrate the conventional expectations of the reader. A reader's wish for a firm sense of his bearings as he progresses into a narrative may be regarded as a frailty, but it is certainly frustrated in the first half of the novel as he is bewilderingly swung about in time and space; and if his desire (when he at last begins to comprehend what is happening) for the excitement of an action which seems to be working up to a grand climax is similarly repre-hensible, it is as surely thwarted.

In discussing the effect of the time-shifts, Douglas Hewitt says that 'by the deliberate disappointment of expectations they force us to think more clearly about the meaning of [the] story'; and, with specific reference to the shift which occurs in Mitchell's narrative, that it makes 'more 'emphatic' that Conrad's theme is 'not revolution and physical action'.[6] This is doubtless the case, but I think the effect of the time-shifts is more far-reaching. The form of the novel may be said to point to its fundamental thematic concerns – to the thwarting of the conventional expectations that are aroused by the reactivation of the San Tomé mine; and the thwarting, as far as almost all the main characters are concerned, of the expectations that are bred by their assumption of conventional roles. *Nostromo* may, in this respect, be compared to Jane Austen's *Emma*, which, dealing with deception, itself deceives the reader in such a way as to make him feel on his own pulses what it is like to be deceived. And *Nostromo* has its own appropriate emblem for the great expectations it depicts: when she first perceives the 'secret mood' governing her husband-to-be, the 'delight in him' of 'the future Mrs. Gould', which has been 'lingering with half-open wings like those birds that cannot rise easily from a flat level', is said to have 'found a pinnacle from which to soar up into the skies' (p. 59). But, in its presentation of the relationship of the Goulds, it is with the bitter frustration of that desire to soar that the novel actually deals. Virtually all the characters in the novel are grounded, as it were, with their wings no more than half-open.

II

It is revelatory of the animating principle of *Nostromo* that, when the action finally gets under way with the attempt by Nostromo and Decoud to save the consignment of silver that has been brought down to Sulaco on the day the rioting begins, their intentions should be thwarted by Sotillo's steamer running into their lighter in the darkness of the gulf. The scene in the gulf is the finest in the novel and, functioning as a central epiphany, it makes manifest most of the important aspects of Conrad's theme of 'material interests'. It is these interests that are seen to be para-mount in the life of Costaguana; and what is involved in the attempt to safeguard them is symbolized by the attempt to save the silver, for to the Europeans who rally round Gould in the emergency and help load the lighter 'with their own hands' it is as if the silver is 'the emblem of a common cause, the symbol of the supreme importance of material in-terests' (p. 260). Before he leaves Sulaco, Decoud writes to his sister that the silver 'must be saved at all costs' (p. 244). The venture ultimately costs him his life, and his death is a striking indication of the kind of price paid by those who lend themselves to material interests. Conrad's overt concern in *Nostromo* might be described as the fixing of this price on both a social and personal level – though his fundamental preoccupations, I shall argue, are in line with those revealed in his earlier work.

'At night,' we are told in the opening pages of the novel, 'the body of clouds advancing higher up the sky smothers the whole quiet gulf below with an impenetrable darkness' (p. 6); and indeed as Nostromo and Decoud move out into the gulf it is so dark that they are 'unable to see each other' (p. 261), and 'even the lighter's sail' is 'invisible' (p. 269). An immediate consequence of this is that they cannot tell whether they are moving – 'Do we move at all, Capataz?' Decoud asks (p. 263) – and it is neatly implied that the habitual assumption of progress as a concomitant of material advance is open to question. It is a question that has been much argued by critics; Robert Penn Warren, for instance, maintaining that Albert J. Guerard's view that the mine brings civil war rather than progress is 'far too simple': 'we must admit that the society at the end of the book is preferable to that at the beginning.'[7] Conrad himself on one occasion even uses the word 'progress' as a synonym for 'material interests', and it seems to me he is throughout less concerned with doubts as to its actuality than with reservations as to its cost – as he makes clear on the same occasion:

> the sparse row of telegraph poles strode obliquely clear of the town, bearing a single, almost invisible wire far into the great campo – like a slender, vibrating feeler of that progress waiting outside for a moment of peace to enter and twine itself about the weary heart of the land. (p. 166)

If the onward stride of the telegraph poles is a forceful image of material progress, Conrad simultaneously contrives with the simile of the feeler to subvert the image into one of constriction, and to suggest that the cost of such progress, undoubted though it may be, is a contraction of the inner vitality of the country.[8] And the final view we have of Sulaco is of 'material changes' sweeping along to such effect 'in the train of material interests' that for the city it is 'like a second youth, like a new life'; but we are also told that 'the hidden treasures of the earth' on which it grows rich are 'hovered over by the anxious spirits of good and evil', and that the new life to which it has progressed is full of 'unrest' and 'toil' as well as 'promise' (p. 504).

If the lighter, then, does make progress, even though it is only by 'feeling the water slip though his fingers' that Decoud can convince himself they are moving (p. 277), an obvious further consequence of their being in the dark is that they cannot see where they are going, cannot tell where they are heading. Trying to make a course, Nostromo calls down 'the curse of Heaven' on 'this blind gulf' (p. 269), though we have earlier been told that 'the eye of God Himself . . . could not find out what work a man's hand is doing in there; and you would be free to call the devil to your aid with impunity if even his malice were not defeated by such a blind darkness' (p. 7). Nor is the blinding darkness confined to the gulf: sitting in the Goulds' drawing-room, Captain Mitchell is a representative figure, for he is said to be 'utterly in the dark' though 'imagining himself to be in the thick of things' (p. 112) – a condition even more strongly exemplified by the man who is really at the centre of events.

Charles Gould '[pins his] faith to material interests' because he believes they are 'bound to impose the conditions on which alone they can continue to exist', and so will perforce bring to Costaguana what is most needed there – 'law, good faith, order, security' (p. 84). Gould, as Royal Roussel has pointed out,[9] is in this respect a Kurtz, a civilizer confidently carrying his torch into the heart of darkness; and, like Kurtz, he succumbs to the customs of the land that confront him. It is 'the bitter fate of any idea', Conrad comments elsewhere, 'to lose its royal form and power, to lose its "virtue" the moment it descends from its solitary throne to work its will among the people';[10] and in trying to ensure the security of his mine, Gould finds himself compelled to resort first to wide-spread bribery and then to direct interference in the politics of Costaguana, lending his support to the 'armed struggle' that brings the Ribierist party to power (pp. 142–4). Far from bringing law and order to the country, therefore, Gould helps to perpetuate the corruption which is at the heart of its lawlessness and the political instability which underlies the prevailing disorder.

That the mine is hardly likely to be a force for peace is indicated when the very first consignment of silver is brought down to Sulaco: on that occasion 'the charge of the San Tomé silver escort' through the city suggests 'the reckless rush and precise driving of a field battery hurrying into action' (p. 114). And for the Goulds 'each passing of the escort under the balconies of the Casa Gould' is 'like another victory gained in the conquest of peace for Sulaco' (p. 115). I think we are justified in believing Conrad intended a wider reference here. In Richard Curle's copy of *Nostromo* he wrote that it was his ambition 'to render the spirit of an epoch in the history of Sth. America';[11] but he would seem to have cast his net even wider, as a prescient passage in 'Autocracy and War' (1905) reveals:

> Industrialism and commercialism . . . stand ready, almost eager, to appeal to the sword as soon as the globe of the earth has shrunk beneath our growing numbers by another ell or so. And democracy, which has elected to pin its faith to the supremacy of material interests, will have to fight their battles to the bitter end, on a mere pittance – unless, indeed, some statesman . . . succeeds in carrying through an international understanding for the delimitation of spheres of trade all over the earth, on the model of the territorial spheres of influence marked in Africa to keep the competitors for the privilege of improving the nigger (as a buying machine) from flying prematurely at each other's throats.[12]

And in the same essay he remarked that 'Germany's attitude proves that no peace for the earth can be found in the expansion of material interests which she seems to have adopted exclusively as her only aim, ideal, and watchword' (p. 113). There is a clear logical continuity between the views expressed in these passages and Dr. Monygham's contention that 'there is no peace and no rest in the development of material interests':

'They have their law, and their justice. But it is founded on expediency, and is inhuman; it is without rectitude, without the continuity and the force that can be found only in a moral principle. Mrs. Gould, the time approaches when all that the Gould Concession stands for shall weigh as heavily upon the people as the barbarism, cruelty, and misrule of a few years back.' (p. 511)

There is nothing in the novel to offset the doctor's prognostication, which crushingly predicates the utter frustration of the noble aims with which Gould started on the mining venture. But to all this Gould is quite blind; he '[can] not see', as his wife does in a final horrifying vision, that the mine is 'more soulless than any tyrant, more pitiless and autocratic than the worst Government; ready to crush innumerable lives in the expansion of its greatness' (p. 521). This view of material progress is striking in its radicalism – and it is a view that the large prophetic tenor of *Nostromo* leads us to believe is also that of the supposedly conservative novelist.

Unable to tell whether they are making any progress or to see where they are heading, but knowing that 'to come to the land anywhere in a hundred miles along [the] coast with [the] silver in [their] possession is to run the naked breast against the point of a knife', Nostromo and Decoud realize that 'the possession of [the] treasure is very much like a deadly disease' for men situated as they are (p. 264). It is not merely in terms of random simile that we are to register their decision to put the silver first as subjecting them, so to speak, to the working of a deadly disease, to a process of corruption, for it is such a process that the novelist patiently traces in the lives of the main characters, and the darkness into which they have plunged becomes a concretization of what Antonia Avellanos later thinks of as 'the moral darkness of the land' (p. 354). This darkness is depicted as being as far-reaching as that in the gulf appears to be, but the particular moral vice discernible in Costaguana (on both a national and personal level) is that of betrayal – and this too is adumbrated in the scene in the lighter. When Nostromo and Decoud discover that they have a stowaway aboard, the Capataz remarks that Hirsch's being there is 'a miracle of fear', and he adds: 'There is no room for fear in this lighter' (p. 274). Whether there is room or not, it is vividly suggested that those responsible for the preservation of material interests willy-nilly carry fear with them, the specific fear to which they are exposed being that of betrayal, for we are told that 'the mere presence of a coward, however passive, brings an element of treachery into a dangerous situation' (p. 274).[13] Hirsch's presence in the lighter, which is of crucial importance in the development of the action, is thus also given an effective symbolic dimension, but it must be objected that Conrad has earlier had recourse to the worst type of stock characterization in order to prepare for it. We are not to query Hirsch's somewhat improbable behaviour because he, after all, is a Jew, and his cowardice therefore self-explanatory. Conrad, indeed, wastes no time on subtleties in his presentation of Hirsch. He is a 'little hook-nosed man from Esmeralda', the fact of his 'hooked beak' apparently being sufficient warrant both for his 'mercantile soul' and for his cowardice. His fear, we are to understand, is so deep-seated – racially innate, it would appear – that it even infects his speech under normal circumstances, for he speaks with 'a strange, anxious whine', thus 'degrading . . . the sonority of the Spanish language', and the very 'jargon' he uses, for of course he does not speak Spanish like a Spaniard, is said to be 'cringing' (pp. 201–3).

III

If the form of the narrative adverts us to the motif of thwarting, the central action of the novel is presented as a drama of possession. The political conflicts, which affect the lives of all the main characters, may be seen as revolving round the desire of one 'gang' after another to remain 'in possession of the Presidential Palace' (p. 56). After one such gang confers on Mr. Gould, senior, 'the perpetual possession of [the] desolate locality' which contains the abandoned silver mine (p. 54) and so makes possible the reactivation of the mine by his son, the mine becomes so important a factor in the political life of Costaguana that it is its support which brings Ribiera to power and its possession which becomes a major objective of the disaffected Monterist faction. The action of *Nostromo*, indeed, ultimately resolves itself into a complex struggle for possession of the silver that is brought down to Sulaco on the same day the defeated Ribiera reaches it. No one who can get his hands on the silver, like Nostromo, or believes he may be able to, like Sotillo, can bear to let go. What they enact, accordingly, like the gringos in the legend of Azuera whose 'souls cannot tear themselves away from their bodies mounting guard over the discovered treasure' (p. 5), is an ironic story of possession – of the possessor (or would-be possessor) possessed.

It would seem, therefore, that the motif of possession should be added to that of thwarting if we are to get at Conrad's fundamental preoccupations in the novel. As we might expect, it is with possession of self that he is most vitally concerned, though this is closely bound up with the possession of power or wealth. It is notable, however, that a capacity for physical self-possession in an emergency seems now, with regard to the main characters, almost to be taken for granted, and is not an issue of consequence in *Nostromo*. When the steamer strikes the lighter, for instance, all Decoud's sensations remain clear: 'he had kept complete possession of himself; in fact, he was even pleasantly aware of that calmness at the very moment of being pitched head first over the transom, to struggle on his back in a lot of water' (p. 292). As events move to a crisis in Sulaco 'with Sotillo expected from one side, and Pedro Montero from the other', the engineer-in-chief cannot help commenting 'appreciatively' on the fact that Charles Gould is 'calmness personified', and he adds: 'He must be extremely sure of himself.' Dr. Monygham caustically remarks that this is 'the last thing a man ought to be sure of' (pp. 308–10) – but in fact Gould retains his calm surety throughout the troubled period. Captain Mitchell, we are told, 'for all his pomposity in social intercourse', can 'meet the realities of life in a resolute and ready spirit'; and when he gets over the shock of 'the abominable treatment' he receives at the hands of Sotillo, is 'cool and collected enough' (p. 335). Dr. Monygham, on his first encounter with Sotillo, remains 'observant and self-possessed' (p. 343), and he continues to be so throughout the long and dangerous game he plays with him. Nostromo's actions during the period of riot and disorder bespeak his self-possession; and later, even when he is led to look 'suicide deliberately in the face' in the despairing belief that nothing can save his theft of the silver from detection, he does not '[lose] his head' (p. 525).

Conrad himself, as he remarked later in the Author's Note (1917) to *Nostromo*, became aware of 'a subtle change in the nature of [his] inspiration' (p. xv) after he had completed the *Typhoon* volume of stories. This should not only be taken to refer to an obvious change in the direction of his work, the change from his earlier depiction in relatively small compass of life at sea or in the jungle to the large-scale presentation of the functioning of whole societies in *Nostromo*, *The Secret Agent*, and *Under Western Eyes*. It has its bearing too on a new conception of the ways in which a man many lose full possession of himself, of a spiritual disintegration which – though less outwardly apparent – may be as devastating as a Willems's succumbing to sexual passion or a Jim's to physical panic. Conrad's concern with the consequences of abandon, that is to say, modulates from an interest in the abandon of passion to that of despair to that of obsession. In *Nostromo*, in the case of major characters such as Gould, Nostromo, and Decoud, the assumption of a conventional role deteriorates into the fixation of obsession and these characters are all ultimately thwarted in the aims they set themselves. Only Dr. Monygham, who at the outset of the action has been deprived of a sense of wholeness, may be said to come into possession of himself – to open his wings, as it were, and soar up into the skies.

The way in which Conrad sets off the lives of his major characters in an elaborate and harmonious counterpoint is a remarkable feat. Caught up in a large action of national consequence, they act out their individual destinies in a manner that not only offers a Tolstoyan comment on the nature of history but also reveals, with a subtle and satisfying comprehensiveness, varied dimensions of personal obsession. The intricate organization of *Nostromo*, we come to realize, is much more than a matter of its involved time-scheme. But the final effect of the novel is peculiar. It must undoubtedly be seen as Conrad's most complex achievement – his major work – but it seems to me that it is also in some essentially limiting way a cold work. As I trust will be evident in the ensuing analysis, there is in *Nostromo* a profound understanding of the working of character and an imaginative flair for the revelatory action in which this issues, but we are kept at such a distance from the characters and see them in so remorselessly cold and intellectual a light that, while everything is plausible, there is little that has the warmth, the crucial emotional force, of the greatest art – or that can compare among his own works with the impact, in this respect, of *Lord Jim* or *Under Western Eyes*.

*   *   *

Charles Gould's conscious motives for attempting the rehabilitation of the San Tomé mine in defiance of his father's wishes are varied. The project clearly holds a special attraction for his youth, presenting the kind of challenge and offering the sort of 'strange life' that enable him to transform a business venture into an adventure. He is swayed too by 'a subtle thought of redress', by the belief that he can make up for the suffering of his father by giving it meaning through the rehabilitation. Much aware, moreover, that the mine has been 'the cause of an absurd moral disaster' in reducing his father to despair, he is drawn to the idea of making it 'a serious and moral success' (pp. 65–6); it is as if he and his young wife-to-be feel 'morally bound to make good their vigorous view of life against the unnatural error of weariness and despair' (p. 74). He also believes, as has been remarked earlier, that the reactivation of the mine will be for the good of the whole country, helping to ensure the law and order it so badly needs. But Gould would seem to remain unconscious of the major force that drives him to make his decision:

> It hurt Charles Gould to feel that never more, by no effort of will, would he be able to think of his father in the same way he used to think of him when the poor man was alive. His breathing image was no longer in his power. This consideration, closely affecting his own identity, filled his breast with a mournful and angry desire for action. In this his instinct was unerring. Action is consolatory. It is the enemy of thought and the friend of flattering illusions. Only in the conduct

of our action can we find the sense of mastery over the Fates. For his action, the mine was obviously the only field. It was imperative some-times to know how to disobey the solemn wishes of the dead. He resolved firmly to make his disobedience as thorough (by way of atonement) as it well could be. . . . (pp. 65–6)

The passage indicates that the most important consequence for Gould of his father's death is that it closely affects his sense of his own identity. With his father's 'breathing image . . . no longer in his power', Gould has to face the fact of the finality of his separation from him – has to face the fact, that is, that he is no longer a son but a man on his own. If Gould in his grief instinctively seeks the consolation and relief of action, his conviction that 'for his action' the mine is 'obviously the only field' suggests in its arbitrariness his overriding need to disobey his father's wishes in order to assert his own independent life. The reactivation of the mine, in other words, is the means by which he seeks to establish his selfhood. But Gould, as Decoud sees, is the kind of man who 'cannot act or exist without idealizing every simple feeling, desire, or achievement' (pp. 214–15); and the San Tomé project consequently spawns its sincere but deceptive motivations. The particular 'flattering illusion' that this 'action' inspires is the unformulated belief that it is possible to reconcile overt aims that are idealistic and altruistic with a venture that is essentially materialistic and egoistic.

The kind of self that Gould succeeds in establishing in Sulaco is vividly imaged early in the novel:

His way would lie along the old Spanish road – the Camino Real of popular speech – the only remaining vestige of a fact and name left by that royalty . . . whose very shadow had departed from the land; for the big equestrian statue of Charles IV at the entrance of the Alameda . . . was only known to the folk from the country and to the beggars of the town that slept on the steps around the pedestal, as the Horse of Stone. The other Carlos, turning off to the left . . . – Don Carlos Gould, in his English clothes, looked as incongruous, but much more at home than the kingly cavalier . . .

The weather-stained effigy of the mounted king . . . seemed to present an inscrutable breast to the political changes which had robbed it of its very name; but neither did the other horseman . . . wear his heart on the sleeve of his English coat. His mind preserved its steady poise as if sheltered in the passionless stability of private and public decencies at home in Europe. He accepted with a like calm the shocking manner in which the Sulaco ladies smothered their faces with pearl powder . . . , the peculiar gossip of the town, and the continuous political changes . . . (pp. 48–9)

We have earlier been told that Gould rides 'like a centaur' (p. 48), and this evocation of his natural and effortless poise on horseback is matched by the description of his habitual mental composure, the 'steady poise' and 'calm' of his mind. Gould, that is to say, is presented as showing all the inner and outer signs of a perfect self-possession. The self of which he has now taken possession, moreover, would seem to be of majestic and powerful proportions, as the implied comparison in the reference to 'the other Carlos' suggests – as does his nickname, 'King of Sulaco'. His composure is the more noteworthy in that it is maintained amid the confusion and disorder of 'the continuous political changes', and we realize it is 'sheltered' not alone by the 'private and public decencies' in which he has been nurtured in Europe but also by 'the passionless stability' he contrives to create around himself even in troubled Costaguana. He creates this by successfully projecting an image of himself that is so rock-like in its imperturbability – Don José comments on his 'rock-like quality of character' (p. 86) – that it dispels, by a kind of legerdemain, all surrounding agitation. The 'provincial Excellency', for instance, whom he has to bribe in connection with the mine, attempts 'the assault of Charles Gould's polite silence' only to give up suddenly as though he has been 'beaten off from a fortress' (p. 91); and in his dealings with Gould, Pedrito Montero concludes that he is a 'stony fiend of a man' (p. 403). Pedrito thus feels what has been earlier implied by the analogy between Don Carlos on horseback and the equestrian statue of Charles IV, which is known to the countryfolk and the beggars only as 'the Horse of Stone': they leave out the man, that is, and in the case of the King of Sulaco too the man is not there, as it were. The secret of Gould's imperturbability, we realize, is that there is nothing left in him of the human to ruffle. He, like Kurtz before him, is a hollow man, for his stony fortress is empty. But Conrad does not now simply take the idea of hollowness for granted; he knows now what can make a man hollow at the core.

Cold and impervious though he may be, Gould is the victim of passion. Decoud sees, and remarks on the fact in his letter to his sister, that Gould holds to his mine 'as some men hold to the idea of love or revenge':

> A passion has crept into his cold and idealistic life. A passion which I can only comprehend intellectually. A passion that is not like the passions we know, we men of another blood. But it is as dangerous as any of ours. (p. 245)

Gould's passion proves to be dangerous in a number of respects. First, it is dangerous to his wife, for it destroys her happiness. She dreads his 'cold and overmastering passion' more than 'if it were an infatuation for another woman' (p. 245); but she is powerless to deflect it, and to her he seems 'to dwell alone within a circumvallation of precious metal, leaving her outside . . . ' (p. 222). It is not only to strangers, it appears, that Gould seems stony. He uses the mine to keep her out too, shutting her out of his emotions and encasing himself in his devotion to it as in a fort. Decoud views this as a 'sentimental unfaithfulness', which we see is even more crushing to Mrs. Gould than sexual infidelity, for it 'surrenders her happiness, her life, to the seduction of an idea' (p. 245). We are to infer that it surrenders her sexual well-being too, and it is no doubt significant, as Juliet McLauchlan remarks, that they have no children, for this symbolizes 'the deeper sense in which [their marriage] is sterile'.[14] Towards the end of the novel, when Mrs. Gould wistfully watches Basilio carrying his child, 'careful of his light burden' (p. 519), it is suggested that the servant knows more of the simple joy of life and of its fundamental fulfilments than the First Lady of Sulaco – or the King of Sulaco.

The insistent analogies between the nature of Gould's passion and that of sexual passion imply that, when he is 'over-mastered' by his feeling for the mine, he succumbs to an abandon that is as thoroughgoing as that of Willems when he is overcome by his desire for Aïssa. What Gould abandons himself to, however, is an obsession – his will is 'haunted by a fixed idea' – and his passion is seen to be dangerous in a further respect, for 'a man haunted by a fixed idea is insane': 'He is dangerous even if that idea is an idea of justice; for may he not bring the heaven down pitilessly upon a loved head?' (p. 379). Conrad's vision is such that we suddenly see through the immaculate and highly civilized mine-owner the savages who burst out of the jungle in 'Heart of Darkness', suggesting in the wildness of their abandon, an 'outbreak in a madhouse'.[15]

But it is of course to himself that Gould's passion is ultimately dangerous. When he lets go of everything but the mine, he also loses possession of the self he aspired to establish in undertaking the mining venture. And by an inexorable logic he thereby opens himself to a counter-possession: Mrs. Gould '[sees] clearly the San Tomé mine possessing, consuming, burning up the life of the last of the Costaguana Goulds' (p. 522). Possessed and consumed by his obsession, Gould disintegrates spiritually behind his fortress-like exterior, reduced to a nullity that is manifested in the moral nihilism of his attitudes where the mine is concerned.

Having decided 'to accommodate himself to existing circumstances of corruption' in Costaguana, Gould may be said to embark on his mining venture as a moral relativist, for though he refuses 'to discuss the ethical view with his wife', he trusts that, even if she is 'a little disenchanted', she will be 'intelligent enough to understand that his character [safeguards] the enterprise of their lives as much or more than his policy' (pp. 142–3). The policy of the Gould Concession is 'to fight for life with such weapons as [can] be found at once in the mire of corruption that [is] so universal as to almost lose its significance'; and Gould is 'prepared to stoop for his weapons'. That his character is not as effective a safeguard as he supposes – and his stooping into the mire more like a fall – is indicated when he begins at the same time to feel that 'the worthiness of his life' is 'bound up with success' (p. 85). The weapon he uses is 'the wealth of the mine', and this is said to be 'more dangerous to the wielder' than 'an honest blade of steel', for it is 'steeped in all the vices of self-indulgence as in a concoction of poisonous roots' (p. 365). Equating worth with success, Gould comes to believe – with a poisonous self-indulgence which insidiously destroys the self he is intent to expand – that anything is permitted him, slipping in the mud from a position of moral relativism to one of moral nihilism. 'There is no going back now,' he tells his wife:

'I don't suppose that, even from the first, there was really any possible way back. And, what's more, we can't even afford to stand still.'

'Ah, if one only knew how far you mean to go,' said his wife, inwardly trembling, but in an almost playful tone.

'Any distance, any length, of course,' was the answer, in a matter-of-fact tone, which caused Mrs. Gould to make another effort to repress a shudder. (pp. 207–8)

Gould's readiness to go to any lengths to preserve the Gould Concession is corrupted further into a determination to destroy the mine rather than surrender it, and full preparations are made to blow it up in an emergency. To the end Gould remains blind to the more profound implications of his condition, unable to see how far he has gone – just as Nostromo and Decoud in the lighter cannot tell their position – but he does begin to have an inkling:

After all, with his English parentage and English upbringing, he perceived that he was an adventurer in Costaguana . . . For all the uprightness of his character, he had something of an adventurer's easy morality which takes count of personal risk in the ethical appraising of his action. He was prepared, if need be, to blow up the whole San Tomé mountain sky high out of the territory of the Republic. This resolution expressed the tenacity of his character, the remorse of that subtle conjugal infidelity through which his wife was no longer the sole mistress of his thoughts, something of his father's imaginative weakness, and something, too, of the spirit of a buccaneer throwing a lighted match into the magazine rather than surrender his ship. (pp. 365–6)

Just prior to this Gould has been struck by 'the truth of the comparison' when the emissary of the bandit Hernandez asks whether 'the master of the mine' has a message for 'the master of the Campo' (p. 360). Perceiving that he, like Hernandez, has in effect become a law unto himself, he is able to acknowledge that, for all his pretensions, he is 'an adventurer in Costaguana'. It is to 'an adventurer's easy morality', to a concern with prowess rather than principle, that his morality has degenerated; and he is thus not only like a bandit but also like the violent and primitive men 'but little removed from a state of utter savagery' who ride triumphantly into Sulaco with Pedrito Montero, and are 'artless in their recognition of success as the only standard of morality' (pp. 385-6). The play of analogy in the novel being insistent, we see that Gould is also like Nostromo, for his readiness in giant egotism to blow up the mine not only reveals 'the spirit of a buccaneer' but recalls the determination of the Capataz to sink the silver entrusted to his care 'rather than give it up to any stranger' (p. 267). Gould's determination to blow up the mine if necessary may express 'the tenacity of his character', but in its egotism and irresponsibility it is utterly subversive of the altruism in the name of which he has supposedly been labouring. And if it is also expressive of 'remorse' for his 'subtle conjugal infidelity', it is furthermore intimated that – in the last resort – he is not only guiltily ready to destroy the object which has seduced his affections from his wife but also himself, for, having surrendered himself to the mine, he can have no life apart from it. Gould's obsession should thus ultimately be seen as having a self-destructive tendency. And his moral nihilism not only links up with that of Kurtz, who contemplates the extermination of numberless brutes in Africa, but anticipates that of the Professor (in *The Secret Agent*), who is ready to blow himself up together with countless others rather than submit.[16]

*   *   *

Nostromo cultivates a style as much as Gould, and the people of Sulaco defer to it no less:

> He turned his horse slowly, and paced on between the booths, checking the mare almost to a standstill now and then for children, for the groups of people from the distant Campo, who stared after him with admiration. The Company's lightermen saluted him from afar; and the greatly envied Capataz de Cargadores advanced, amongst murmurs of recognition and obsequious greetings, towards the huge circus-like erection. . . . a man, wrapped up in a faded, torn poncho, walked by his stirrup, and, buffeted right and left, begged 'his worship' insistently for employment on the wharf. He whined, offering the Señor Capataz half his daily pay for the privilege of being admitted to the swaggering fraternity of Cargadores; the other half

would be enough for him, he protested. But Captain Mitchell's right-hand man – 'invaluable for our work – a perfectly incorruptible fellow' – after looking down critically at the ragged mozo, shook his head without a word in the uproar going on around. (pp. 126–7)

Mingling with the crowd, Nostromo is clearly 'a man of the People', as Conrad describes him in his Author's Note (p. xix); yet at the same time, and not merely by virtue of his being on horseback, he is raised above them. As he is admiringly stared after, saluted, and obsequiously greeted, there is even something regal about his progress that recalls the description of the mounted King of Sulaco making his way past the royal equestrian statue, the resemblance to Gould being further suggested by his aloofness amid the uproar and by his disdainful imperviousness to the pleas of the ragged mozo. This implicit pictorial juxtaposition of Nostromo and Gould also highlights the contrast between them, their obvious differences within the imposed frame of likeness, and indeed Conrad refers to them in the same Note as 'the two racially and socially contrasted men' who are 'both captured by the silver of the San Tomé Mine' (p. xix). It is possible to view them, therefore, as exemplifying alternative and contrasted forms of a subjection to material interests and of a corruption by silver (with Captain Mitchell's blazoning of Nostromo's integrity taking on the appropriate irony); but it seems to me more rewarding to regard Nostromo's story, though enacted on a lower level, as being parallel to that of Gould. It too is a story of an assertion and loss of self.

Giorgio Viola's wife, Teresa, is the first character in the novel to be critical of Nostromo, and the terms of her indignation prove suggestive. She is dying, and just before Nostromo is about to set out with Decoud in the attempt to save the silver, asks him to bring her a priest, but he refuses to go both because he does not believe in priests 'in their sacerdotal character' and because he has already given her 'the very last moment' he can spare:

'You refuse to go?' she gasped. 'Ah! you are always yourself, indeed.'

'Listen to reason, Padrona,' he said. 'I am needed to save the silver of the mine. Do you hear? A greater treasure than the one which they say is guarded by ghosts and devils in Azuera. It is true. I am resolved to make this the most desperate affair I was ever engaged on in my whole life.'

She felt a despairing indignation. The supreme test had failed. Standing above her, Nostromo did not see the distorted features of her face, distorted by a paroxysm of pain and anger. Only she began to tremble all over. Her bowed head shook. The broad shoulders quivered.

'Then God, perhaps, will have mercy upon me! But do you look
to it, man, that you get something for yourself out of it, besides the
remorse that shall overtake you some day.'

She laughed feebly. 'Get riches at least for once, you indispensable,
admired Gian' Battista, to whom the peace of a dying woman is less
than the praise of people who have given you a silly name – and
nothing besides – in exchange for your soul and body.' (pp. 255–6)

It is interesting, in the light of Conrad's earlier work, that it is Teresa's
request to Nostromo – and not his desperate effort to save the silver –
that is presented as constituting his 'supreme test'. The 'subtle change' in
Conrad's inspiration, that is, would seem to involve a corresponding
change in his conception of the test, it being now an emotional rather than
a physical capacity that is exposed to sudden stress. It is the strength of
Nostromo's personal loyalties that is tested here, Teresa implicitly calling
on him to put his loyalty to her before that to 'the silver of the mine'. His
failure to pass the test, moreover, is seen (in the world of the mine) to
be representative, for it is a strikingly analogous test that Gould is required
to meet and cannot. To Nostromo the issues are clear-cut, his appeal 'to
reason' reflecting his belief that from any rational point of view the silver
must come first, that a man's loyalty is due to that which is bigger than
the individual – a rationalization to which Razumov also succumbs in
Under Western Eyes. But Teresa, though she gives her intuition quaint
expression, penetrates to a more profound view of what it is that moves
the Capataz. 'You are always yourself,' she tells him, having previously
said (and so providing us with a gloss on her words): 'You never change,
indeed . . . Always thinking of yourself and taking your pay out in fine
words from those who care nothing for you' (p. 253). Teresa, that is, sees
that Nostromo fails to put her first because he puts himself first, that
behind his apparent concern for the silver there lurks (as we have seen in
the case of Gould) a compulsive egotism, and that he has contrived to
reduce a matter of supposedly national importance to 'the most desperate
affair' he personally 'was ever engaged on'. She sees, furthermore, that
the self which he puts first is, paradoxically, no longer his, for he has
given it 'soul and body' to those whom she imagines run him. In this she
would appear to err, for we become aware that it is not as 'Captain
Mitchell's right-hand man', as she supposes, that Nostromo has his being:
indeed it is Nostromo who winds 'round his little finger, almost daily, the
pompous and testy self-importance of the old seaman' (p. 419). It is,
however, as 'the greatly envied Capataz de Cargadores' that he exists; and
if he is content to take his pay out 'in fine words' or in 'praise' from those
who 'care nothing' for him, it is because he has given himself body and
soul, as surely as if into the cannon's mouth, to bubble reputation.

Nostromo, that is to say, has abandoned himself to popular fame, and is as obsessively a prey to success as Gould.

When Sotillo's steamer smashes into the lighter, Nostromo makes his way back to Sulaco. He has failed in his mission and is forced to lie low, but, with the silver safely landed on the island, he makes up his mind that 'the treasure should not be betrayed':

> The word had fixed itself tenaciously in his intelligence. His imagination had seized upon the clear and simple notion of betrayal to account for the dazed feeling of enlightenment as to being done for, of having inadvertently gone out of his existence on an issue in which his personality had not been taken into account. A man betrayed is a man destroyed. Signora Teresa (may God have her soul!) had been right. He had never been taken into account. Destroyed! . . . (pp. 419–20)

That Nostromo seizes on the 'notion of betrayal' to account for his dazed and complex feelings on his return to Sulaco reflects his conviction that 'a man betrayed is a man destroyed', for he knows only that in some unfathomable way he has been destroyed. His sense of this is so strong that he not only feels 'done for' but as if he has 'gone out of his existence'. Nostromo, that is, though he remains physically calm and collected, here confusedly registers the loss of a more profound possession of self. His sense of personal disintegration is intimately connected with a feeling that the world to which he is accustomed has dissolved around him: having 'lived in splendour and publicity up to the very moment, as it were, when he took charge of the lighter . . . ,' the realization that it is 'no longer open to him to ride through the streets, recognized by everyone, great and little', makes Sulaco 'appear to him as a town that [has] no existence' (pp. 414–15); and, given the 'strong check to [his] ruling passion', he is beset by 'confused and intimate impressions of universal dissolution' (p. 417). Nostromo's ruling passion, his obsession, is of course for the adulation of success; and having given himself to fame, living only as a public persona, he finds that he is reduced to nothing when suddenly deprived of both.

Nostromo's feeling of dissolution is associated with death when an owl ('whose appalling cry: "Ya-acabo! Ya-acabo! – it is finished; it is finished" – announces calamity and death in the popular belief') drifts 'like a large dark ball across his path' (p. 418). Earlier, 'the first thing' he sees on waking after his long sleep is a vulture, which has taken up its position within three yards of him, a 'patient watcher for the signs of death and corruption' (p. 413). What we watch is the way in which Nostromo's spiritual dissolution, his inability to keep hold of himself, is followed by the corruption of his moral being. This process, as in the case of Gould, is seen in terms of a demonic counter-possession, Nostromo's obsessive concern with reputation being transformed into an obsession with the six-month consignment of silver he has hidden on the island. His knowledge of the treasure '[possesses] his whole soul'; and its existence confuses his thoughts 'with a peculiar sort of anxiety, as though his life [has] become bound up with it' (p. 424). Postulating the way in which Sotillo might be expected to respond to hopes of obtaining the silver, Nostromo later tells Dr. Monygham that 'there is something in a treasure that fastens upon a man's mind'; and he addds that 'there is no getting away from a treasure that once fastens upon your mind' (p. 460). The immediate form his obsession with the silver takes is a determination that it should not be betrayed; and, since he cannot bring himself to trust anyone with the true story of what has happened, he says nothing about Decoud either and so in effect abandons him to his fate – as he recognizes later: 'And he wondered how Decoud had died. But he knew the part he had played himself. First a woman, then a man, abandoned each in their last extremity, for the sake of this accursed treasure. It was paid for by a soul lost and by a vanished life' (p. 502).

The actual moment of Nostromo's corruption is strikingly depicted. Returning by sea with Barrios after his famous ride to Cayta, he suddenly sees the dinghy of the lighter adrift in the gulf. Leaping overboard, he swims out to it, clambers over the stern, and, after 'a minute examination', discovers 'a brown stain on the gunwale':

> And now, with the means of gaining the Great Isabel thrown thus in his way at the earliest possible moment, his excitement had departed, as when the soul takes flight leaving the body inert upon an earth it knows no more. Nostromo did not seem to know the gulf. For a long time even his eyelids did not flutter once upon the glazed emptiness of his stare. Then slowly, without a limb having stirred, without a twitch of muscle or quiver of an eyelash, an expression, a living expression came upon the still features, deep thought crept into the empty stare – as if an outcast soul, a quiet, brooding soul, finding that untenanted body in its way, had come in stealthily to take possession. (p. 493)

Though he is already obsessed by thoughts of the treasure, it is of course Nostromo's realization that Decoud (who has left behind him only a bloodstain and an empty dinghy) must be assumed to be dead, that is the immediate cause of his falling – like an overripe fruit – into corruption, for with this realization there comes the overwhelming knowledge that he is the only man alive who knows about the silver. As he succumbs to the temptation of the treasure, he lets go of his integrity in more than one sense, and it is significant that his condition at this point is imaged as one of spiritual vacancy or nullity: it is as if his 'soul takes flight', revealing its departure in 'the glazed emptiness' of his stare. His earlier and inchoate experience of a loss of self, of having gone out of his existence, is now re-enacted with even greater force in the dinghy; and it is as if a corrupt or 'outcast' soul now stealthily fills the vacuum and 'takes possession' of his 'untenanted body'. It is this moment of loss of self and counter-possession that is the turning-point in Nostromo's life – and that gives the lie to his deathbed justification of his theft of the silver: 'How could I give back the treasure with four ingots missing? They would have said I had purloined them' (p. 559); for Nostromo, as the scene in the dinghy shows, is corrupted before he even knows the ingots are missing. And the experience leaves its marks on him, as Captain Mitchell intuitively registers: he later reports that Nostromo 'seemed quite overcome' when he told him of having found the dinghy, and that he could see at once Nostromo 'was another man': 'He seemed absolutely indifferent to what went on. I asked him on the wharf, "When are you going to take hold again, Nostromo? There will be plenty of work for the Cargadores presently" ' (pp. 487–8).

Just as Gould is consumed by the mine that takes possession of him and reduces him to a fortified hollowness, so Nostromo is eaten up by the criminality that takes hold of him. 'A transgression, a crime, entering a man's existence,' we are told, 'eats it up like a malignant growth, consumes it like a fever'; and so 'the genuineness of all [Nostromo's] qualities' is 'destroyed': 'He felt it himself, and often cursed the silver of San Tomé' (p. 523). Like Gould's, furthermore, Nostromo's obsession is seen in terms of a passion that is as insistent in its promptings as the most imperative sexual lust: 'He yearned to clasp, embrace, absorb, subjugate in unquestioned possession this treasure, whose tyranny had weighed upon his mind, his actions, his very sleep' (p. 529). Though he ardently desires Giselle, and, 'masterful and tender', begins '[to enter] slowly upon the fulness of his possession' when he first kisses her (p. 538), the subsequent action makes it clear that his real passion, like that of Gould, is not for a woman but the silver.

Thomas Moser has remarked that Conrad's handling of the love affair between Nostromo and Giselle 'very nearly wrecks the last few chapters; the prose describing it falls far below the standard of the rest of the novel'.[17] It is indeed part of the inscrutability of the creative process that a man capable of the achievement of the scenes with the lighter in the gulf could remain indifferent to the level of the prose in the following passage:

He broke out –

'Your hair like gold, and your eyes like violets, and your lips like
the rose; your round arms, your white throat.' . . .
    Imperturbable in the indolence of her pose, she blushed deeply all
over to the roots of her hair. She was not conceited. She was no more
self-conscious than a flower. But she was pleased. And perhaps even
a flower loves to hear itself praised. He glanced down, and added
impetuously –
    'Your little feet!' (pp. 535–6)

But the love affair is nonetheless necessary to the design, for it makes clear
the extent of Nostromo's corruption. This is registered not only as a
thoroughgoing criminality but also as a spiritual emptiness that in its
evocation of the absence of the man recalls the Horse of Stone. When
Giorgio Viola, who has been like a father to Nostromo (and whom he has
already used to assure his access to the silver), assumes it is Linda he
wishes to marry and Nostromo says nothing because he is 'afraid of being
forbidden the island' (p. 531), his failure to speak is eloquent of a nullity
that is appalling in its inhumanity to Giorgio and Giselle as well as
Linda. It is also, as Giselle tells him, a 'blind, mad, cruel, frightful thing'
to do (p. 538); but if Nostromo – as on an earlier and momentous occasion
– cannot see where he is heading, it is clearly indicated to us:

> [Giselle's] form drooped consolingly over the low casement towards
> the slave of the unlawful treasure. The light in the room went out,
> and weighted with silver, the magnificent Capataz clasped her round
> her white neck in the darkness of the gulf as a drowning man clutches
> at a straw. (pp. 544–5)

The analogy with the suicide of Decoud that is set up by the description
of Nostromo's embracing of Giselle suggests that the course followed by
the Capataz is strongly self-destructive in tendency – as was the case with
Gould too. And indeed, though it is Giorgio who in the end actually kills
Nostromo, we realize that he in effect kills himself when he first succumbs
to the temptation of the silver and his soul takes flight, leaving an untenanted body in the dinghy of the lighter.

*   *   *

The story of Decoud also makes manifest the self-destructive implications
of a loss of self. There is an immediately apparent analogy between the
experiences of Decoud and Nostromo. In the lighter with Nostromo,
Decoud has to contend with the blind darkness that smothers the gulf:

> The Isabels were somewhere at hand. 'On your left as you look
> foward, señor,' said Nostromo, suddenly. When his voice ceased, the

enormous stillness, without light or sound, seemed to affect Decoud's senses like a powerful drug. He didn't even know at times whether he were asleep or awake. Like a man lost in slumber, he heard nothing, he saw nothing. Even his hand held before his face did not exist for his eyes. The change from the agitation, the passions and the dangers, from the sights and sounds of the shore, was so complete that it would have resembled death had it not been for the survival of his thoughts. In this foretaste of eternal peace they floated vivid and light, like unearthly clear dreams of earthly things that may haunt the souls freed by death from the misty atmosphere of regrets and hopes. Decoud shook himself, shuddered a bit, though the air that drifted past him was warm. He had the strangest sensation of his soul having just returned into his body from the circumambient darkness in which land, sea, sky, the mountains, and the rocks were as if they had not been. (p. 262)

The 'enormous stillness, without light or sound', that Decoud confronts calls to mind the core of darkness (though confined and disturbed by an echo) that Mrs. Moore peers into in the Marabar Caves in E. M. Forster's *A Passage to India*.[18] Both Decoud and Mrs. Moore, that is to say, are suddenly made to look into a void, but where the consequence of this for Mrs. Moore is a loss of faith, for Decoud it is a loss of self. He is 'like a man lost in slumber'; and he is overcome (like Nostromo on his return to Sulaco after the collision with Sotillo's steamer) by a sense of dissolution: his very hand 'held before his face' does 'not exist for his eyes', and but for 'the survival of his thoughts', the experience 'would have resembled death'. It is an experience, at all events, that closely resembles that of Nostromo on another occasion when his untenanted body is left in the dinghy of the lighter, for Decoud has 'the strangest sensation of his soul having just returned into his body from the circumambient darkness'. And if, for Decoud, the experience provides a 'foretaste of eternal peace', for us it is both a preparation for his response to the ordeal that awaits him on the island and an adumbration of the ultimate loss of self in which that culminates.

The cause of Decoud's sense of dissolution is not unlike that of Nostromo's in the instance referred to. Decoud, we are told, is a man 'with no faith in anything except the truth of his own sensations' (p. 229), and therefore he may be said to live on his sensations in much the same way that Nostromo was accustomed to live on public adulation. Consequently, when his senses appear unable to function in the soundless darkness of the gulf, he feels unaccountably deprived of life. But his lack of faith in anything apart from his own sensations also makes him a thoroughgoing sceptic or, as the novelist refers to him, an 'imaginative materialist' (p.

364). It is a neat phrase, and it deftly relates Decoud as an ideological instance of material interest to the more common commercial varieties that are depicted on another level of the novel. He is even more significantly related to the magnate of San Tomé, however – and on the level on which the drama of self is enacted – for his scepticism or materialism is as obsessive a passion as that of Gould for the mine.

Decoud is placed for us by his own view of himself in relation to Father Corbelàn:

> [Father Corbelàn] rolled his black eyes upwards. By the side of the frail diplomatist [i.e. Don José Avellanos] – the life and soul of the party – he seemed gigantic, with a gleam of fanaticism in the glance. But the voice of the party, or, rather, its mouthpiece, the 'son Decoud' from Paris, turned journalist for the sake of Antonia's eyes, knew very well that it was not so, that he was only a strenuous priest with one idea, feared by the women and execrated by the men of the people. Martin Decoud, the dilettante in life, imagined himself to derive an artistic pleasure from watching the picturesque extreme of wrong-headedness into which an honest, almost sacred, conviction may drive a man. 'It is like madness. It must be – because it's self-destructive,' Decoud had said to himself often. It seemed to him that every conviction, as soon as it became effective, turned into that form of dementia the gods send upon those they wish to destroy. But he enjoyed the bitter flavour of that example with the zest of a connoisseur in the art of his choice. Those two men got on well together, as if each had felt respectively that a masterful conviction, as well as utter scepticism, may lead a man very far on the by-paths of political action. (p. 200)

Decoud sees clearly that the Father, for all his magnificence of bearing, is in his single-minded devotion to the church, a pitiable prey to obsession. His obsessiveness reveals itself in the 'gleam of fanaticism' in his glance, and in the monomania which dictates his actions: he is a man 'with one idea', a 'masterful conviction', that leads him to an 'extreme of wrong-headedness'. In relation to Gould, it will be recalled, we were told that 'a man haunted by a fixed idea is insane', for he might well 'bring the heaven down pitilessly upon a loved head'; Decoud considers that the Father's obsession is 'like madness . . . because it's self-destructive', thus making explicit what remains implicit in the case of Gould. But Decoud's sceptical estimate of the priest obviously has an application not only to Gould. He is 'a connoisseur' of the Father's particular kind of frailty because he finds himself on home ground, as it were, 'in the art of his choice'; and though he has a taste for such analysis, he cannot help registering 'the bitter flavour' of its application to himself. For his own 'utter scepticism' is not only grammatically juxtaposed with the Father's 'masterful conviction'; it is an obsession of a like order, a passion that (as in the case of both Gould and Nostromo) proves to be stronger than his feeling for a woman, and it is literally self-destructive. Father Corbelàn, just prior to Decoud's contemplation of him, says he is 'the victim of this faithless age' (p. 198); it would be more accurate to view him, as the novelist does at the end of his tale, as a victim of 'the self-destructive passion of . . . utter scepticism' (p. 537).

Albert J. Guerard has interestingly suggested that there is 'a marked discrepancy between what Decoud does and says and is, and what the narrator or omniscient author says about him'; and he maintains that 'if we subtract the ironic epithets, authorial summaries, and solitary suicide, a quite different person emerges'.[19] But I do not think that Conrad, in presenting Decoud as a lover or as an active participant in Costaguanan affairs, is inconsistent. Decoud's exclusive belief in his own sensations is shown to fail to provide a lasting basis for his love for Antonia, which accordingly proves to be unable to sustain him in his hour of need; and, in putting an end to his own life, he does not show much concern with hers. His giving himself to his scepticism, moreover, is not inconsistent with the type of activity he engages in since this allows full play for his cynicism; and the nullity which is a consequence of such a surrender of self reveals itself in an idiosyncratic but unmistakable moral nihilism: the only idea he cares for, he tells Mrs. Gould, is 'not to be separated from Antonia', and he adds: 'I am not deceiving myself about my motives. She won't leave Sulaco for my sake, therefore Sulaco must leave the rest of the Republic to its fate. . . . I cannot part with Antonia, therefore the one and indivisible Republic of Costaguana must be made to part with its western province' (p. 215). And we can hardly subtract the solitary suicide, for that is of the essence.

Decoud's response to the solitude he experiences on the island on which Nostromo leaves him is in line with his earlier reaction to the darkness of the gulf: he finds himself 'solitary on the beach like a man in a dream' (p. 301), and he becomes 'oppressed by a bizarre sense of unreality affecting the very ground upon which he [walks]' (p. 302). This sense of unreality is intensified to a point where he ultimately '[dies] from solitude' (p. 496):

The brilliant 'Son Decoud', the spoiled darling of the family, the lover of Antonia and journalist of Sulaco, was not fit to grapple with himself single-handed. Solitude from mere outward condition of existence becomes very swiftly a state of soul in which the affectations of irony and scepticism have no place. It takes possession of the mind, and drives forth the thought into the exile of utter unbelief. After three days of waiting for the sight of some human face, Decoud caught himself entertaining a doubt of his own individuality. It had merged into the world of cloud and water, of natural forces and forms of nature. . . . (p. 497)

On the island Decoud is 'not fit to grapple with himself single-handed' because he discovers that, in effect, he has no self left to take hold of. Having surrendered himself to his scepticism, having 'recognized no other virtue than intelligence and . . . erected passions into duties' (p. 498), he is reduced to nothing when deprived of objects on which his intelligence and passion can play, when deprived, that is, of what he habitually lives by. In 'a state of soul' which is thus a state of vacancy, he is open to a counter-possession; and it is the solitude that 'takes possession of [his] mind', driving out the last vestiges of his belief in himself or others. His spiritual disintegration manifests itself in his feeling that his individuality has 'merged into the world of cloud and water'. At this point, and in a way which strikingly recalls the response of Jim on board the *Patna*, he begins to give way to the abandon of hopelessness and despair, seeing the universe as a 'succession of incomprehensible images' and converting possibility into abysmal fact: 'Nostromo was dead. Everything had failed ignominiously. He no longer dared to think of Antonia. She had not survived. But if she survived he could not face her. And all exertion seemed senseless' (p. 498). Before he kills himself on the tenth day of his isolation on the island, with the solitude (as previously the case with the darkness) appearing 'like a great void' and himself feeling quite 'impalpable', Decoud begins to long for the end, for the peace of death (pp. 498–9). It is by a spreading 'soft spot' (though explicitly undiscerned) that he is finally undone.

*   *   *

Dr. Monygham serves as a foil to Gould and Nostromo and Decoud, the essential features of his story offering a mirror-image of theirs. He also starts where they end. His collapse goes back to the days of Guzman Bento when he was imprisoned 'at the time of the so-called Great Conspiracy' and 'betrayed some of his best friends amongst the conspirators' (p. 312):

> The doctor had been a very stubborn prisoner, and, as a natural consequence of that 'bad disposition' (so Father Beron called it), his subjugation had been very crushing and very complete. That is why the limp in his walk, the twist of his shoulders, the scars on his cheeks were so pronounced. His confessions, when they came at last, were very complete, too. Sometimes on the nights when he walked the

floor, he wondered, grinding his teeth with shame and rage, at the fertility of his imagination when stimulated by a sort of pain which makes truth, honour, self-respect, and life itself matters of little moment. . . .

When making his extorted confessions to the Military Board, Dr. Monygham was not seeking to avoid death. He longed for it. Sitting half-naked for hours on the wet earth of his prison, and so motionless that the spiders, his companions, attached their webs to his matted hair, he consoled the misery of his soul with acute reasonings that he had confessed to crimes enough for a sentence of death – that they had gone too far with him to let him live to tell the tale. (pp. 373–4)

Given the doctor's stubborn resistance to torture, his determination not to let go, it takes a lot to make him confess; but when he finally breaks down, his subjugation is so 'crushing and . . . complete' as to posit a nullification of the self he has hitherto possessed. The nullity issues in a moral nihilism which regards 'truth, honour, self-respect, and life itself' as 'matters of little moment'. And it typically manifests itself, furthermore, in a physical paralysis of non-being, for he sits 'so motionless' that the spiders attach their webs to his hair, and in a spiritual despair that makes him 'long' for the release of death.

Nor does the restoration of his freedom bring a spiritual liberation. On the contrary, he has become 'in a manner, the slave of a ghost', for years later he is haunted by the idea that he 'would have quailed' before Father Beron had he met him in the street; and, though the Father is dead by then, the 'sickening certitude' prevents the doctor from 'looking anybody in the face' (pp. 373–4). Dr. Monygham, in other words, having once lost possession of himself, is subsequently possessed by his disgrace. With his 'outcast spirit', he is steadily consumed by it too, and is left with a 'withered soul' (p. 369). Seen (even during the process of his redemption) as a lonely figure, 'hopping amongst the dark bushes like a tall bird with a broken wing' (p. 411), the doctor is an image of that frustration of being which is a common affliction in the novel.

But the doctor is redeemed – and by passion, following a path which is the reverse of that taken by Gould, Nostromo, and Decoud:

The doctor was loyal to the mine. It presented itself to his fifty-years' old eyes in the shape of a little woman in a soft dress with a long train, with a head attractively overweighted by a great mass of fair hair and the delicate preciousness of her inner worth, partaking of a gem and a flower, revealed in every attitude of her person. As the dangers thickened round the San Tomé mine this illusion acquired force, permanency, and authority. It claimed him at last! This claim, exalted by a spiritual detachment from the usual sanctions of hope and reward, made Dr. Monygham's thinking, acting, individuality extremely dangerous to himself and to others, all his scruples vanishing in the proud feeling that his devotion was the only thing that stood between an admirable woman and a frightful disaster.

It was a sort of intoxication which made him utterly indifferent to Decoud's fate, but left his wits perfectly clear for the appreciation of Decoud's political idea. It was a good idea – and Barrios was the only instrument of its realization. The doctor's soul, withered and shrunk by the shame of a moral disgrace, became implacable in the expansion of its tenderness. . . . (p. 431)

It is the doctor's passion for Mrs. Gould, we see, his loyal devotion to her, that steadily begins to fill the void of his being, the soul 'withered and shrunk by the shame of a moral disgrace'. His feeling for her issues no doubt in a number of illusory qualities that he bestows on her, but for him it is no illusion; on the contrary, it gradually acquires 'force, permanency, and authority', and finally, when 'it [claims] him at last', takes possession of him. The nature of his passion is notable. First, his passion in the world of San Tomé (as that of Dickens's heroes in the Victorian world of the late novels) postulates the existence of another kind of wealth, for Monygham gives his devotion to 'the delicate preciousness' of Mrs. Gould's 'inner worth'. In striking contrast to Nostromo, therefore, he is ultimately able to live 'on the inexhaustible treasure of his devotion drawn upon in the secret of his heart like a store of unlawful wealth' (p. 504). Second, since his passion is unrequited, and since he accepts that it offers him neither the hope nor the reward of reciprocation, it is essentially selfless and disinterested. As such it is markedly different from the passions of Gould, Nostromo and Decoud; and where they are undone by theirs, Monygham is 'exalted', having attained to 'spiritual detachment'. Like theirs, however, his passion is also 'extremely dangerous' since, in his determination to save Mrs. Gould from 'a frightful disaster', it dispels 'all his scruples', making him let go of all customary restraints as in 'a sort of intoxication'. But this, we see, is the kind of losing of self that is also a finding, for if the doctor's withered and shrunken soul becomes 'implacable', it also 'expands' in its tenderness. It is significant that Conrad should first depict the paradox of the loss that is a finding in this context, for though Monygham's passion is not consummated, it is sexual in origin, and it is sexual intercourse that most readily offers an instance of the phenomenon. It is because the passions of Gould, Nostromo and Decoud are not turned outward to another person but inward on the self that they prove to be so destructive.

Like theirs, moreover, the doctor's passion has an obsessive dimension. When he undertakes to play his game with Sotillo in an effort to save the situation at Sulaco, he does so 'in a fanatical spirit' (p. 439), being urged on by 'the fanaticism of his devotion' (p. 453) to Mrs. Gould and so to the mine. But, once again, it is not with himself that he is obsessively concerned, and consequently he is able to regain or reconstitute the self that disintegrated under torture. 'Absorbing all his sensibilities', his devotion leaves 'his heart steeled against remorse and pity' (p. 438), but the possession of a steeled heart, it will be recalled, is also the saving counter to a manifestation of the soft spot. And indeed, strong in heart, the doctor is calmly ready to risk his life in attempting to deceive Sotillo, being prepared to keep the game up for 'as long as [he lives]' (p. 437) and to make 'the sacrifice of his life' (p. 458). It is with a justifiable pride that he says to Nostromo: 'You are not the only one here who can look an ugly death in the face' (p. 437). As events turn out, he is taken at his word, Sotillo having led him out to be hung when the arrival of Barrios fortuitously saves him. It is because he is 'possessed by the exaltation of self-sacrifice' (p. 461) that Monygham is ready to give 'himself up for lost' (p. 484); but such a readiness is quite different from the despair in which Decoud takes his life – and it is rewarded by a recrudescence of self that absorbs and dissipates the sense of disgrace that was previously consuming him. He tells Mrs. Gould that he feels 'rewarded beyond [his] deserts', and refers to the career he has made as Inspector-General of State Hospitals, but he keeps secret his real reward which (in addition to his inexhaustible treasure) is the recovery of his 'self-respect', a development that is 'marked inwardly by the almost complete disappearance from his dreams of Father Beron' (pp. 507–8).

It is in *Nostromo*, then, that Conrad would seem for the first time to recognize clearly that a capacity to let go may be a virtue. It is precisely at this point, indeed, that his theme of material interests meets that of possession. In this respect the scene is set in the opening pages when we are told of the gringos of Azuera, whose 'souls cannot tear themselves away from their bodies mounting guard over the discovered treasure': 'They are now rich and hungry and thirsty – a strange theory of tenacious gringo ghosts suffering in their starved and parched flesh of defiant heretics, where a Christian would have renounced and been released' (p. 5). It is not until near the end of the novel that there is an analogous moment in the lives of the possessed of Costaguana. When the dying Nostromo, despite an 'involuntary reluctance' that he cannot overcome, tries to dispossess himself of the secret of the treasure and offers to tell Mrs. Gould where it is hidden, she will not let him: ' "No, Capataz," she said. "No one misses it now. Let it be lost for ever" ' (p. 560). This is a renunciation, no doubt, but it remains no more than a gesture, for on leaving Nostromo Mrs. Gould settles once more for her emptily conventional role as 'the first lady of Sulaco, the wife of the Señor Administrador of the San Tomé mine' (p. 561). Life in the Occidental Republic goes on, that is to say, though we cannot help wondering what it will profit its citizens if they gain the whole world and lose their own souls. It is Dr. Monygham alone who – through his self-effacement – establishes the profit of loss.

CHAPTER SIX

The Secret Agent

I

JOCELYN BAINES roundly declares that *The Secret Agent*, 'unlike most of Conrad's work, [lacks] a unifying theme, and when it is carefully examined falls apart into a succession of only superficially related scenes'.[1] But the fact that the novel has perhaps the most compact unity of plot of any of Conrad's books, presenting us with an action in which every incident and every character has its meticulously ordained place, should incline us to believe that it is not notably different from his other work in respect of a unifying theme. Form in Conrad, as we have seen, is not readily detachable from substance. What Baines's view suggests, however, is that the unifying theme is not clearly apparent on the surface of the action, and that there is no convenient tag – such as that of 'material interests' in *Nostromo* – to provide us with a quick principle of organization. If the succession of scenes appears to be only superficially related, we are perhaps challenged to perceive unity in unexpected relations. Not that we are today without help in the matter, for, in what must be the most revealing preface he ever wrote, Conrad in 1920 indicated where we might look.

In describing the gestation of the novel, Conrad relates how 'at last the story of Winnie Verloc stood out complete from the days of her childhood to the end', and he emphatically adds: '*This* book is *that* story, reduced to manageable proportions, its whole course suggested and centred round the absurd cruelty of the Greenwich Park explosion' (p. xii). This statement confronts us with two problems. It challenges us, first, to define the sense in which the book that is nominally about Winnie's husband, the secret agent who is certainly at the centre of the action, is actually about her; and so to characterize her story with the utmost precision. The experience of reading *Nostromo* before *The Secret Agent* is of help here, for Winnie's story, in its own appropriate terms, turns out to follow the same pattern as the stories of Gould, Nostromo and Decoud. Our awareness of this is of considerable aid in understanding what happens to Winnie since Conrad, drawing with swift assurance on the insights of the earlier work, is more indirect in his presentation of her. Second, though the sense in which Winnie's story may be said to 'centre round . . . the Greenwich Park explosion' is clear enough, we are further challenged, if the novel does indeed have a unifying theme, to establish a relation between her story and other stories which likewise centre in the explosion – between it and that of her brother Stevie, who is killed in the explosion, for instance, or that of the Professor, the anarchist who provides the explosives, or that of the police, who speedily solve the Greenwich Park mystery.

Winnie's story may be called A Tale of Two Boats:

> But this vision [i.e. of her dreary life with her mother and brother in their Belgravian boarding house] had a breath of a hot London summer in it, and for a central figure a young man wearing his Sunday best, with a straw hat on his dark head and a wooden pipe in his mouth. Affectionate and jolly, he was a fascinating companion for a voyage down the sparkling stream of life; only his boat was very small. There was room in it for a girl-partner at the oar, but no accommodation for passengers. He was allowed to drift away from the threshold of the Belgravian mansion while Winnie averted her tearful eyes. He was not a lodger. The lodger was Mr. Verloc, indolent and keeping late hours, sleepily jocular of a morning from under his bed-clothes, but with gleams of infatuation in his heavy-lidded eyes, and always with some money in his pockets. There was no sparkle of any kind on the lazy stream of his life. It flowed through secret places. But his barque seemed a roomy craft, and his taciturn mag-nanimity accepted as a matter of course the presence of passengers.
>
> Mrs. Verloc pursued the visions of seven years' security for Stevie loyally paid for on her part; of security growing into confidence, into a domestic feeling, stagnant and deep like a placid pool, whose guarded surface hardly shuddered on the occasional passage of Comrade Ossipon, the robust anarchist with shamelessly inviting eyes, whose glance had a corrupt clearness sufficient to enlighten any woman not absolutely imbecile. (p. 243)

In letting the butcher boy drift away in his small boat and in choosing the more accommodating craft of Mr. Verloc, Winnie is of course actuated by one primary consideration – the attainment of 'security for Stevie', though she is glad to be able to provide for her mother too. Stevie's security, indeed, is her obsession, her wish to protect him giving her a 'singleness of purpose' that has 'the unerring nature and the force of an instinct' (p. 179), and making her life 'of single purpose and of a noble unity of inspiration, like those rare lives that have left their mark on the thoughts and feelings of mankind' (p. 242). Winnie's feeling for Stevie, moreover, provides her with 'what there [is] of the salt of passion in her tasteless life – the passion of indignation, of courage, of pity, and even of self-sacrifice' (p. 174). Her attitude might thus at first seem to be both soundly natural and nobly self-sacrificial, but the abandon of obsession – as *Nostromo* repeatedly shows – has other and more compromising attributes. Her self-sacrifice is not analogous to the self-effacement of a Dr. Monygham, for instance, since it calculatingly encompasses the deception and exploitation of another person. To the bitter end the magnanimous Verloc holds to the belief that he is 'loved for himself', whereas the truth is that it is not only his magnanimity that is consistently and shamelessly played on. Though Winnie, in 'her respectability and her ignorance', is initially a sexual innocent, she soon learns an easy way to her husband's heart, mastering the sort of glance – 'half arch, half cruel, out of her large eyes' – of which 'the Winnie of the Belgravian mansion days would have been incapable' (p. 196); and for seven years she plays up to his love though, after his death, she implies that she even felt physical revulsion from him: 'Seven years – seven years a good wife to him,' she says to Ossipon, 'the kind, the good, the generous, the – And he loved me. Oh, yes. He loved me till I sometimes wished myself – ' (p. 276). Winnie's self-sacrifice, therefore, should be sharply distinguished from that of her mother, who, actuated by the same concern for Stevie, is completely disinterested and exploits only the resources of charity when – an 'heroic old woman' – she resolves 'on going away from her children as an act of devotion and as a move of deep policy' (p. 162), and takes herself off to an almshouse. Such self-effacement is viewed as heroic, it being repeatedly referred to in such terms (pp. 161, 162, 163); and it is this quality, standing out in a novel whose perspective is otherwise ironic,[2] that would seem to account for a puzzling reference to Winnie's mother in a letter of Conrad's to Edward Garnett: 'I am no end proud to see you've spotted my poor old woman. You've got a fiendishly penetrating eye for one's most secret intentions. She *is* the heroine.'[3]

Winnie's self-sacrifice, furthermore, must be seen as a perverse denial of self and of life. The reference in the previously quoted passage to the young man she loves presenting himself as a companion 'for a voyage down the sparkling stream of life' associates life with sparkle; and so her choice of Verloc, when there is 'no sparkle of any kind on the lazy stream of his life', suggests a resigned acceptance on her part of non-being, of vacancy, as it were. If her 'domestic feeling' is 'like a placid pool', it is also 'stagnant', the placidity of torpor. Winnie's choice is the more perverse in that she clearly has a strong sexuality: she is 'a young woman with a full bust, in a tight bodice, and with broad hips' (p. 5); she has 'glossy dark hair' and a 'full, rounded form' (p. 6). All her passion, however, is deflected into her feeling for her brother: in bed with her husband, it is her 'ardour o protecting compassion' for Stevie that tinges Winnie's 'sallow cheeks with a faint dusky blush' and makes 'her big eyes gleam under the dark lids' as she hangs over Mr. Verloc's recumbent form 'in her anxiety that he should believe Stevie to be a useful member of the family'; it is then that Mrs. Verloc looks 'as young as Winnie used to look, and much more animated than the Winnie of the Belgravian days had ever allowed herself to appear to gentlemen lodgers' (p. 58).

Winnie herself, of course, has no doubt about the morality of her conduct. Mr. Verloc provides accommodation in his barque for her and her family, and she 'loyally pays' for this, giving herself to him, and barely allowing herself to notice the 'shamelessly inviting eyes' of Comrade Ossipon. (In passing, it should be noted how well Conrad suggests sexual tensions in this novel, his reliance on implication and understatement proving far more effective than the overblown rhetoric he customarily employs for such purposes.) But it is clear that Winnie's morality of the market-place has created an existence which, if 'admirable' in its 'continuity of feeling and tenacity of purpose', is 'foreign to all grace and charm, without beauty and almost without decency' (p. 244). And it is not only her husband whom she in fact cheats. Her obsessive self-sacrifice results as surely in a loss of self as the obsessive self-aggrandizement of a Gould or a Nostromo. Her 'protecting passion' (p. 195), moreover, aligns her with other protectors in the novel, notably her husband and a policeman such as Chief Inspector Heat, both 'pro-tectors of society'; and it becomes apparent that her state of vacancy, her nullity of being, should ultimately be related to a moral nihilism that is similar to theirs (we shall see) in its exclusive concern with an end and its bland indifference to the means employed to achieve it.

Winnie contrives, however, to maintain 'an equable soul', and to remain blind to her own inner hollowness – as to most other things – by making 'her force and her wisdom' of the 'instinct' that 'things do not stand much looking into' (p. 177), that it is preferable to be in the dark. Her eyes are opened to the true nature of her husband on the day of the Greenwich Park explosion when she discovers that he has used the half-witted Stevie for his own devious purposes, and that the boy has been killed in the process. This atrociously presents itself to her mind as the murder of her brother: 'And she thought without looking at Mr. Verloc: "This man took the boy away to murder him. He took the boy away from his home to murder him. He took the boy away from me to murder him!" ' (p. 246) – and she at last realizes that she has been 'a blind fool' (p. 247). But the effect of the discovery, as her habitual world seems to disintegrate around her, is to plunge her into a still more appalling darkness: 'She kept still as the population of half the globe would keep still in astonishment and despair, were the sun suddenly put out in the summer sky by the perfidy of a trusted providence' (p. 244). Her sense of the collapse of her world is but the prelude to a personal disintegration: 'her personality' seems to have been 'torn into two pieces' (p. 254); her 'moral nature' is 'subjected to a shock of which, in the physical order, the most violent earthquake of history could only be a faint and languid rendering' (p. 255); and, in the face of her despair, all her husband can do is to reiterate that she try 'to pull herself together' (pp. 232, 240, 247).

The kind of shock Winnie is subjected to is great enough and terrible enough to account for her collapse, but it is also implied that her disintegration is so complete because of her habitual vacancy, the empty vessel shattering more incontinently than a solid one might be expected to. The connection, in Winnie's case, between breakdown – or madness – and vacancy is at any rate implied by a vivid image: as she listens at the keyhole to the conversation between Chief Inspector Heat and her husband that reveals the truth to her, her eyes are said to be 'like two black holes' in her 'pale face' – the eyes, that is, that are 'crazed eyes' (p. 210). Forcibly deprived of her old obsession, Winnie is at this point possessed by a new one that rushes in to fill the void: 'Mrs Verloc's mental condition had the merit of simplicity; but it was not sound. It was governed too much by a fixed idea. Every nook and cranny of her brain was filled with the thought that this man, with whom she had lived without distaste for seven years [the revulsion pushing into consciousness still being repressed here], had taken the "poor boy" away from her in order to kill him – . . .' (p. 249); and so she lets most of what Verloc says go by her, for 'what could words do to her for good or evil in the face of her fixed idea?' (p. 250)

Winnie's derangement and prolonged immobility, it becomes clear, are likely to issue in violence, though it is a moot point against whom this will be directed. At first it seems as if it will be directed against herself, for, no longer able to see what there is 'to keep her in the world at all', she begins 'to look upon herself as released from all earthly ties', her 'contract with existence', as represented by Verloc, being 'at an end' (p. 251). We recall that Nostromo, when deprived of what he has habitually lived by, feels as if he has gone out of his existence. But then Verloc caps his earlier crassness – 'Do be reasonable, Winnie. What would it have been if you had lost me?' (p. 234) – by asking her to come to him as he lies on the sofa, using 'a peculiar tone, which might have been the tone of brutality, but was intimately known to Mrs. Verloc as the note of wooing' (p. 262). She comes to him then, but it is to stab him to death with the carving knife she has snatched up, Verloc having time to take in that she has 'gone raving mad – murdering mad', that she is an 'armed lunatic', but no more. It is the madness, not a mystical or poetic justice, that accounts for her resemblance to Stevie as she moves towards Verloc: 'As if the homeless soul of Stevie had flown for shelter straight to the breast of his sister, guardian, and protector, the resemblance of her face with that of her brother grew at every step, even to the droop of the lower lip, even to the slight divergence of the eyes' (p. 262). Dreading to be hung for the murder, Winnie within three minutes forms 'the resolution to drown herself in the Thames' (p. 269). Though 'the instinct of self-preservation' (p. 273) leads her to cling to Ossipon when he fortuitously presents himself, she cannot cope with his desertion of her and takes her own life.

If we try to sum up Winnie's story, then, the story that *is The Secret Agent*, we may say that it is essentially a story of disintegration, the disintegration that follows a prolonged state of nullity or vacancy, and issues in the violence of murder and self-destruction. But Winnie's story is also, in a sense, Stevie's story; and the presentation of Stevie accordingly offers us a ready check on the validity of our view of Winnie.

From the outset one fact about Stevie is stressed over and over again. He is not all there, and this is repeatedly viewed as a state of vacancy: he is 'delicate and, in a frail way, good-looking, too, except for the vacant droop of his lower lip' (p. 8); when he remains 'very good and quiet', he '[stares] vacantly' (p. 39); on the memorable occasion when he and Winnie escort their mother to the almshouse, 'his vacant mouth and distressed eyes [depict] the state of his mind', and 'on the box', Stevie shuts 'his vacant mouth first' in order to tell the driver not to whip the horse (pp. 156, 157); in a later exchange with the driver, he looks 'vacantly into [his] fierce little eyes', but in response to his vehemence, 'Stevie's vacant gaze' changes slowly 'into dread' (p. 166), and when he is finally left alone, he glares 'with vacant sulkiness' (p. 169); it is 'with an aspect of hopeless vacancy' that he gives up the 'intellectual enterprise' of thinking intensely (p. 172); and when Mr. Verloc directs 'a casual and somnolent glance at Stevie', he registers him as 'delicate, pale-faced, his rosy mouth open vacantly' (p. 183).

Following his indoctrination of Stevie and having 'gauged the depth of [his] fanaticism', Verloc relies on the boy's 'blind docility' and 'blind devotion' (for Stevie is in the dark about most things) to bring their Greenwich Park enterprise to a successful conclusion (p. 229). But 'within five minutes of being left to himself', Stevie stumbles and – in the central epiphany of the novel – blows himself up (p. 230). The novelist seems to go out of his way to convey the extent of Stevie's disintegration. The constable, who was 'the first man on the spot after the explosion', tells Chief Inspector Heat that he was forced to use a shovel in order to collect all the remains; and though Heat is 'shocked' by his inspection of those remains in the hospital mortuary, it is (to say the least) prolonged by the novelist. The Inspector stands his ground before the sight of 'a heap of rags, scorched and bloodstained, half concealing what might have been an accumulation of raw material for a cannibal feast' (p. 86). Stooping over the remains, Heat has to fight down an 'unpleasant sensation in his throat':

> The shattering violence of destruction which had made of that body a heap of nameless fragments affected his feelings with a sense of ruthless cruelty, though his reason told him the effect must have been as swift as a flash of lightning. The man, whoever he was, had died instantaneously; and yet it seemed impossible to believe that a human body could have reached that state of disintegration without passing through the pangs of inconceivable agony. (p. 87)

And while he broods about 'the inexplicable mysteries of conscious existence', the Chief Inspector goes on 'peering at the table with a calm face and the slightly anxious attention of an indigent customer bending over what may be called the by-products of a butcher's shop with a view to an inexpensive Sunday dinner' (p. 88). Stevie's story, too, the novelist seems emphatically and repeatedly to suggest, is one of vacancy leading to disintegration – leading even, if we take Verloc's harsher view of the matter, to self-destruction: 'If only that lad had not stupidly destroyed himself!' (p. 253), he mournfully reflects.

II

A number of critics have commented on the various ways in which Dickens's influence makes itself felt in *The Secret Agent*, Frederick R. Karl's account being perhaps the most comprehensive:

> It soon becomes apparent that Conrad's London is a direct outgrowth of Dickens', with perhaps overtones of the Paris of Baudelaire. In regard to Dickens, I have in mind a book like *Our Mutual Friend*, in which the scrubby side of London is the very stuff of the story . . . or a novel like *Little Dorrit*, in which the Marshalsea becomes the equivalent of prison-London in *The Secret Agent*. Even Conrad's eccentrics are not far removed from the character creations of Dickens – the Professor, for instance, is obviously a caricature of an idea. Further, the scene between the Assistant Commissioner and Sir Ethelred . . . is Dickensian humor; and the scenes involving Winnie's mother and brother have Dickensian grotesqueness. . . .[4]

To this list of resemblances we might add a young man taken straight out of Dickens, down to his very name, Toodles; and similarities of style and organization. The stylistic echoes of Dickens are on occasion so uncanny as to suggest a reincarnation rather than an influence: 'Vast in bulk and stature, with a long white face, which, broadened at the base by a big double chin, appeared egg-shaped in the fringe of thin greyish whisker, the great personage seemed an expanding man' (p. 136); 'Sir

Ethelred opened a wide mouth, like a cavern, into which the hooked nose seemed anxious to peer' (p. 138); 'Mr. Verloc went on divesting himself of his clothing. . . . All was so still without and within that the lonely ticking of the clock on the landing stole into the room as if for the sake of company' (p. 179); '. . . she turned on and lighted . . . one of the two gas-burners, which, being defective, first whistled as if astonished, and then went on purring comfortably like a cat' (p. 191). Dorothy Van Ghent, one likes to think, might well have given us an interesting view of the Conradian world from Todgers's. Dickens's stylistic influence, at all events, is salutary; and, in combination with the muscular discipline imparted by the ironic method, may perhaps help account for the fact that *The Secret Agent* is by far the most well written of Conrad's books – and the most enjoyable. Indeed, though it clearly does not have the majestic scope of *Nostromo*, it seems to me that, in the smooth assurance of its effects – it is the only Conrad novel that does not offend by even a momentary lapse – in its striking economy of means, and in the force of its vision, it is his finest artistic achievement.[5] It is one of those rare books that hides its complexities beneath a surface simplicity, but these, I shall try to show, are well worth digging for.

It is perhaps because London was foreign territory to Conrad the writer, *The Secret Agent* being his first major work to be set in the city, that he used Dickens as a guide, getting at his own London, as it were, through the London of novels such as *Bleak House*, *Little Dorrit* and *Our Mutual Friend*. In doing so he would seem to have divined and appropriated some of Dickens's structural principles, for while *The Secret Agent* is unlike Conrad's other work in its method of organization, it is strikingly similar to that of Dickens in the novels referred to. I have argued elsewhere at length[6] that Dickens, within the framework of a unifying plot, points to thematic correspondences through the extensive use of analogies that are established by the recurrence of poetic images. This is precisely what Conrad does with consummate skill in *The Secret Agent*, combining the poetic and ironic methods to unique effect in his work.

An awareness of the method employed helps us tackle the second problem posed by Conrad's placing of Winnie's story at the centre of the novel: the discovery of a relation between her story and that of the anarchists and policemen and government minister and society hostess by which it is surrounded. Conrad is instructive here, for in a fascinating account of how he came to conceive the novel, he also reveals how he himself suddenly perceived a central relation. In his preface to *The Secret Agent* he recounts how, in 'a casual conversation about . . . anarchist activities' with a friend (Ford Madox Ford), he commented on the 'perverse unreason' of the attempt, some years earlier, 'to blow up the Greenwich Observatory'. To this his friend replied, 'in his characteristically casual and omniscient manner: "Oh, that fellow was half an idiot. His sister committed suicide afterwards." ' Though Conrad says he did not 'even attempt to perceive anything' for some time, he was obviously struck by 'the illuminating quality' of those facts:

It was only the illuminating impression that remained. It remained satisfactory but in a passive way. Then, about a week later, I came upon . . . the rather summary recollections of an Assistant Commissioner of Police . . . The book was fairly interesting, very discreet of course; and I have by now forgotten the bulk of its contents. . . . I won't even try to explain why I should have been arrested by a little passage . . . in which the author . . . reproduced a short dialogue held in the Lobby of the House of Commons after some unexpected anarchist outrage, with the Home Secretary. I think it was Sir William Harcourt then. He was very much irritated and the official was very apologetic. The phrase, amongst the three which passed between them, that struck me most was Sir W. Harcourt's angry sally: 'All that's very well. But your idea of secrecy over there seems to consist of keeping the Home Secretary in the dark.' Characteristic enough of Sir W. Harcourt's temper but not much in itself. There must have been, however, some sort of atmosphere in the whole incident because all of a sudden I felt myself stimulated. And then ensued in my mind what a student of chemistry would best understand from the analogy of the addition of the tiniest little drop of the right kind, precipitating the process of crystallization in a test tube containing some colourless solution.

It was at first for me a mental change, disturbing a quieted-down imagination, in which strange forms, sharp in outline but imperfectly apprehended, appeared and claimed attention as crystals will do by their bizarre and unexpected shapes. One fell to musing before the phenomenon – even of the past: of South America, a continent of crude sunshine and brutal revolutions, of the sea, the vast expanse of salt waters, the mirror of heaven's frowns and smiles, the reflector of the world's light. Then the vision of an enormous town presented itself, of a monstrous town more populous than some continents and in its man-made might as if indifferent to heaven's frowns and smiles; a cruel devourer of the world's light. There was room enough there to place any story, depth enough there for any passion, variety enough there for any setting, darkness enough to bury five millions of lives. (pp. ix–x, xi–xii)

This remarkable description reveals how Conrad, having been struck by the illuminating possibilities in his friend's account of the personal facts relating to the Greenwich explosion, suddenly saw in the anecdote of the Home Secretary a link between them and the public realm in which he ultimately set them in the novel. It was his own seeing of a connection that was like 'the addition of the tiniest little drop of the right kind' and precipitated crystallization, that suddenly energized the images of the half-idiot fellow and his sister who committed suicide which had been lying 'passive' in his mind. Given the anecdote, it would seem to be Conrad's sense of how the fellow and his sister and the Home Secretary were all equally 'in the dark' that suddenly struck him as a liberating possibility. And then there followed a vision of darkness as the appropriate setting for the action, the darkness of a 'monstrous town' which was dark enough 'to bury five millions of lives'. It is images of darkness that are the key to the finished work as they are to its conception.

Conrad's implicit comparison of the novel in embryo with his own past work intensifies the impression of how the former took form and definition in darkness, for it is of course before his own artistic 'past' that he 'fell to musing', the immediately preceding past of *Nostromo* and *The Mirror of the Sea*. It is surprising but significant that he should associate both these works with sun and light – *Nostromo* with the 'crude sunshine' of South America, and *The Mirror of the Sea* with the sea that is 'the reflector of the world's light' – for though this is apt enough in regard to *The Mirror of the Sea*, it hardly accords with our sense of the darkness (culminating in the magnificent scenes set in the dark gulf) that in a number of respects may be said to be at the centre of *Nostromo*. As he brooded over the new work (or reviewed it later in 1920), his sense of its all-encompassing darkness must have been so strong as to differentiate it antipodally from *Nostromo*. His description of the monstrous town of *The Secret Agent* as 'a cruel devourer of the world's light' in contrast to the sea as 'the reflector of the world's light', moreover, suggests a further dimension of this placing of his own work. The contrast between land values and sea values was first tentatively pointed to, as we have seen, when Singleton of the *Narcissus* stepped ashore; and it would seem to be true to say that in the Conradian world life at sea – for all its exposure of hidden weakness – is consistently depicted as a support of enlightened values. In *The Secret Agent* Conrad undertakes to explore some of the darker implications of life ashore, setting his scene neither in the jungle nor in an underdeveloped country but in the heart of civilization – in urban England.

Various features of the form of the novel would seem to body forth the innate darkness of its substance. First, the plot, regarded as a system of relationships, seems to have been devised to emphasize that all the major characters are in the dark about a centrally important aspect of their main relationships. The Verloc family may be taken as being representative in this respect. Winnie, who anyway does not like looking too deeply into things, is quite in the dark about her husband's secret connections with both the embassy and the police. Verloc is throughout in the dark about the nature of Winnie's feelings for him, not doubting for a moment that he is loved for himself. Stevie remains in the dark about most of the things that go on round him; and the whole family is in the dark as to the motives of Winnie's mother when the old woman leaves the Verloc home. Or we may consider as representative Verloc's relationships outside the home: his anarchist friends, like Winnie, are in the dark about his contacts with the embassy and the police; Vladimir is in the dark about his relationship with Chief Inspector Heat, who in turn keeps his connection with Verloc quite dark. And if we consider the plot as an action, as the 'tenebrous affair' (p. 279) it is said to be, then the detail on which the whole plot turns, the label which Winnie has sewn in Stevie's coat, is something about which she has kept Verloc in the dark.

Conrad's dislocation of chronology, so fundamental to the conception of *Nostromo*, here quietly underpins the effect of the plot. There is only one major time-shift in *The Secret Agent*, that in Chapters VIII and IX when, having previously reached the day of the Greenwich Park explosion in Chapters IV–VII, we are taken back to a time some weeks prior to the explosion. The dislocation of the chronology has the effect of keeping the reader in the dark about the identity of the man who has been blown up at Greenwich, for we are first led to believe that it is Verloc (pp. 70, 74), though it then appears that this is apparently not the case (p. 88); and it is only after some hundred pages that we can first possibly suspect it is Stevie (pp. 186, 188, 189), the actual revelation being still further delayed (p. 205).

*   *   *

In 'The Informer', a story completed (in December 1905) shortly before Conrad began work on *The Secret Agent*, an anarchist's pronouncement that 'there's no amendment to be got out of mankind except by terror and violence' causes the narrator to have 'a disturbing vision of darkness, full of lean jaws and wild eyes'.[7] The sense of anarchist lawlessness, that is to say, triggers a direct image of the darkness of the jungle. In the novel the darkness which settles with fine impartiality on all the citizens of London, the law-abiding as well as the revolutionary, has more complex implications. The monstrous city seems to be so much a power of darkness that, even when it does not completely devour the light, it dims or tarnishes it: the 'peculiarly London sun' is said to look 'bloodshot' (p. 11), for instance, or generates a 'rusty London sunshine' (p. 26). The Verloc shop is infested with a darkness that both devours and tarnishes: 'In that shop of shady wares fitted with deal shelves painted a dull brown, which seemed to devour the sheen of the light, the gold circlet of the wedding ring on Mrs.

Verloc's left hand glittered exceedingly with the untarnished glory of a piece from some splendid treasure of jewels, dropped in a dust-bin' (p. 213). But the tarnishing that takes place in a dust-bin is a foul dirtying or sullying; and this idea is reiterated in relation to the darkness that lies beyond the shop when Winnie, after the murder, goes outside and is given 'a foretaste of drowning': 'a slimy dampness enveloped her, entered her nostrils, clung to her hair. It was not actually raining, but each gas lamp had a rusty halo of mist. The van and horses were gone, and in the black street the curtained window of the carters' eating-house made a square patch of soiled blood-red light glowing faintly very near the level of the pavement' (p. 269). It is not only the 'slimy dampness' that takes us back to the dust-bin; in that black street the light (perhaps too insistently coloured 'blood-red' in one instance) is both 'rusty' and 'soiled'. The same sort of association is made in the description of the 'gloom' of a spring day: 'In front of the great doorway a dismal row of newspaper sellers standing clear of the pavement dealt out their wares from the gutter. It was a raw, gloomy day of the early spring; and the grimy sky, the mud of the streets, the rags of the dirty men harmonized excellently with the eruption of the damp, rubbishy sheets of paper soiled with printers' ink. The posters, maculated with filth, garnished like tapestry the sweep of the curbstone' (p. 79). It is such a darkness, too, that falls on Winnie's mother as she makes her way to the almshouse: 'Night, the early dirty night, the sinister, noisy, hopeless, and rowdy night of South London, had overtaken her on her last cab drive' (p. 159). In *The Secret Agent*, it is apparent, the unclean darkness is imaged as a corrupting force, and the prevalence of this line of imagery reveals Conrad's preoccupation in the novel with urban corruption.

The particular aspect of corruption he is concerned with is itself suggested by other images of darkness. One of the most vivid of these describes the Assistant Commissioner's departure from his office: 'He left the scene of his daily labours quickly like an unobtrusive shadow. His descent into the street was like the descent into a slimy aquarium from which the water had been run off. A murky, gloomy dampness enveloped him' (p. 147). If the slime and the murk and the gloom are a familiar combination, the image of the drained aquarium adds a new dimension to the prevailing view. What it suggests, among other things (such as the dampness) that might first come to mind, is emptiness, vacancy – and we recall that we have already encountered this aspect of the darkness in the crazed black holes that are Winnie's eyes. The darkness, indeed, is repeatedly associated with a void. In the following passage, for instance, people are described as disappearing into the darkness as if into some bottomless pit, the darkness seeming to devour men as well as the light:

Brett Street was not very far away. It branched off, narrow, from the side of an open triangular space surrounded by dark and mysterious houses, temples of petty commerce emptied of traders for the night. Only a fruiterer's stall at the corner made a violent blaze of light and colour. Beyond all was black, and the few people passing in that direction vanished at one stride beyond the glowing heaps of oranges and lemons. No footsteps echoed. They would never be heard of again. (p. 150)

After the murder Winnie feels as if she has been plunged into such a void: 'She was alone in London: and the whole town of marvels and mud, with its maze of streets and its mass of lights, was sunk in a hopeless night, rested at the bottom of a black abyss from which no unaided woman could hope to scramble out' (pp. 270–1); but even when Ossipon appears and seems to offer the necessary aid, the feeling is not notably different: 'Winnie Verloc turning about held him by both arms, facing him under the falling mist in the darkness and solitude of Brett Place, in which all sounds of life seemed lost as if in a triangular well of asphalt and bricks, of blind houses and unfeeling stones' (p. 276).

I shall return to the sense in which emptiness may be regarded as a corruption; but, if the images of the aquarium, the pit, the abyss and the well all variously evoke the void in which the citizens of dark London exist, the likely consequence of such emptiness is early intimated: 'On one side the low brick houses had in their dusty windows the sightless, moribund look of incurable decay – empty shells awaiting demolition' (p. 82). What demolition effects, however, is a sudden accentuation of the emptiness, particularly when it is of an explosive kind. As Conrad remarked to Edward Garnett some ten years before he wrote the novel: 'An explosion is the most lasting thing in the universe. It leaves disorder, remembrance, room to move, a clear space. Ask your Nihilist friends.'[8] The master of explosives in *The Secret Agent*, of course, is the Professor; and when he tells Ossipon that nobody in 'the beer saloon in the basement of the renowned Silenus Restaurant' could 'hope to escape' were he to press the india-rubber ball that he has in his pocket, the robust anarchist is momentarily overwhelmed by the demolition he imagines:

For a moment Ossipon imagined the overlighted place changed into a dreadful black hole belching horrible fumes choked with ghastly rubbish of smashed brickwork and mutilated corpses. He had such a distinct perception of ruin and death that he shuddered again. (p. 67)

The 'black hole', into which Ossipon imagines 'the overlighted place' is converted, may be thought of as the central image of darkness in the novel, for lines from it radiate to key points in the pattern of the imagery. The 'ghastly rubbish' it contains leads us to the soiling, corrupting darkness of the dust-bin; the clear space evoked by the hole in contradistinction to the bustling restaurant seems to have an illogical imagistic life of its own – for it persists despite our impression of the litter with which the hole is said to be filled – and to lead us to the dark vacancy of Winnie's eyes that are 'like two black holes' in her 'pale face' which feels to her 'as if it were enveloped in flames' (p. 210); and, finally, the 'smashed brickwork and mutilated corpses' of the exploded ruin evoke the idea of disintegration and so make us aware of a new but crucial aspect of the imagery of darkness.

We are now in a better position to attempt to resolve the two problems posed by Conrad's insistence that *The Secret Agent* is Winnie's story. In its movement from vacancy to disintegration, Winnie's story, we see, runs parallel not only to the story of Stevie but also to the predominant pattern of imagery. This should not be found altogether unexpected, for Winnie's story would seem to have been given point and direction in the image of darkness that is basic to the conception of the whole novel. The rest of the novel, indeed, may be said to have taken shape around it, and in that sense it is at its centre. The darkness, however, encompasses not only Winnie and Stevie – and the Home Secretary – but a whole city; and, given the remarkable tightness of the novel, we might further expect its citizens also to be exposed to that which the darkness signifies. Winnie's story, in other words, may be thought of as the paradigmatic centre of a series of concentric circles. The larger vacancy with which the novelist is concerned is a social vacancy, a social loss of self, as it were, that expresses itself in the nullity of a pervasive and darkly corrupting moral nihilism and is itself a form of social madness or breakdown. What Winnie's story prognosticates, as we watch the pattern repeated in different social circles, is the violent disintegration of such a society.[9] *The Secret Agent*, that is to say, should be viewed as one of the four major English novels that envision the disintegration of the society that in fact collapsed in 1914. Superior to H. G. Wells's *Tono-Bungay* and E. M. Forster's *Howards End*, it is smaller than D. H. Lawrence's *Women in Love*[10] but not diminished by it.

III

Conrad was concerned it should not be thought he was offering a serious critique of anarchism in *The Secret Agent*:

> In such a tale one is likely to be misunderstood. After all, you must not take it too seriously. The whole thing is superficial and it is but a tale. I had no idea to consider Anarchism politically, or to treat it seriously in its philosophical aspect; as a manifestation of human

nature in its discontent and imbecility. . . . As to attacking Anarchism as a form of humanitarian enthusiasm or intellectual despair or social atheism, that – if it were worth doing – would be the work for a more vigorous hand and for a mind more robust, and perhaps more honest than mine.[11]

He told another correspondent that the novel is 'based on the inside know-ledge of a certain event in the history of active anarchism', but he insisted that 'otherwise it is purely a work of imagination'.[12] Conrad, that is to say, uses his anarchists for his own imaginative purposes, even if that entails a radical simplification of anarchist ideas. It is a broad tendency he seizes on, projecting it almost symbolically as symptomatic of proclivities more deviously present in the society he portrays. A novelist's sociology may be open to objection in regard to its surface truth – but it may also penetrate to a deeper imaginative truth.

The Professor, who makes an embryonic appearance in 'The Informer', where he is said to have 'the true spirit of an extreme revolutionist' since it is explosives that are 'his faith, his hope, his weapon, and his shield' (p. 88), develops into 'the perfect anarchist' (p. 95) of the novel – and, despite the irony, he is the most interesting figure in the anarchist group. On the day of the Greenwich Park explosion, Ossipon criticizes him for being too free with his 'stuff', for being ready to hand it over 'to the first fool that comes along' (p. 71), and provokes the following reply:

> 'To break up the superstition and worship of legality should be our aim. Nothing would please me more than to see Inspector Heat and his likes take to shooting us down in broad daylight with the approval of the public. Half our battle would be won then; the distintegration of the old morality would have set in in its very temple. That is what you ought to aim at. But you revolutionists will never understand that. You plan the future, you lose yourselves in reveries of economical systems derived from what is; whereas what's wanted is a clean sweep and a clear start for a new conception of life. That sort of future will take care of itself if you will only make room for it. Therefore I would shovel my stuff in heaps at the corners of the streets if I had enough for that; and as I haven't, I do my best by perfecting a really depend-able detonator.' (p. 73)

It is clear how the anarchists are related to the theme of the novel: they are the group that is avowedly dedicated to the disruption of the estab-lished social order, to the violent 'breaking up' or 'disintegration' of legality and morality. They believe in 'the destruction of what is' (p. 306), in 'making room' (or a clear space) for 'a new conception of life', and so explosives are their appropriate weapon. The Professor would accordingly be pleased to provoke 'Inspector Heat and his likes' into violent reprisals against anarchists and so undermine their moral position. It is one of the nicer ironies of the novel that the police, who are nominally contra-distinguished from the anarchists – as 'protectors of society' it is their job to defend the established order, to hold it together, as it were, and their appropriate weapon is the lockup – should be shown to have affinities with them. It is a further irony that the anarchists may be said to 'lose them-selves' not 'in reveries of economical systems derived from what is', as the Professor claims, but in a moral nihilism that is so pronounced as to suggest their inner nullity – and so to posit their own ultimate disintegra-tion. The Professor himself is the representative instance here. His readiness to shovel his stuff 'in heaps at the corners of the streets' or, relying on his 'dependable detonator', to blow to pieces not only those rash enough to risk arresting him but anyone else in the vicinity makes tangible what Karl Yundt ('the terrorist') enunciates as a principle: anarchists should be 'absolute in their resolve to discard all scruples in the choice of means' and strong enough to have 'no pity for anything on earth, including themselves' (p. 42).

What is ultimately implied by an absolute indifference to the means employed in pursuit of a desired end emerges in the Professor's conception of a better world. It is a dream of 'a world like shambles', where the weak are 'taken in hand for utter extermination':

> 'Do you understand, Ossipon? The source of all evil! They are our sinister masters – the weak, the flabby, the silly, the cowardly, the faint of heart, and the slavish of mind. They have power. They are the multitude Theirs is the kingdom of the earth. Exterminate, exter-minate! That is the only way of progress. It is! Follow me, Ossipon. First the great multitude of the weak must go, then the only relatively strong. You see? First the blind, then the deaf and the dumb, then the halt and the lame – and so on. Every taint, every vice, every prejudice, every convention must meet its doom.' (p. 303)

It is not only with the hollow Kurtz's 'Exterminate all the brutes' that we make a connection here. If Conrad's portrayal in *Nostromo* of material progress has a remarkably prophetic quality, so too does his sense of what men like the Professor would be capable of in the 'way of progress'. It is easy to dismiss the Professor as a caricature; when we bear in mind how flexible are the categories, once they are established at all, of human beings fit for extermination, it is perhaps more discerning to regard him as a prefigurement.[13] Within the more limited perspective of the novel what he ironically prefigures is his own disintegration, for, with his hand on the india-rubber ball in his pocket as he passes on 'unsuspected and deadly, like a pest in the street full of men' (p. 311), he is primed for explosion. It is not without significance, moreover, that Conrad should have chosen to end the novel on that note.

The Professor, as the india-rubber ball indicates, is also a prey to obsession. On an ideological level, his wish 'to destroy public faith in legality' is 'the imperfect formula of his pedantic fanaticism' (p. 81). But a man who is obsessed, it was repeatedly insisted in *Nostromo*, is in effect insane; and Chief Inspector Heat certainly thinks of the Professor as a 'lunatic' (p. 97). It is illustrative of the intense imaginative cohesion of the novel that it should be the feeble-minded Stevie who is blown up by the Professor's explosives – and that the attack on Greenwich Observatory should have been conceived as a deliberately mad act by Mr. Vladimir. 'Madness alone is truly terrifying,' he tells Verloc, and so decides that he needs for his purposes 'an act of destructive ferocity so absurd as to be incomprehensible, inexplicable, almost unthinkable; in fact, mad' (p. 33). Vladimir's plan, of course, is to provoke the English government into repressive measures against the anarchists, but Chief Inspector Heat can only marvel at Verloc for having agreed to carry it out: 'He [i.e. Stevie] may've been half-witted,' he says to Verloc, 'but you must have been crazy. What drove you off your head like this?' (p. 212). As we watch irrationality multiply, spreading out in ever widening circles round the prototypic Stevie, the impression grows of a general vacancy, settling over the main action like a darkness.

Madness is given a further dimension in Michaelis's view of 'the madness of self-aggrandizement' that is capitalism:

> He saw Capitalism doomed in its cradle, born with the poison of the principle of competition in its system. The great capitalists devouring the little capitalists, concentrating the power and the tools of production in great masses, perfecting industrial processes, and in the madness of self-aggrandizement only preparing, organizing, enriching, making ready the lawful inheritance of the suffering proletariat. (p. 49)

If the devouring of little capitalists by great capitalists recalls Dickens's speculative birds of prey in *Our Mutual Friend*, it is also an activity that clearly has a place in the monstrous town that is a devourer of the world's light. As an evocation of cannibalistic activity, at any rate, it badly frightens Stevie, who overhears the anarchist discussion, the more so when Yundt follows this up with some particularizing detail: 'Do you know how I would call the nature of the present economic conditions? I would call it cannibalistic. That's what it is! They are nourishing their greed on the quivering flesh and the warm blood of the people – nothing else' (p. 51). The irony, of course, is that Stevie himself, as we have already seen, is soon reduced to 'what might have been an accumulation of raw material for a cannibal feast'. He too may be said to have been devoured, the victim of the combined madness of the Professor and Vladimir and Verloc. The vacancy of Kurtz, a hollow man at the heart of another darkness, ended in a literal cannibalism; the metaphoric cannibalism in the dark and vacant city is premonitory of the madness of self-destruction – for, amid general discord, the universal wolf will at last eat up himself.

*   *   *

The anarchists are connected, through Verloc, with the police (not to mention foreign governments); and, through Michaelis, with Society (with a capital S, as Dickens liked to say). Verloc is a man of passion: 'His idleness was not hygienic, but it suited him very well. He was in a manner devoted to it with a sort of inert fanaticism, or perhaps rather with a fanatical inertness. Born of industrious parents for a life of toil, he had embraced indolence from an impulse as profound as inexplicable and as imperious as the impulse which directs a man's preference for one particular woman in a given thousand' (p. 12). In a world where small capitalists are devoured by big ones, the indolence which he embraces issues, not irrationally, in a desire for easy money, and leads in the end to his getting his living as a secret agent in the pay of a foreign embassy. But this makes him a middleman, so to speak, poised between the anarchists and the embassy; and, when Chief Inspector Heat gets on to his track and begins to use him for his own purposes, between Heat and the anarchists and between Heat and the embassy. The middle ground he occupies and which seems best to accommodate his idleness is nicely figured by the kind of business he chooses to run as the supposed means by which he earns his livelihood. He is 'a seller of shady wares' (p. 5), the purveyor of rubber goods and pornography, and as such he keeps to the dim reaches between the light of the law-abiding and the darkness of the underworld – or of the underground to which he nominally belongs.

In both capacities, as agent and shopkeeper, Verloc stands between society and its corruptions, as the novelist takes the opportunity to tell us in relation to one of Verloc's noble utterances – when he says to Winnie: 'Don't you make any mistake about it: if you will have it that I killed the boy, then you've killed him as much as I':

> In sincerity of feeling and openness of statement, these words went far beyond anything that had ever been said in this home, kept up on the wages of a secret industry eked out by the sale of more or less secret wares: the poor expedients devised by a mediocre mankind for preserving an imperfect society from the dangers of moral and physical corruption, both secret, too, of their kind. They were spoken because Mr. Verloc had felt himself really outraged; but the reticent

decencies of this home life, nestling in a shady street behind a shop where the sun never shone, remained apparently undisturbed. (p. 258)

The secret moral corruption from which the 'secret industry' preserves society is, of course, that which the anarchists hope insidiously to inculcate; the secret physical corruption is, presumably, of the kind spread by venereal disease, the contraceptives among Verloc's 'secret wares' being the defensive expedient in this connection. Since social disintegration is the ultimate aim of the anarchists and physical distintegration the ultimate consequence of the disease, the irony becomes the more biting when we reflect that the redoubtable Verloc, a bulwark if not a pillar of society, is unable to protect his own family from a similar fate: the subject of his remarks is the disintegrated Stevie, and the result of the boy's untimely end is the death of his wife and himself. But it is his own corruption which is responsible for the violent break-up of the family barque, and consequently Verloc's shadiness – associated with that of the street in which he has his shop and his home, the street where the sun never shines – turns out to have darker implications. His household is not only 'hidden in the shades of the sordid street seldom touched by the sun' but also 'behind the dim shop with its wares of disreputable rubbish' (pp. 38–9), and Verloc's shadiness is thus further associated with the corruptions of the dust-bin.

The novelist early on gives a name to the particular kind of corruption to which Verloc is subject. If he is 'undemonstrative and burly in a fat-pig style', we are also told that 'his general get-up' is that of 'a well-to-do mechanic in business for himself':

> But there was also about him an indescribable air which no mechanic could have acquired in the practice of his handicraft however dishonestly exercised: the air common to men who live on the vices, the follies, or the baser fears of mankind; the air of moral nihilism common to keepers of gambling hells and disorderly houses; to private detectives and inquiry agents; to drink sellers and, I should say, to the sellers of invigorating electric belts and to the inventors of patent medicines. . . . (p. 13)

Verloc's moral nihilism, brutally demonstrated in his use of Stevie and his response to his death, is the prime cause of the main action of the novel, and so may be regarded as being at its centre. As such it is linked radially not only to that of the anarchists but also, the quoted passage suggests, to that of the police, who are institutionalized 'private detectives and inquiry agents', so to speak. And indeed Verloc is directly, if ironically, aligned with the police, for his 'vocation' is described as being that of 'a protector of society' (p. 5). His moral nihilism is also the cause of his own nullity, his loss of self being symbolized by his lack of a firm identity: he himself would be hard put to it to select as central any one of his manifold activities as informer, *agent provocateur*, police spy, anarchist, seller of pornography – and husband of Winnie (beloved for himself). In the end we begin to feel that he, like Stevie, is not really there. It is not merely another irony in this book of ironies that, after the explosion and the revelation of his part in it, Verloc should be said to feel 'terribly empty physically' (p. 232). There is nothing that can now fill that emptiness, certainly not the meat he devours, and Winnie's knife-thrust goes in easily.

*　　*　　*

Michaelis, 'the ticket-of-leave apostle of humanitarian hopes', is taken up by the 'great lady' who becomes his 'patroness' (p. 104). An eccentric and unusual lady, she has a large social range, and her drawing-room is said to be 'probably the only place in the wide world where an Assistant Commissioner of Police could meet a convict liberated on a ticket-of-leave on other than professional and official ground' (p. 105):

> . . . she amused her age by attracting within her ken through the power of her great, almost historical, social prestige everything that rose above the dead level of mankind, lawfully or unlawfully, by position, wit, audacity, fortune or misfortune. Royal Highnesses, artists, men of science, young statesmen, and charlatans of all ages and conditions, who, unsubstantial and light, bobbing up like corks, show best the direction of the surface currents, had been welcomed in that house, listened to, penetrated, understood, appraised, for her own edification. In her own words, she liked to watch what the world was coming to. . . . (p. 105)

At first sight it appears that the great lady, whose chief amusement is to watch the world by watching those who have made themselves prominent in some way, may be held accountable for nothing more vicious than a refined and intellectual sensationalism. But a lightweight herself, she too bobs up like a cork and shows 'the direction of the surface currents' in the flux of her times. Her sensationalism, we see, is grounded in a moral indifference which in the world of *The Secret Agent* is at once suspect, for, interested only in those who have risen above 'the dead level of mankind', she is not concerned how they have become conspicuous, whether 'lawfully or unlawfully', or whether they are men of ability or charlatans. The corollary of such indifference is nicely suggested in her idiosyncratic response to Michaelis's anarchist views:

163

She had come to believe almost his theory of the future, since it was not repugnant to her prejudices. She disliked the new element of plutocracy in the social compound, and industrialism as a method of human development appeared to her singularly repulsive in its mechanical and unfeeling character. The humanitarian hopes of the mild Michaelis tended not towards utter destruction, but merely towards the complete economic ruin of the system. And she did not really see where was the moral harm of it. It would do away with all the multitude of the 'parvenus', whom she disliked and mistrusted, not because they had arrived anywhere (she denied that), but because of their profound unintelligence of the world, which was the primary cause of the crudity of their perceptions and the aridity of their hearts. With the annihilation of all capital they would vanish, too; but universal ruin (providing it was universal, as it was revealed to Michaelis) would leave the social values untouched. The disappearance of the last piece of money could not affect people of position. She could not conceive how it could affect her position, for instance. . . . (pp. 110–111)

Michaelis's mild hope for 'the complete economic ruin of the system' is of course simply a variant of the Professor's desire for the disintegration of the old morality; and what their mutual conviction of the need for a clear space evokes is a black hole. The lady patroness's failure to see 'the moral harm' of this is evocative in turn, though in a tentative and genteel fashion, of their more unambiguous moral nihilism; and indeed her readiness to countenance 'the annihilation of all capital' because it will 'do away with' the parvenus, whom she dislikes for 'the crudity of their perceptions and the aridity of their hearts', suggests nothing so much as the Professor's advocacy of the extermination of the blind and the deaf and the dumb, as a preliminary to that of the halt and the lame. Her blind supposition, moreover, that the ruin of the system cannot affect her position of moneyed ease is so perversely irrational as to appear demented. In the end, the lady patroness seems to be morally ready to condone not only that violent disruption of the established order at which the anarchists aim but also her own destruction. Society (with a capital S), we see, is deeply implicated in its own threatened disintegration.[14]

*   *   *

Conrad had not ventured hitherto into the upper reaches of Society, and it must have been with some trepidation that he undertook the depiction not only of a great lady but also of a great man, the Home Secretary, Sir Ethelred. He wrote later to R. B. Cunninghame Graham that he was 'extremely flattered' to have secured his 'commendation' for his 'Secretary of State and for the revolutionary Toodles', and he added: 'It was very easy there (for me) to go utterly wrong.'[15] Graham's commendation was certainly judicious, for Conrad's portrayal of the scenes between the Home Secretary and the Assistant Commissioner of Police (not to mention that of the encounters between the Commissioner and Toodles) is both assured and delightful, one of his finest comic achievements. But these scenes are not merely evidence of a creative fertility and exuberance, for they are firmly integrated within the work as a whole, and it is with this aspect that I wish to deal.

The Home Secretary, we are told, looks like an oak, yet some of his attitudes suggest that, amid the prevailing darkness and emptiness, he is not quite as solid as he seems:

> He stood on the hearthrug in big, roomy boots, and uttered no word of greeting.
>
> 'I would like to know if this is the beginning of another dynamite campaign,' he asked at once in a deep, very smooth voice. 'Don't go into details. I have no time for that.'
>
> The Assistant Commissioner's figure before this big and rustic Presence had the frail slenderness of a reed addressing an oak. And indeed the unbroken record of that man's descent surpassed in the number of centuries the age of the oldest oak in the country.
>
> 'No. As far as one can be positive about anything I can assure you that it is not.'
>
> 'Yes. But your idea of assurances over there,' said the great man, with a contemptuous wave of his hand towards a window giving on the broad thoroughfare, 'seems to consist mainly in making the Secretary of State look a fool. I have been told positively in this very room less than a month ago that nothing of the sort was even possible.'
>
> The Assistant Commissioner glanced in the direction of the window calmly.
>
> 'You will allow me to remark, Sir Ethelred, that so far I have had no opportunity to give you assurances of any kind.'
>
> The haughty droop of the eyes was focused now upon the Assistant Commissioner.
>
> 'True,' confessed the deep, smooth voice. 'I sent for Heat. You are still rather a novice in your new berth. And how are you getting on over there?'
>
> 'I believe I am learning something every day.'
>
> 'Of course, of course. I hope you will get on.' (pp. 136–7)

In the discussion of the two men responsible for dealing with the anarchists, potentially explosive recrimination is contained in gentlemanly innuendo. The minister's resentment at being made to 'look a fool' is largely expressed in the 'contemptuous wave of his hand'; and the Assistant Commissioner's protest at the minister's impropriety in having bypassed him in consulting with Chief Inspector Heat on a matter concerning his department is politely confined to the quiet remark he allows himself. Its import, however, is not lost on the minister, as the sudden focusing on the Commissioner of 'the haughty droop' of his eyes indicates. He is sufficiently 'the great man' to 'confess' to his lapse, but he cannot help trying to justify himself; and his justification reveals the general drift of relations not only between himself and the Commissioner but also between the Commissioner and the Chief Inspector. It is a lack of confidence or trust in the Commissioner, whom he regards as 'rather a novice' in his 'new berth', that has led the minister to break established forms and turn to the old hand, Heat. But in breaking established forms in this manner, the Home Secretary is startlingly aligned with the anarchists – and his doing so proves to have a subtly disintegrative effect on the Assistant Commissioner's department: it leads Heat to believe, as the Commissioner has already discovered, that he can act as a law unto himself in the department and with impunity keep the Commissioner in the dark about his findings in regard to the Greenwich explosion. The upshot, in this instance, is that instead of working together the Commissioner and the Inspector have been set against each other. In the circumstances, the way in which the great man turns the subject with his enquiry as to how the new man is getting on 'over there' is the perfection of nonchalance.

As the interview proceeds, the minister will not allow the Commissioner to expatiate on the nature of 'an imperfect world', but insists that he 'be lucid':

'Yes, Sir Ethelred – An imperfect world. Therefore directly the character of this affair suggested itself to me, I thought it should be dealt with with special secrecy, and ventured to come over here.'

'That's right,' approved the great Personage, glancing down complacently over his double chin. 'I am glad there's somebody over at your shop who thinks that the Secretary of State may be trusted now and then.'

The Assistant Commissioner had an amused smile.

'I was really thinking that it might be better at this stage for Heat to be replaced by – '

'What! Heat? An ass – eh?' exclaimed the great man, with distinct animosity.

'Not at all. Pray, Sir Ethelred, don't put that unjust interpretation on my remarks.'

'Then what? Too clever by half?'

'Neither – at least not as a rule. All the grounds of my surmises I have from him. The only thing I've discovered by myself is that he has been making use of that man [i.e. Verloc] privately. Who could blame him? He's an old police hand. He told me virtually that he must have tools to work with. It occurred to me that this tool should be surrendered to the Special Crimes division as a whole, instead of remaining the private property of Chief Inspector Heat. I extended my conception of our departmental duties to the suppression of the secret agent. But Chief Inspector Heat is an old departmental hand. He would accuse me of perverting its morality and attacking its efficiency. He would define it bitterly as protection extended to the criminal class of revolutionists. It would mean just that to him.' (pp. 139–40)

It is not only the Assistant Commissioner's replacement of Heat that shows he is adept at making a clear space for himself to work in but also his settling of scores with both the minister and his own subordinate in a manner which is a civilized – but almost as deadly – variant of the Professor's shovelling of his stuff at street corners. He does not let the minister off with the 'amused smile' he allows himself in response to his apparently insensitive reference to the question of trust, but quietly beards him with the repeatedly derogatory references to the 'old hand' he has seen fit to put before himself. That the minister is now disposed to regard Heat 'with distinct animosity', and that the Commissioner on going back to his office finds he in turn has been the subject of Heat's 'mistrust', for the Inspector has barefacedly carried off from his superior's desk 'the only piece of material evidence' in the Greenwich case (p. 147), is illustrative of the terms on which the men in the higher echelons of the state are bound together.

The Assistant Commissioner hints to Sir Ethelred that he has had to worm out of Heat the information concerning Verloc; we know that, 'debarred by his position from going out of doors personally in quest of secrets locked up in guilty breasts', he has 'a propensity to exercise his considerable gifts for the detection of incriminating truth upon his own subordinates', that this 'peculiar instinct' feeds, since it cannot 'roam abroad', on 'the human material which [is] brought to it in its official seclusion' (pp. 117–18) – and that Heat has just made one such meal for it. The Commissioner may be said to inter the remains of Heat when he now proceeds to put the dirt in for him, though he first makes a show of being scrupulously fair to him. He shovels the dirt with some scrupulosity too, since the Inspector does in fact regard Verloc as his 'private property', and does actually wish to cover up for him in order to ensure his continued usefulness. He proceeds to tell the minister that a natural consequence of Heat's attitude is that he wants 'to fasten the guilt upon as many prominent anarchists as he can' on whatever pretext offers, while he in contradistinction is 'bent upon vindicating their innocence' (p. 142). It is an obvious irony that the Commissioner should have been made to feel that in so wishing he is 'perverting [the] morality' of the police department he heads. It is a further irony, of which the minister remains unaware, that the Assistant Commissioner is not actuated merely by a concern for police morality: he knows that one of the anarchists Heat would like to get his hands on is Michaelis, and he knows, furthermore, that if he is 'laid hold of again', then 'the distinguished and good friend of his wife', who happens to be the lady patroness of Michaelis, 'will never forgive' him (p. 112). 'If that infernal Heat has his way,' he has thought earlier, 'the fellow'll die in prison smothered in his fat, and she'll never forgive me' (p. 113). It is a final irony that, asking for 'a free hand' in the space he has cleared for his own operations, the Assistant Commissioner receives the minister's permission to give Verloc 'such assurances of personal safety' as he may think proper (pp. 142–3); for, wanting to get at the foreign embassy, he intends to engage in the same protection racket with Verloc that he has just condemned Heat for privately indulging in. This is the kind of protection, we see, that is proffered by the 'protectors of society'. The cluster of familiar motifs that emerges in this scene between the minister and the Assistant Commissioner is so striking that we now respond somewhat differently to the Professor's earlier and contemptuous collocation of anarchists and policemen: 'Like to like. The terrorist and the policeman both come from the same basket. Revolution, legality – counter moves in the same game; forms of idleness at bottom identical' (p. 69).[16]

The Professor does not think of himself as participating in the same game – 'I don't play,' he says; 'I work fourteen hours a day . . .' (p. 69) – but, if he thus excludes himself from the comparison with policemen, Chief Inspector Heat is nonetheless seen to be not only his immediate opponent but his direct counterpart. When the Assistant Commissioner finally gets Heat to admit to Verloc, the Inspector cannot help boasting a little of the usefulness of his connection with him – but he is brought up short by the Commissioner's 'significant remark':

'He failed you this time.'

'Neither had I wind of anything in any other way,' retorted Chief Inspector Heat. 'I asked him nothing so he could tell me nothing. He isn't one of our men. It isn't as if he were in our pay.'

'No,' muttered the Assistant Commissioner. 'He's a spy in the pay of a foreign government. We could never confess to him.'

'I must do my work in my own way,' declared the Chief Inspector. 'When it comes to that I would deal with the devil himself, and take the consequences. There are things not fit for everybody to know.'

'Your idea of secrecy seems to consist in keeping the chief of your department in the dark. That's stretching it perhaps a little too far, isn't it?' (p. 132)

Heat, we see, is a man of the mould of Charles Gould, with an 'adventurer's easy morality' and the 'spirit of a buccaneer'. When he says that he must do his work in his own way, he clearly believes with some confidence that the end justifies the means; but that this in effect signifies his acceptance of a moral nihilism as radical as that of the Professor's is revealed in his expressed readiness to 'deal with the devil himself'. Like the Professor, moreover – and, ironically enough, in direct relation to him – he is also led in the arrogance of his similar spiritual nullity to establish categories of those not fit to live: 'To the vigorous, tenacious vitality of the Chief Inspector, the physical wretchedness of that being [i.e. the Professor], so obviously not fit to live, was ominous; for it seemed to him that if he had the misfortune to be such a miserable object he would not have cared how soon he died' (p. 94).

It is interesting that Conrad should have chosen to give the Home Secretary's seminal lament about being kept 'in the dark' to the Assistant Commissioner. In doing so he transforms a failure of communication between a policeman and a minister into a darker condition of divided interests and disunity within the police department itself. Heat's moral position, indeed, is subversive of all sense of solidarity, and the logical consequence of his attitudes is that he is ultimately led to work actively against the Assistant Commissioner:

On the other side of the door, Chief Inspector Heat was saying to Mr. Verloc, the secret agent:

'So your defence will be practically a full confession?'

'It will. I am going to tell the whole story.'

'You won't be believed as much as you fancy you will.'

And the Chief Inspector remained thoughtful. The turn this affair was taking meant the disclosure of many things – the laying waste of fields of knowledge, which, cultivated by a capable man, had a distinct value for the individual and for the society. It was sorry, sorry meddling. It would leave Michaelis unscathed; it would drag to light the Professor's home industry; disorganize the whole system of supervision; make no end of a row in the papers . . .

'You will be preached to, no doubt,' [said the Chief Inspector],

'before they put you into the dock. And in the end you may get let
in for a sentence that will surprise you. I wouldn't trust too much the
gentleman [i.e. the Assistant Commissioner] who's been talking to
you.'
> Mr. Verloc listened, frowning.
> 'My advice to you is to clear out while you may. . . .' (pp. 210–11)

As Heat reflects on the turn the affair is taking, his spontaneous verbal
collocations are neatly revelatory of his position. For him the possibility
of exposure – the 'disclosure of many things', the 'dragging to light' of
the Professor's industry – is associated with disruption – the 'laying waste
of fields of knowledge', the 'disorganizing' of the 'system of supervision'.
The Chief Inspector, that is to say, has a vested interest in the darkness.
And in defending his own interests, Heat has no inhibitions: he is not
only ready to tell a wanted criminal that he should not trust the Assistant
Commissioner of Police but also, in advising him 'to clear out', to conspire
with him against the Commissioner. It is, of course, above all a desire to
protect himself that leads the Inspector to behave in this way, an anxiety
to ensure that his own inglorious role in relation to the Professor as well
as Verloc be kept in the dark. In his readiness to stick at nothing in protecting himself, that is to say, Chief Inspector Heat resembles nobody so
much as the Professor, who (with his india-rubber ball) is like a pest
among men. That, finally, is the ironic perspective in which he is placed.

Since Conrad's irony is so unremitting throughout the novel, however,
The Secret Agent is sometimes regarded as a work of unrelieved cynicism.
Conrad himself is on record as saying that he always shrank instinctively
'from a charge of cynicism': 'It is like a charge of being blind in one eye,
a moral disablement, a sort of disgraceful calamity that must be carried
off with a jaunty bearing – a sort of thing I am not capable of.'[17] And even
when the relentless irony has not been regarded as a sign of cynicism, it
has been viewed as an artistic defect:

> What one misses in *The Secret Agent* is some dramatic principle of
> contradiction, some force of resistance; in a word, a moral positive to
> serve literary ends. Conrad's ironic tone suffuses every sentence,
> nagging at our attention to the point where one yearns for the relief
> of direct statement almost as if it were an ethical good.[18]

To this the short answer is that Conrad's ironic method, like that of an
eighteenth-century satirist, constantly does posit the norm in relation to
which his irony functions. The whole novel makes it clear that his moral
positive, in a word (though in a number of senses), is integrity.

CHAPTER SEVEN

A. 'The Secret Sharer'

IN HIS 'Author's Note' (1920) to the three stories ('A Smile of Fortune', 'The Secret Sharer', and 'Freya of the Seven Isles') published together as *'Twixt Land and Sea* (1912), Conrad refers to *The Nigger of the 'Narcissus'* and 'Typhoon' as his 'two Storm-pieces', and to 'The Secret Sharer' and *The Shadow-Line* (1917) as his 'two Calm-pieces' (p. ix). This 'classification by subjects' emphasizes an obvious affinity between the paired works;[1] but we have seen that 'Typhoon' is most closely connected to *Lord Jim*, and I believe that the significant relation of 'The Secret Sharer' is to *Under Western Eyes*. The circumstances in which the story was composed lend some support to this view. By the end of 1909 Conrad was under considerable pressure by J. B. Pinker, his agent, to complete *Under Western Eyes*, which he had been working at for the past two years. It was then, however, that he put the novel aside to write 'The Secret Sharer', which he began towards the end of November 1909 and completed in early December.[2] He thereupon finished *Under Western Eyes*, the typescript of the novel bearing the inscription, 'End. 22 Jan. 1910 J. C.'[3] There would appear to be grounds for supposing, therefore, that Conrad urgently needed to write the story as a preliminary to undertaking the conclusion of the novel.

Conrad's modification of the real-life occurrences on which the story is based – the killing of a member of the crew of the *Cutty Sark* in 1880 – perhaps indicates what it was that was preoccupying him at the end of 1909. The most interesting change he makes is not, it seems to me, in his conception of Leggatt, who is presented as a more admirable kind of man than his prototype, Sidney Smith, the mate of the *Cutty Sark*; or in his accentuation of the mitigating circumstances in which Leggatt is led to kill a member of his crew as compared with those in which Smith killed the Negro, John Francis. What is particularly striking is Conrad's transformation of the fate of the men who, in each case, help the guilty mate to escape. Captain Wallace of the *Cutty Sark* helped Smith to transfer secretly to the American ship *Colorado* – and then committed suicide four days later.[4] The captain-narrator in 'The Secret Sharer' helps Leggatt to escape, and this act is significantly related to his ceasing to be 'a stranger' to himself. Conrad, that is, transformed an occasion for the destruction of self into one for the discovery of self. It is this, I believe, that has a direct bearing on the conclusion of *Under Western Eyes*, for which 'The Secret Sharer' (after the unmitigated disintegration of self in *The Secret Agent*) may be seen as a short trial run.

In 'The Secret Sharer', furthermore, the *Cutty Sark* material is grafted on to episodes directly related to Conrad's own life, specifically to his maiden voyage as a captain. It is again striking that Conrad should have adapted the *Cutty Sark* story in a way that enabled him to draw on a somewhat dubious personal experience for the climax of the tale. When the captain-narrator in 'The Secret Sharer' takes his ship dangerously close to Koh-ring in the Gulf of Siam in order to help Leggatt to escape (an incident which had no parallel in the flight of Smith), he engages in the kind of 'manoeuvring' that Captain Korzeniowski indulged in when he launched his first command – as the following passage from *The Mirror of the Sea* indicates:

> ... there were moments when I detested Mr. B—[i.e. Born, Conrad's chief officer] exceedingly. From the way he used to glare sometimes, I fancy that more than once he paid me back with interest. It so happened that we both loved the little barque very much. And it was just the defect of Mr. B—'s inestimable qualities that he would never persuade himself to believe that the ship was safe in my hands. To begin with, he was more than five years older than myself at a time of life when five years really do count, I being twenty-nine and he thirty-four; then, on our first leaving port (I don't see why I should make a secret of the fact that it was Bangkok), a bit of manoeuvring of mine amongst the islands of the Gulf of Siam had given him an unforgettable scare. Ever since then he had nursed in secret a bitter idea of my utter recklessness. ... (p. 19)[5]

Conrad, too, that is to say, would seem – like the young captain in the story – to have risked not only his own life but also the lives of his crew in the Gulf of Siam. It is suggestive, therefore, that, at the very end of a period of intense creative activity in which he had been consistently concerned with various manifestations of a loss of self, he should have recurred to this exploit and imaginatively recreated it in a context of the finding of self.

*   *   *

There would appear to be two main ways in which Leggatt may be regarded. Albert J. Guerard maintains that 'in broad terms "The Secret Sharer" concerns the classic night journey and willed descent into the unconscious'.[6] According to this view, Leggatt is seen as 'criminally impulsive' and as an embodiment of the captain-narrator's 'own potential criminality'; the captain, therefore, is said to 'travel through Leggatt' – through his identification with the second self that Leggatt represents – into 'the primitive and unconscious sources of being', and so (having come to know himself) into manhood and maturity.[7] Daniel Curley, however, has set out a number of objections to such a view of Leggatt, maintaining that he 'cannot be considered a "murderous ruffian" but must on the contrary be held to be what the story itself clearly suggests him to be: the ideal conception of himself that the captain has set up for himself secretly'.[8] It seems to me that Conrad at least intended us to regard Leggatt in these terms rather than those proposed by Guerard. One indication of this, as Curley has pointed out, is his sense of outrage at a reviewer's treatment of Leggatt:

> I can't tell you [i.e. John Galsworthy] what pleasure you have given me by what you say of the 'Secret Sharer', – and especially of the swimmer. I haven't seen many notices, – three or four in all: but in one of them he is called a murderous ruffian, – or something of the sort. Who are these fellows who write in the Press? Where do they come from? I was simply knocked over, – for indeed I meant him to be what you have seen at once he was. And as you have seen, I feel altogether comforted and rewarded for the trouble he has given me in the doing of him, for it wasn't an easy task. It was extremely difficult to keep him true to type, first as modified to some extent by the sea life and further as affected by the situation.[9]

But Lawrence Graver, neatly occupying a middle position between Guerard and Curley, has stated that 'just as there is adequate evidence to deny Leggatt's villainy, so there is proof to smudge his status as an ideal figure'; and he goes on to say that 'one thing can be said with certainty about Leggatt: he is neither higher nor lower, only different'.[10] It is precisely because Leggatt is smudged in 'the doing of him' that such opposed views may be taken of him; and he is smudged because the moral perspective in which he is placed is blurred. The facts of his story are such, as we shall see, that we cannot unreservedly accept the captain-narrator's easy condonation of him; but this is the judgement that the author, limited here to the point of view of his narrator and not having any recourse to irony, would appear to want us to make. Given the fineness of Conrad's moral discrimination, it is difficult to account for his apparent unawareness of some of the moral obliquities of Leggatt's position, but it would seem at least in part to be due to a carrying over into the art of a bluff and lax view of the *Cutty Sark* material incorporated in the story, as the phrases 'had the misfortune' and 'had the decency' in the following extract from a letter suggest:

The Swimmer himself was suggested to me by a young fellow who was 2d mate (in the '60) of the *Cutty Sark* clipper and had the misfortune to kill a man on deck. But his skipper had the decency to let him swim ashore on the Java Coast as the ship was passing through Anjer Straits.[11]

The moral blurring, however, may rather be attributed to Conrad's preoccupation with the psychological aspects of his story, the preoccupation clearly revealing itself in the title of the story and the numerous references in the tale itself to second selves and doubles. His concern, indeed, is with the coexistence in the individual psyche of radically opposed qualities; and such an apprehension of being, as D. H. Lawrence was to state a few years later, makes it impossible 'to conceive a character in a certain moral scheme and make him consistent'. In 'The Secret Sharer' Conrad's imagination seems to have seized on the fact that ideal seamanship may depend on the integration of qualities that are potentially subversive of it.

Leggatt would certainly seem to be strikingly endowed with the quality that is the first condition of good service. From the start, it is his self-possession that most strongly characterizes him. At the end of his tether physically after his two-mile swim, holding on to the ladder in exhaustion and incapable of swimming even round the ship (p. 110), and at the mercy of the captain, who has detected him, he exudes an almost hypnotically potent sense of the quality: 'The voice was calm and resolute. A good voice. The self-possession of that man had somehow induced a corresponding state in myself' (p. 99). Throughout the period of his secret confinement in the captain's cabin he continues to exhibit this quality, being at once 'in the full possession of his senses' when suddenly woken (p. 114), looking 'always perfectly self-controlled, more than calm – almost invulnerable' (p. 127), and giving a notable demonstration of the quality in action when he jumps into the bath and so avoids detection by the steward. On that occasion the captain cannot help 'marvelling at that something unyielding in his character' which is 'carrying him through so finely' (p. 131). The 'something unyielding' in Leggatt's character implies he possesses that 'blessed stiffness before the outward and inward terrors' or 'steeled soul' that Jim lacked; and indeed that Leggatt is a harking back to Jim is suggested by the fact that his father, like Jim's, is a parson, and that he, like both Jim and the captain-narrator, has started his career as a boy on a 'training-ship for officers of the mercantile marine'.

Unlike Jim, Leggatt has earlier shown, moreover, that he gives way neither to despair nor panic when put to the test at sea. Aboard the *Sephora* in 'a sea gone mad', it is Captain Archbold who gives up hope when the main topsail blows away and, with 'all his nerve [gone] to pieces altogether' (p. 107), fails to give the order to set the foresail; it is Leggatt who, realizing what should be done, gives the necessary order, sees that it is carried out, and saves the ship (pp. 106, 124). But it is also on that occasion that he kills an unruly member of the crew, as he tells the narrator:

'It happened while we were setting a reefed foresail, at dusk. Reefed foresail! You understand the sort of weather. The only sail we had left to keep the ship running; so you may guess what it had been like for days. Anxious sort of job, that. He gave me some of his cursed insolence at the sheet. I tell you I was overdone with this terrific weather that seemed to have no end to it. Terrific, I tell you – and a deep ship. I believe the fellow himself was half crazed with funk. It was no time for gentlemanly reproof, so I turned round and felled him like an ox. He up and at me. We closed just as an awful sea made for the ship. All hands saw it coming and took to the rigging, but I had him by the throat, and went on shaking him like a rat, the men above us yelling, "Look out! look out!" Then a crash as if the sky had fallen on my head. They say that for over ten minutes hardly anything was to be seen of the ship – just the three masts and a bit of the fore-castle head and of the poop all awash driving along in a smother of foam. It was a miracle that they found us, jammed together behind the forebits. It's clear that I meant business, because I was holding him by the throat still when they picked us up. He was black in the face. . . .' (p. 102)

The vivid picture we are given here of Leggatt at the man's throat, frozen in that posture, as it were, since we are to understand that he 'was holding him by the throat' for 'over ten minutes', provides us with one of the most significant images – and epiphanies – in all Conrad. For what Leggatt's posture symbolizes is a holding on that is simultaneously a letting go. The letting go is implicit in his having maintained such a grip for so long a time; and when he says, in retrospect, that it was clear he 'meant business', he seems to recognize how he in fact abandoned himself to his impulse, even though he may have had no conscious intention of killing the man when he sprang at him.

The young captain-narrator, in his response to Leggatt's story, uses an image which helps us to clarify the implications of a holding on that is also a letting go. He tells Leggatt that he 'quite [understands]':

It was all very simple. The same strung-up force which had given twenty-four men a chance, at least, for their lives, had, in a sort of recoil, crushed an unworthy mutinous existence. (pp. 124–5)

The way in which the captain envisages Leggatt as having let go is vividly evoked by the image of the 'recoil' of the 'strung-up force'; but that it is 'the same force' which saves life and destroys life suggests that the force is itself a tension of opposites, that the quality of self-possession, which, strung-up to a pitch, saves the ship, contains or controls the quality of abandon, which, released in recoil, kills the man. But then the force may be said to contain the abandon in another sense – to contain it as a constituent; and Conrad, after ten years of sustained grappling with the problem, had thus articulated an intuition that he seemed to be groping after in 'Heart of Darkness', where the self-possession of Kurtz's savage woman, it will be recalled, appeared to be founded on a capacity for abandon. The novelist's unexpected return to the question of physical self-possession, therefore, may be seen as an attempt to take the matter further than he had been able to by the end of *Lord Jim* and 'Typhoon'; it may also be explained by a need, at the point he had reached in *Under Western Eyes*, to substantiate a similar intuition that he had been moving towards in the intangible sphere of the spirit in the more palpable terms of the flesh – and of the life at sea that he knew so well.

Such paradoxes of being, however, are not easily accommodated by a conventional morality, whether of the formally strict or practically tolerant variety. Captain Archbold, for instance, at once concludes that Leggatt's action has made him morally unfit to retain his position as an officer aboard the *Sephora* – 'Mr. Leggatt, you have killed a man. You can act no longer as chief mate of this ship,' he is reported to have said (p. 103) – and though he may be formally correct, we are aware that during the storm Leggatt has in fact proved himself better fitted to command than the captain himself. The captain-narrator, on the other hand, concludes that Leggatt was morally justified in doing what he did because of the danger that threatened the ship; and though this is the more lenient judgement that we are implicitly asked to accept as final, we cannot but be aware that, when he says 'it was all very simple', he is ignoring some of the disturbing implications of the thrusts of force he has so vividly discerned. A concern for life, for example, which may be assumed to have impelled Leggatt in his desire to save it, would seem to coexist with a contempt for life – or, at any rate, for certain manifestations of it – that is seen to lurk behind his readiness to destroy it. It is no chance comparison he uses when he relates how he had the man by the throat and was 'shaking him like a rat'; he has just previously referred to him as an 'ill-conditioned snarling cur' and as one of those 'miserable devils that have no business to live at all' (p. 101). When the captain-narrator, moreover, talks of the recoiling force 'crushing an unworthy mutinous existence', he may be taken to be not only echoing this view but endorsing it. It is an attitude that implies there is no real cause for regret at the sailor's death – it is notable that Leggatt at no point expresses any regret at what has happened

– because neither Leggatt nor the captain thinks of him as fully human◗ the captain's 'crushing' also implying it is a lower, insect-like 'existence' that is stamped out. The sailor, in other words, was neither significant nor good enough to live; but such a view smacks disquietingly of the Professor's final solution for the halt and the lame in *The Secret Agent*.

Leggatt bears an unexpected resemblance to the Professor in another respect. This emerges when he explains to the narrator why he did not try to break out of the cabin in which he was locked aboard the *Sephora*, and why, when he finally seized a chance to escape, he did not stay on the nearby island on which he landed rather than attempt the two-mile swim to the young captain's ship:

'. . . I wouldn't think of trying to smash the door. There would have been a rush to stop me at the noise, and I did not mean to get into a confounded scrimmage. Somebody else might have got killed – for I would not have broken out only to get chucked back, and I did not want any more of that work. . . .' (pp. 106–7)

'. . . I landed on the nearest islet before the boat left the ship's side. I heard them pulling about in the dark, hailing, and so on, but after a bit they gave up. . . . I felt certain they would start searching for me at daylight. There was no place to hide on those stony things – and if there had been, what would have been the good? But now I was clear of that ship, I was not going back. . . . No. Do you see me being hauled back, stark naked, off one of these little islands by the scruff of the neck and fighting like a wild beast. Somebody would have got killed for certain, and I did not want any of that. . . .' (pp. 108–9)

Referring to these passages, Daniel Curley says that Leggatt 'twice renounces violence as a way out'; and he adds that 'Leggatt specifically renounces violence when only his personal freedom or his life is at stake'.[12] Both statements are no doubt factually correct, but what the passages strongly imply is that Leggatt eschews the possibility of violence in these instances not because of a self-denying ordinance when it is only his own life that is at stake but because of a realization of the inevitability of his recapture in the event of his having followed either of the two courses he imagines. It is clear, moreover, that the 'something unyielding' in his character which the young captain admires (and which manifests itself alike in his saving of the *Sephora* and in his determination not to go back to it after his escape) betokens – as he himself realizes full well – that, were he to find himself in a position where his bid for freedom were threatened, he would be ready both to kill and be killed rather than submit. Contemplating that possibility, Leggatt is not very far removed from the Professor with his hand on the india-rubber ball.

Aboard the *Sephora* during the storm, Leggatt is distinguished by another quality – his capacity to take responsibility. It is when his captain goes to pieces after the main topsail has blown away and is reduced to an impotent whimpering about the loss of their last hope – Leggatt recalls how he 'positively whimpered about it and nothing else' – that the mate takes matters 'into [his] own hands' – and saves the ship (p. 124). But this high-mettled readiness to assume responsibility coexists with an arrogant refusal to accept it in respect of the death of the sailor. At first it seems that his flight is from the humiliation for his family and himself that his trial in a court of law would entail, for he says to the captain-narrator: 'My father's a parson in Norfolk. Do you see me before a judge and jury on that charge? For myself I can't see the necessity' (p. 101). If the parson-father recalls Jim, as I have remarked, Leggatt's flight from a public investigation of his actions is in striking contrast to Jim's facing of the court of inquiry. But it is not merely that Leggatt shrinks from the humiliation. When he says that he 'can't see the necessity' of a trial, he indicates his belief that, in the circumstances, he should not be held legally – let alone morally – accountable for the killing. What such a view implies emerges in a subsequent conversation that he has with the narrator:

> 'You don't suppose I am afraid of what can be done to me? Prison or gallows or whatever they may please. But you don't see me coming back to explain such things to an old fellow in a wig and twelve respectable tradesmen, do you? What can they know whether I am guilty or not – or of *what* I am guilty, either? That's my affair. What does the Bible say? "Driven off the face of the earth." Very well. I am off the face of the earth now. As I came at night so I shall go.'
> (pp. 131–2)

The arrogance that is revealed in Leggatt's view of the unruly sailor as a rat or a cur who is not fit to live emerges here in his contemptuous assumption that the 'old fellow in a wig and twelve respectable tradesmen' are not fit to judge him. His arrogance, indeed, is so far-reaching that it leads him to assert he is accountable for his actions only to himself, the killing of the sailor being '[his] affair' alone. Leggatt's acceptance of the 'brand of Cain', therefore, should be seen as a consequence of his flight from responsibility rather than his assumption of it, as the captain-narrator believes. Given his refusal to face the courts, he has no other alternative. When he tells the narrator that he is 'ready enough to go off wandering on the face of the earth', and adds that that is 'price enough to pay for an Abel of that sort' (p. 107), we see that, if the sailor's unruliness has cost him his life, it is Leggatt who has arrogated to himself the right to fix the price not only for his insolence but also for his death. At the end of the story, the captain-narrator thinks of Leggatt's having 'lowered himself into the water to take his punishment: a free man, a proud swimmer striking out for a new destiny' (p. 143); we cannot help feeling that he has stolen away, like a thief in the night.

*   *   *

The captain-narrator begins his story at the moment the tug disappears and he is 'left alone' with his ship:

> She floated at the starting-point of a long journey, very still in an immense stillness, the shadows of her spars flung far to the eastward by the setting sun. At that moment I was alone on her decks. There was not a sound in her – and around us nothing moved, nothing lived, not a canoe on the water, not a bird in the air, not a cloud in the sky. In this breathless pause at the threshold of a long passage we seemed to be measuring our fitness for a long and arduous enterprise, the appointed task of both our existences to be carried out, far from all human eyes, with only sky and sea for spectators and for judges. . . .
>
> In consequence of certain events of no particular significance, except to myself, I had been appointed to the command only a fortnight before. . . . All these people had been together for eighteen months or so, and my position was that of the only stranger on board. I mention this because it has some bearing on what is to follow. But what I felt most was my being a stranger to the ship; and if all the truth must be told, I was somewhat of a stranger to myself. The youngest man on board (barring the second mate), and untried as yet by a position of the fullest responsibility, I was willing to take the adequacy of the others for granted. They had simply to be equal to their tasks; but I wondered how far I should turn out faithful to that ideal conception of one's own personality every man sets up for himself secretly. (pp. 92–4)

The 'immense stillness' in which the ship floats is suggestive of a suspension of life, for 'nothing [moves], nothing [lives]', and the 'breathless pause' seems accordingly to mark a still point not only before the journey (or between day and night) but between two phases of existence. The narrator, of course, is about to enter literally on a new phase of existence as a captain, and he appears to believe that the 'long and arduous enterprise' of the coming voyage will measure his fitness not only to command but to live since to command is 'the appointed task' of his existence. He regards the voyage, that is to say, as a test of himself both as a man and a captain, and what he consequently '[feels] most' before its start is his being 'a stranger to the ship' and 'somewhat of a stranger' to himself. At the outset, therefore, he finds himself in a paradoxical situation: in order to be sure of being able to meet the test he must know both the ship and himself, to a degree that he may take both its adequacy and his own 'for granted'; he can only achieve such knowledge, however, by testing himself and his ship to the utmost. In the event, it is this that he soon proceeds to do. And he may then be assumed to be seeking to live up to 'that ideal conception' of his personality which he has 'set up for himself secretly'.

The fact that the young captain has set up such a shadow figure suggests he has a secret sharer even before Leggatt appears on the scene. When Leggatt comes aboard, the captain not only identifies with him but would seem to regard him as an embodiment of his own ideal conception of self. His 'feeling of identity' with Leggatt is so strong that he dreads the captain of the *Sephora* will ask him 'point-blank' whether he has seen his mate: 'I could not, I think, have met him by a direct lie . . . for psychological (not moral) reasons' (p. 120). To deny having seen Leggatt would, for the captain, be tantamount to denying his own existence – to denying that his ideal could be embodied. Whereas he is intent on giving it embodiment in himself, on fleshing it out in a unified self: 'This is not the place to enlarge upon the sensations of a man who feels for the first time a ship move under his feet to his own independent word. In my case they were not unalloyed. I was not wholly alone with my command; for there was that stranger in my cabin. Or rather, I was not completely and wholly with her. Part of me was absent' (p. 125).

The main test the young captain has to face is that of responsibility. As he himself reflects in the quoted passage, he is 'untried as yet by a position of the fullest responsibility'; and he knows it is 'the novel responsibility of command' that will alone be unfamiliar to him on the coming voyage (p. 96). To be vested with such responsibility, however, is also to be free to 'do what [he likes], with no one to say nay to [him] within the whole circle of the horizon' (p. 113); and it is clear that, at the outset of the voyage, he has no conception of the possible complexities of such freedom: 'And suddenly I rejoiced in the great security of the sea as compared with the unrest of the land, in my choice of that untempted life presenting no disquieting problems, invested with an elementary moral beauty by the absolute straightforwardness of its appeal and by the singleness of its purpose' (p. 96). The captain's choice of an 'untempted life' at sea is suggestive not only of a preference for a life of moral simplicity but also of a flight from the 'disquieting problems' that present themselves amid 'the unrest of the land'. If so, he is brought sharply back to earth, as it were, when Leggatt appears.

The captain's initial response is to temporize in regard to the moral problem posed by Leggatt's tacit appeal to him for help:

'Do you think they [i.e. men from Leggatt's ship] will be round here presently?' I asked with some incredulity.

180

'Quite likely,' he said, faintly.

He looked extremely haggard all of a sudden. His head rolled on his shoulders.

'H'm. We shall see then. Meantime get into that bed,' I whispered. 'Want help? There.' (p. 111)

If the captain does not at once commit himself to protecting Leggatt, he responds with an immediate humanity and compassion to his need of physical help. His fellow-feeling for Leggatt, which rapidly expands into a sense of identification with him, imposes on him a choice between loyalty to the man, which requires his continued aiding of him, and fidelity to the social and legal code, which necessitates his surrendering him to the captain of the *Sephora* when he arrives. The young captain's dilemma, that is, is analogous to that which confronts Razumov in *Under Western Eyes* when he finds Haldin in his room; and it is striking that Conrad, while still working on the novel, should in the tale have imagined a resolution of the dilemma which is the reverse of that arrived at by Razumov. The captain has so strong a sense of the mitigating circumstances of Leggatt's crime that it outweighs the kind of 'pitiless obligation' which the captain of the *Sephora* feels he must adhere to; and, in deciding to stand by Leggatt, he comes to regard Captain Archbold's tenacious anxiety to give him up 'to the law' as having in it 'something incomprehensible and a little awful; something, as it were, mystical, quite apart from his anxiety that he should not be suspected of "countenancing any doings of that sort" ' (pp. 118–19). In protecting Leggatt, therefore, the captain stands by his own moral judgement, accepting the obligation not of the law but of an individual moral responsibility. The undeviating firmness with which he follows this course points to his possession of the kind of blessed stiffness that is required for the successful undertaking of the 'arduous enterprise'. But his firmness of attitude and readiness to act in terms of an individual moral responsibility coexist, as we have seen, with a response to Leggatt that is morally lax, if not irresponsible.

The captain's story is illustrative, we begin to realize, of paradoxes of being that are analogous to those dramatized in the case of Leggatt. And just as Leggatt is most notably characterized by the image of him at the sailor's throat, so the quality of the young captain is epitomized for us in the picture we are given of his handling of his ship when he helps Leggatt to escape. He tells Leggatt he has decided to 'edge [the ship] in to half a mile [of the shore], as far as [he] may be able to judge in the dark – ' (p. 135) in order to give him a chance to swim for the island of Koh-ring:

I came out on deck slowly. It was now a matter of conscience to shave the land as close as possible – for now he must go overboard whenever the ship was put in stays. Must! There could be no going back for him. After a moment I walked over to leeward and my heart flew into my mouth at the nearness of the land on the bow. Under any other circumstances I would not have held on a minute longer. The second mate had followed me anxiously. (p. 139).

It is evident it is not out of a sense of obligation to Leggatt that the captain regards it as 'a matter of conscience' to take his ship so dangerously close to the shore, for he knows that Leggatt is a strong swimmer, and the mate has earlier told him that, in covering the distance of two miles between the *Sephora* and the captain's ship, he swam the 'last spell' of 'over a mile' without any rest (p. 109). Nor does it seem adequate to say, as Albert J. Guerard does, that the captain is 'evidently compelled to take an extreme risk in payment for his experience',[13] it not being clear to whom he owes such a debt. He would seem to be driven rather by a need to put both himself and his ship to an extreme test as a necessary preliminary to his taking effective possession of it as its captain. It is striking, in this respect, that the test should be depicted (as in the case of Leggatt's killing of the sailor) in terms of a holding on that is simultaneously a letting go: 'under any other circumstances', the captain reflects, he 'would not have held on a minute longer', but he does in fact hold on, letting the ship go closer and closer, giving it its head, as it were, until the 'black southern hill of Koh-ring' seems 'to hang right over the ship like a towering fragment of the everlasting night' and to be 'gliding irresistibly' towards it (p. 139). The watch gaze 'in awed silence', but the captain lets the ship go on, ordering the crew not to 'check her way', until it seems as if the ship is 'in the very blackness' of the land, 'swallowed up as it were, gone too close to be recalled, gone from [the captain] altogether' (pp. 139–40).

Unlike Leggatt at the sailor's throat, however, the captain never loses his self-control, and at the last moment succeeds in bringing the ship round:

> Already the ship was drawing ahead. And I was alone with her. Nothing! no one in the world should stand now between us, throwing a shadow on the way of silent knowledge and mute affection, the perfect communion of a seaman with his first command. (p. 143)

Though the captain may start as 'a stranger to the ship', he comes to full knowledge of it as a result of this experience, the 'silent knowledge' that he has of it evoking, in its context of 'mute affection' and 'perfect communion', the sort of knowledge that a man may take of a woman. The captain, that is, sees himself as having fully taken possession of his ship; we see, furthermore, that he has ceased to be 'somewhat of a stranger' to himself, and that, having learnt to know his own resources, he has also taken full possession of himself. During the manoeuvre, the self-possession he demonstrates in snatching the ship from disaster is shown to coexist with a capacity for letting go; just as his fitness for the responsibility of command (which he proves at the same time) is seen to coexist, given the way in which he risks the safety of his ship and the lives of his crew, with a pronounced tendency to irresponsibility.[14] But the sort of knowledge he comes to as a result of the experience suggests the integration of these dark Dionysian qualities in a self that will henceforth be proof against their disruptive influence, for we are told that nothing can now 'throw a shadow' on his seamanship, on his 'perfect communion' with his 'first command'.

As the captain waits 'helplessly' to see whether the ship will come round, he reflects that what he needs is 'something easily seen, a piece of paper, which [he] could throw overboard and watch'; but he has nothing on him, and has no time 'to run down for it'. Suddenly he makes out 'a white object floating within a yard of the ship's side', and recognizes his 'own floppy hat', which he has earlier given Leggatt and realizes 'must have fallen off his head':

> And I watched the hat – the expression of my sudden pity for his mere flesh. It has been meant to save his homeless head from the dangers of the sun. And now – behold – it was saving the ship, by serving me for a mark to help out the ignorance of my strangeness. Ha! It was drifting forward, warning me just in time that the ship had gathered sternway.
>
> 'Shift the helm,' I said in a low voice to the seaman standing still like a statue. (p. 142)

Conrad's provision of so fortuitous a saving mark 'to help out the ignorance' of the captain's strangeness is a weakness in the story, for it makes his achievement of knowledge too much a matter of chance – and turns the highest kind of seamanship into a tightrope of contingency. But the terms in which the hat is presented also suggest that it is not by chance alone that we are to see the captain as being saved. The hat which saves him is 'the expression' of his pity; and it is in more than a physical sense that he is saved by his pity, the 'sudden pity for mere flesh' that he feels for Leggatt from the moment he comes aboard, and which (among other things) makes it impossible for him to give Leggatt up to the captain of the *Sephora*. What his pity saves him from, indeed, is depicted at length in the story of Razumov in *Under Western Eyes*.

B. *Under Western Eyes*

I

POSSIBLY following the unusual example of E. M. Forster, who the year before had used the words of one of his own characters as the epigraph to *Howards End*, Conrad in 1911 quoted 'Miss Haldin' in his epigraph to *Under Western Eyes*: 'I would take liberty from any hand as a hungry man would snatch a piece of bread.' Whereas Forster's 'Only connect . . .', however, is not only 'the whole of [Margaret Schlegel's] sermon' but the theme of his novel, Conrad's highlighting of Natalia's dictum has no such obvious relation to the apparent drive of his work. But the remark, in its acceptance of the use of any means to achieve a commendable end, does relate Natalia to an earlier idealist in the Conrad canon, to Charles Gould. He (it will be recalled) was ready to use 'such weapons as could be found at once in the mire of corruption' in Costaguana in order to safeguard 'law, good faith, order, security'; and his belief that 'a better justice [would] come afterwards' (p. 84) is parallel to her assertion, which follows the announcement of her credo, that 'the true progress must begin after' (p. 135). The epigraph also relates Natalia to a character such as the Professor, who similarly has no scruples as to the means to be used in bringing about a desired new order. Her remark thus brings to mind the moral nihilism that pervades the societies depicted in both *Nostromo* and *The Secret Agent* – and would seem further to imply that a moral opportunism is the distinguishing mark of anyone brought up in the Russia of *Under Western Eyes*, even as positive (and generally idealized) a character as Natalia Haldin.

This is the judgement the novelist would appear to wish us to make in regard to both the sides engaged in the political conflict which is the background to the main action of the novel, for it emerges as a constant amid shifting views of that struggle. Victor Haldin, who initiates the main action when he assassinates the Minister-President, may be regarded as representative of the revolutionists at their best and acts in the name of the liberty so dear to his sister; we note that he does not hesitate to kill at the same time an unspecified number of innocent bystanders – not to mention his fellow-conspirator (pp. 9–10). The narrator holds this assassination to be 'characteristic of modern Russia', and adds that, in its perversion of admirable qualities, it is 'still more characteristic of the moral corruption of an oppressed society where the noblest aspirations of humanity, the desire of freedom, an ardent patriotism, the love of justice, the sense of pity, and even the fidelity of simple minds are prostituted to the lusts of hate and fear, the inseparable companions of an uneasy despotism' (p. 7). Razumov, when he is faced with the fact of the assassination, decides that 'Haldin means disruption', and (associating him with 'volcanic eruption') concludes it is 'better that thousands should suffer than that a people should become a disintegrated mass, helpless like dust in the wind' (p. 34). The revolutionists, that is to say, figure as the same kind of morally corrupt and disintegrative force as the anarchists in *The Secret Agent* – and indeed Natalia, in the conversation with the narrator from which the epigraph is taken, voices a similarly explosive demand for a clear space: 'The degradation of servitude, the absolutist lies must be uprooted and swept out. Reform is impossible. There is nothing to reform . . .' (p. 133). At the same time, since the narrator says it is 'an uneasy despotism' that provokes 'the lusts of hate and fear', the autocratic regime opposed to the revolutionists is itself seen as the source of corruption, and is itself shown to be an anarchic force. As is the case between anarchist and policeman in *The Secret Agent*, there is nothing to choose, morally, between revolutionist and autocrat; and Conrad forcibly insists on this in his Author's Note: 'The ferocity and imbecility of an autocratic rule rejecting all legality and in fact basing itself upon complete moral anarchism provokes the no less imbecile and atrocious answer of a purely Utopian revolutionism encompassing destruction by the first means to hand, in the strange conviction that a fundamental change of hearts must follow the downfall of any given human institutions' (p. x).

Despite the narrator's reiterated assertion that the materials of his narrative are utterly alien to the western world, we thus cannot help noticing that the Russia of his tale is not notably different from the England of *The Secret Agent*. It is clear, moreover, that the novelist's imagination seized on the Russian experience in terms that are remarkably close to those employed in the English novel: London, we remember, the 'monstrous town', is said to be 'a cruel devourer of the world's light'; the narrator's vision of the 'gigantic shadow of Russian life' would seem to be related to the London image, for he visualizes it as 'deepening around [Natalia] like the darkness of an advancing night' which will 'devour her presently', and considers her mother to be another 'victim of the deadly shade' (p. 202). The narrator's insistent comments make the imagery of darkness significant in this novel too: he maintains that the 'shadow of autocracy' lies on 'Russian lives in their submission or their revolt' (p. 109), and that the 'true, kindly face' of Russia is hidden under a 'pestilential shadow' (p. 184); and, when Natalia has heard Razumov's confession, he notices the 'shadows [seem] to come and go' in her eyes 'as if the steady flame of her soul [has] been made to vacillate at last in the cross-currents of poisoned air from the corrupted dark immensity claiming her for its own, where virtues themselves fester into crimes in the cynicism of oppression and revolt' (p. 356). The darkened world depicted by the narrator of *Under Western Eyes*, indeed, makes contact too with that of 'Heart of Darkness' – and in a way that suggests there is little to choose not only between the autocrat and the revolutionist but also between the supposedly civilized and the savage: 'It seems that the savage autocracy, no more than the divine democracy, does not limit its diet exclusively to the bodies of its enemies. It devours its friends and servants as well' (p. 306).

Though political conflict is the immediate stuff of the novel, *Under Western Eyes* is perhaps even less of a 'political novel' than *Nostromo* or *The Secret Agent*, one indication of this being that the final impression made on us is of a Russia dwarfed by Razumov, whereas Costaguana and the monstrous city bulk at least as large as the spiritual dramas enacted in them. Conrad himself said (in his Author's Note) that his work was 'an attempt to render not so much the political state as the psychology of Russia itself' (p. vii); but just as he thought of Jimmy Wait as 'the centre of the . . . collective psychology' of the crew of the *Narcissus*, so, presumably, he must have regarded Razumov as a prototypical Russian – Razumov, it may be noted, wildly says on one impassioned occasion: 'But Russian *can't* disown me. . . . I am *it*!' (p. 209) – for it is the psychology of Razumov that we are actually given.[1]

The immediate clue to Razumov's psychology is that he is alone in the world:

> Officially and in fact without a family . . . , no home influences had shaped his opinions or his feelings. He was as lonely in the world as a man swimming in the deep sea. The word Razumov was the mere label of a solitary individuality. There were no Razumovs belonging to him anywhere. His closest parentage was defined in the statement that he was a Russian. Whatever good he expected from life would be given to or withheld from his hopes by that connexion alone. This immense parentage suffered from the throes of internal dissensions, and he shrank mentally from the fray as a good-natured man may shrink from taking definite sides in a violent family quarrel. (pp. 10–11)

As lonely 'as a man swimming in the deep sea', Razumov, we infer, is concerned exclusively with keeping himself afloat, but it is further suggested that in Russia the limiting condition of such a concern is not only utter isolation but also complete detachment from 'the throes of internal dissensions'. The plot of the novel, however, at once makes it clear that in this Russia it is impossible to maintain such detachment: slipping into Razumov's rooms after the assassination, Haldin silently demonstrates that one cannot close one's door on dissensions in the street. When Razumov returns to his rooms, Haldin's presence there confronts him with a choice between fidelity to an individual and loyalty to the state, a choice which is analogous, as we have seen, to that faced by the captain-narrator once he takes Leggatt aboard in 'The Secret Sharer'. It is a choice which has been repeatedly posed in the large struggles of our time, and Conrad, as in so much of his best work, was foreshadowing a distinctively modern dilemma.[2]

Whereas the captain-narrator in 'The Secret Sharer' comes to identify himself more and more closely with Leggatt and staunchly stands by him, Razumov's most vital 'connexion' (we have been authoritatively told) is with Russia. The fact, moreover, that his 'closest parentage' is his country is not merely an indication of the bitterness of his illegitimacy; it suggests also that he is heir to the 'moral corruption' which pervades Russia. Caught between the moral nihilism of Haldin and that of the state, Razumov succumbs as if to a moral plague, betrays Haldin, and becomes a spy. In the end it is with Verloc, the secret agent, that Razumov has an unexpected affinity. Though connections between *Under Western Eyes* and *The Secret Agent* are manifold, Conrad is concerned in the Russian novel with the effects of moral nihilism on the individual psyche rather than on the body politic, as he was in the earlier work. *Under Western Eyes* is, specifically, a study of the psychology of betrayal, its causes and consequences; and the nature of the theme is clearly relevant to the fact that Razumov is Conrad's most profound and subtle characterization.[3] It is perhaps worth noting, furthermore, that whereas it is Dickens who unofficially presides over *The Secret Agent*, informing its sense of the interconnectedness of society, it is to Dostoevsky that *Under Western Eyes* does unconscious homage as it probes a soul.[4]

Conrad's theme has a bearing too on his narrative method. His use of the teacher of languages as his narrator at the outset of the novel leads us to believe that we will throughout see events through his (western) eyes, and that consequently the point of view will be limited, defined and fixed. This, however, does not prove to be the case. In Part First the teacher of languages swiftly dissolves as a narrating presence, and though in this section there are some instances of commentary which should properly be attributed to him, he is largely forgotten. Instead the device of Razumov's journal (which comes into the narrator's possession) ensures not only that we see events through the Russian's eyes but that he serves as a centre of consciousness for most of this section – as the following representative passage indicates:

Razumov wondered why he had not cut short that talk and told this man to go away long before. Was it weakness or what?

He concluded that it was a sound instinct. Haldin must have been seen. . . .
Everybody Haldin had ever known would be in the greatest danger. Unguarded expressions, little facts in themselves innocent would be counted for crimes. Razumov remembered certain words he said . . . – it was almost impossible for a student to keep out of that sort of thing . . .
Razumov saw himself shut up in a fortress, worried, badgered, perhaps ill-used. He saw himself deported by an administrative order, his life broken, ruined, and robbed of all hope. . . . (pp. 20–21)

In Part Second there is an abrupt shift in point of view. Razumov, making his appearance in Geneva, is no longer the centre of consciousness; instead he is seen consistently in this section from the outside through the eyes of the narrator or of Natalia, as in the following instance which describes his first meeting with Haldin's sister:

She had stood before him speechless, swallowing her sobs, and when she managed at last to utter something, it was only her brother's name – 'Victor – Victor Haldin!' she gasped out, and again her voice failed her.

'Of course,' she commented to me, 'this distressed him. He was quite overcome. I have told you my opinion that he is a man of deep feeling – it is impossible to doubt it. You should have seen his face. He positively reeled. He leaned against the wall of the terrace. Their friendship must have been the very brotherhood of souls! . . ." (p. 172)

The shift in point of view in this section is accompanied by a very special sort of time-shift. In Part First the narrative is clearly retrospective, and the narrator, having read Razumov's journal, is in possession of all the facts relating to his story; in Part Second the narrative is non-retrospective, and the narrator's earlier knowledge of Razumov is simply suspended (though in a few cases it is disconcertingly noted: 'I could almost feel on me the weight of his unrefreshed, motionless stare, the stare of a man who lies unwinking in the dark, angrily passive in the toils of disastrous thoughts. Now, when I know how true it was, I can honestly affirm that this *was* the effect produced on me. It was painful in a curiously indefinite way – for, of course, the definition comes to me now while I sit writing in the fullness of my knowledge. But this is what the effect was at that time of absolute ignorance' (p. 183)). The immediate effect of the shift in point of view is the creation of a powerful dramatic irony, for we know what Natalia and the narrator do not know, and given our knowledge, the outer view of Razumov is strikingly suggestive of his inner condition.

188

In Part Third there is a shift once again to Razumov's point of view, and consequently in the long scenes between him and Peter Ivanovitch or Sophia Antonovna the narrative is filtered through his consciousness. In this section there are also instances of a doubling-back, so that incidents previously witnessed through the eyes of Natalia or the narrator are now reviewed by Razumov:

'It is here!' he thought, with a sort of awe. 'It is here – on this very spot . . .'
He was tempted to flight at the mere recollection of his first meeting with Nathalie Haldin. He confessed it to himself; but he did not move, and that not because he wished to resist an unworthy weakness, but because he knew that he had no place to fly to. . . . Slowly he ascended the stairs of the terrace, flanked by two stained greenish stone urns of funereal aspect. (p. 204)

Finally, in Part Fourth there is no single or steady point of view. In the first part of this section, with the time-shift to the events in Russia that immediately preceded Razumov's arrival in Geneva, the point of view is that of Razumov; when we return to the fictional present in Geneva, the narrator takes over once more, and we continue to see things through his eyes up to and including the scene of Razumov's confession to Natalia (though the retrospective account of Razumov's interview with Mrs. Haldin is presented from the young man's point of view); Razumov is again the centre of consciousness in the scene of his public confession; in the last chapter of the novel the point of view is that of the narrator.

It is clear, therefore, that Conrad has contrived to handle a nominally fixed point of view and a seemingly chronological narrative in such a way as to effect constant switches in perspective, Part Fourth serving in this respect as a model of the method employed throughout. The form of the novel, that is, forces on us the sense of shifting perspectives, and so serves to help us focus the theme, for what Conrad traces in his psychological study of Razumov is his changing view of the act of betrayal. It is more than a quirk of form that Razumov's ultimate repudiation of the act should be recorded in Part Fourth, where all is fluid, and the novelist, seemingly giving way to a narrative abandon, veers from one view to another.

II

Haldin is drawn to seek the aid of Razumov by the sense he has of his strong self-containment: he tells Razumov that, as he 'dodged in the woodyard down by the river-side', he thought of him as a man with 'a strong character', as one who 'does not throw his soul to the winds' (p. 15); and he declares, furthermore, that Razumov is 'collected – cool as a

cucumber. A regular Englishman' (pp. 21–22). It is one of the biting ironies
of the novel, however, that Haldin should be deceived by Razumov's
apparent self-possession. The product of circumstances which deny him
the moral autonomy that grows out of a secure past, Razumov has only a
tenuous identity, and his very name is to him no more than a 'label'.
Like Jim he gives himself to daydreams of the glories that await him,
seeking to fix an identity in ambitious projections of his future. But in
the present his hold on himself (as is soon shown) is dependent on his
hold on routine: 'Razumov was one of those men who, living in a period
of mental and political unrest, keep an instinctive hold on normal,
practical, everyday life' (p. 10). It is Razumov's tragedy, as it is Jim's,
that the everyday should break on unsuspected wrecks, and that, though
safe in his own rooms, 'the Revolution' should seek him out 'to put to a
sudden test his dormant instincts, his half-conscious thoughts and almost
wholly unconscious ambitions . . .' (p. 294). Though he remains outwardly controlled, his inner response to the predicament he finds himself
in is revealing:

> Razumov had listened in astonishment; but before he could open
> his mouth Haldin added, speaking deliberately, 'It was I who
> removed de P— this morning.'
> Razumov kept down a cry of dismay. The sentiment of his life
> being utterly ruined by this contact with such a crime expressed
> itself quaintly by a sort of half-derisive mental exclamation, 'There
> goes my silver medal!' (p. 16)

Razumov's imagination, like that of Jim or Jukes, is readily susceptible
to intimations of disaster: he at once accepts that 'the sentiment of his
life' is 'utterly ruined' and that his silver medal is lost, the former being
his determination to 'convert the label Razumov into an honoured name'
by the sort of 'distinction' that would begin to accrue to him on his
securing the latter for his prize essay (pp. 13–14). His immediate response,
that is, is despairing, but it is also entirely self-centred; and though he
begins to build an elaborate ideological structure to justify and rationalize
his eventual betrayal of Haldin, it is clear from the outset (as has been
remarked) that it is founded on self-interest.[5]

As it turns out, it is his betrayal of Haldin that ruins the sentiment of
his life since the autocratic regime to which he betrays him will not readily
relinquish Razumov to his studies; but he persists in believing that it is
Haldin who, with 'the self-deception of a criminal idealist', has '[shattered]
his existence like a thunder-clap out of a clear sky' (p. 258), and 'robbed'
him of his 'hard-working, purposeful existence' (p. 358). Since his hold
on such a hard-working existence is his sole support in the deep sea into
which he has been cast, Haldin's irruption into his peaceful rooms is

viewed as striking at his very life, and he feels that his 'solitary and laborious existence [has] been destroyed – the only thing he [can] call his own on this earth' (p. 82). If Razumov, therefore, feels – like Nostromo – that he has gone out of his existence, it is because inwardly he loses possession of himself in the crisis. Subsequently, he tries to contain himself when he discovers that Ziemianitch is drunk, 'biting his lip till blood came to keep himself from bursting into imprecations' (p. 28), but he finally lets go when it appears that not even repeated kicks can wake the drunken driver, whom he has come to summon to Haldin's aid:

> He picked up the lantern. The intense black spokes of shadow swung about in the circle of light. A terrible fury – the blind rage of self-preservation – possessed Razumov.
> 'Ah! The vile beast,' he bellowed out in an unearthly tone which made the lantern jump and tremble! 'I shall wake you! Give me . . . Give me . . .'
> He looked round wildly, seized the handle of a stablefork and rushing forward struck at the prostrate body with inarticulate cries. After a time his cries ceased, and the rain of blows fell in the stillness and shadows of the cellar-like stable. Razumov belaboured Ziemianitch with an insatiable fury, in great volleys of sounding thwacks. . . .
> (p. 30)

Razumov's outward loss of control here, so clearly manifested in his wild cries and looks and in the frenzied 'rain of blows', decides his fate. Losing his self-possession, he becomes 'possessed' by 'the blind rage of self-preservation'. Thereafter his main actions until his confession to Natalia are determined by the force which has now taken hold of him. Razumov, that is to say, is – like Jim – an inglorious victim of his own instincts, of the rage for life.[6]

Razumov continues to beat Ziemianitch until the stick he is using breaks in half:

> He flung from him the piece of stick remaining in his grasp, and went off with great hasty strides without looking back once.
> After going heedlessly for some fifty yards along the street he walked into a snowdrift and was up to his knees before he stopped.
> This recalled him to himself; and glancing about he discovered he had been going in the wrong direction. He retraced his steps, but now at a more moderate pace. . . .
> Ziemianitch's passionate surrender to sorrow and consolation had baffled him. That was the people. A true Russian man! Razumov was glad he had beaten that brute – the 'bright soul' of [Haldin]. Here they were: the people and the enthusiast.
> Between the two he was done for. Between the drunkenness of the

peasant incapable of action and the dream-intoxication of the idealist incapable of perceiving the reason of things, and the true character of men. It was a sort of terrible childishness. But children had their masters. 'Ah! the stick, the stick, the stern hand,' thought Razumov, longing for power to hurt and destroy. (p. 31)

The symbolism here, as always when Conrad is at his best, is a natural outgrowth of the action. Up to this point Razumov has been trying to save himself by saving Haldin; with the urge to protect himself made more imperative as a result both of his surrender to that which has now taken possession of him and of the evident failure of his mission to Ziemianitch, he 'discovers' that he has been 'going in the wrong direction,' that the way he has chosen leads only to an impasse. When he 'retraces his steps', Razumov begins unconsciously to move towards betrayal. The unconscious springs of his thought are strikingly suggested when he begins at once to reflect on the necessity for 'the stick' and a 'stern hand' in dealings with a man such as Ziemianitch: since he views the driver as 'a true Russian man' and representative of 'the people', he tacitly aligns himself here with the authoritarian forces of autocracy – and unconsciously begins to ready himself for the betrayal of Haldin on ideological grounds.[7] Conrad's understanding of Razumov's psychology is subtle indeed: he wishes us to regard his authoritarian views as ideologically sincere, a reflection both of the cast of his mind and of his intellectual integrity when confronted with the revolutionary enthusiasm of a man like Haldin; but the novelist also makes it clear that Razumov's views are triggered by less disinterested forces, of which he remains consciously unaware. The same applies to his emotions. When the Prince takes him to the General and he repeats his story about Haldin, he makes up his mind 'to keep Ziemianitch out of the affair completely':

> To mention him at all would mean imprisonment for the 'bright soul', perhaps cruel floggings, and in the end a journey to Siberia in chains. Razumov, who had beaten Ziemianitch, felt for him now a vague, remorseful tenderness. (p. 48)

Razumov's feeling of remorse and tenderness, though 'vague', is no doubt sincere, but, having determined to betray Haldin and suppress any mention of his attempt to aid him to escape, there are other reasons for his deciding to keep Ziemianitch out of it.

After turning back from the snowdrift, Razumov reflects that having Haldin in his rooms is 'like harbouring a pestilential disease that would not perhaps take your life, but would take from you all that made life worth living – a subtle pest that would convert earth into a hell' (p. 32). Both Nostromo and Decoud, we recall, believe that their 'possession of [the silver] is very much like a deadly disease for men situated as [they] are'; and the reminiscence suggests that, if Razumov finds himself called on to safeguard Haldin as they the silver, any corruption attendant on such an effort will be likely in his case – as it was in theirs – to be worked from within, not without. His system, as we know, has already been under-mined; and, casting round for ways of saving himself, he contemplates killing Haldin on his return home, only to reject that course: 'The corpse hanging round his neck would be nearly as fatal as the living man' (p. 32). Ironically, of course, Razumov's betrayal of Haldin hangs his corpse round his neck just as fatally; and like the Ancient Mariner, Razumov carries that corpse with him – until it drops from his neck when he con-fesses. The literary association here provides a frame for the ensuing drama of guilt and expiation, and also points ahead to the change of perspective required for release.

Before he can bring himself to decide to give Haldin up, Razumov experiences an epiphany – and an hallucination. Continuing to make his way home, he suddenly looks up and sees 'the clear black sky of the northern winter, decorated with the sumptuous fires of the stars' – and receives 'an almost physical impression of endless space and of countless millions'. This impression brings with it an image of the snow covering 'the endless forests, the frozen rivers, the plains of an immense country, obliterating the landmarks, the accidents of the ground, levelling every-thing under its uniform whiteness, like a monstrous blank page awaiting the record of an inconceivable history' (p. 33). Razumov's vision of the snow is not unlike that of Gabriel Conway at the end of Joyce's story 'The Dead', but whereas Gabriel is led by his vision to a melancholy acquies-cence in the blurring of lines between the living and the dead on whom the snow falls alike, Razumov is roused to a sense that what the 'immense country' needs is 'a will strong and one . . . not the babble of many voices, but a man – strong and one!' (p. 33). He is strengthened still further, that is, in the authoritarian position he has taken up, the vision leading him indeed to 'the point of conversion', for it would seem to be only a strong man who could leave his mark on the 'monstrous blank page' that is Russia. At the same time the epiphany provides him with an emotional as well as ideological ground for the betrayal since, under the immense and level snow, the human is blotted out and the individual life made to seem utterly insignificant. It is a further irony of the betrayal that his own life is reduced by it to an insubstantial blankness: within a month of the betrayal he recognizes that 'his existence [is] a great cold blank, something like the enormous plain of the whole of Russia levelled with snow and fading gradually on all sides into shadows and mists' (p. 303).

Though Razumov contemptuously contrasts 'the luridly smoky lucubrations' of Haldin with 'the clear grasp' of his own intellect, and determines that, if he is to suffer, it should be for his convictions, not for 'a crime' that his 'cool superior reason' rejects, he is still not emotionally ready for the betrayal: the moment he '[ceases] to think' he becomes the prey of 'a suspicious uneasiness' that seems to well up from the depths, an 'irrational feeling that something may jump upon [him] in the dark – the absurd dread of the unseen' (p. 35). It takes the hallucination to complete the process by which he is led to ignominy:

> Suddenly on the snow, stretched on his back right across his path, he saw Haldin, solid, distinct, real . . . The snow round him was untrodden.
>
> This hallucination had such a solidity of aspect that the first movement of Razumov was to reach for his pocket to assure himself that the key of his rooms was there. But he checked the impulse with a disdainful curve of his lips. He understood. His thought, concentrated intensely on the figure left lying on his bed, had culminated in this extraordinary illusion of the sight. Razumov tackled the phenomenon calmly. With a stern face, without a check and gazing far beyond the vision, he walked on, experiencing nothing but a slight tightening of the chest. After passing he turned his head for a glance, and saw only the unbroken track of his footsteps over the place where the breast of the phantom had been lying.
>
> Razumov walked on and after a little time whispered his wonder to himself.
>
> 'Exactly as if alive! Seemed to breathe! And right in my way too! I have had an extraordinary experience.'
>
> He made a few steps and muttered through his set teeth –
>
> 'I shall give him up.'
>
> Then for some twenty yards or more all was blank. . . .
>
> 'Betray. A great word. What is betrayal? They talk of a man betraying his country, his friends, his sweetheart. There must be a moral bond first. All a man can betray is his conscience. And how is my conscience engaged here; by what bond of common faith, of common conviction, am I obliged to let that fanatical idiot drag me down with him? On the contrary – every obligation of true courage is the other way.' (pp. 36–8)

Razumov, the son of reason, lives up to his name here, and is satisfied he 'understands' how his 'thought' has brought about the 'extraordinary illusion'. We see, however, that the hallucination is the product of an emotional necessity, of his need to prove to himself that he *can* walk over Haldin, as it were, for his decision to give him up, though unconsciously in the making from the moment he finds Ziemianitch drunk, is consciously formulated only after he demonstrates this to himself. It is notable, moreover, that he gazes 'far beyond the vision' when he walks over it, for in so doing he enacts his version of the betrayal, averting his eyes from the trampling on Haldin which the betrayal entails and fixing them on that which lies 'beyond' him – on the ostensible 'act of conscience' (p. 38) undertaken for the larger welfare of his country. Razumov, that is to say, is trapped in the familiar dilemma of means and ends; and the hollowness of his moral position is indicative of the nullity to which he is reduced when he first loses possession of himself. For there *is* 'a moral bond' between Haldin and himself, the bond of fellowship or brotherhood which Haldin asserts in turning to him for help (and indirectly affirms when he constantly refers to Razumov as 'brother'), the bond of their common humanity whose obligations are as strong as those of a 'common faith' or 'common conviction'. That Razumov deliberately walks over 'the place where the breast of the phantom had been lying' brings out the human implications of the betrayal, the willed denial of feeling that it is; just as the fact that he sees Haldin lying 'right across his path', 'right in [his] way', is expressive of his view of Haldin as an obstacle to his own progress – and so of the base self-centredness of his public concern.

Crushingly aware of his own 'moral solitude' and desperately longing for 'moral support' in the position he has taken up (p. 39), Razumov exploits the opportunity of turning to Prince K—, his unacknowledged father, with his tale of Haldin. The Prince treats him considerately, but will have nothing more to do with him; and the betrayal, which is formally committed at this point, accordingly only intensifies Razumov's sense of moral isolation. Not that he is left without his ghosts, for the sights and sounds of Haldin's trusting departure from his rooms remain to haunt him:

> Gazing down into the deep black shaft with a tiny glimmering flame at the bottom, [Razumov] traced by ear the rapid spiral descent of somebody running down the stairs on tiptoe. It was a light, swift, pattering sound, which sank away from him into the depths: a fleeting shadow passed over the glimmer – a wink of the tiny flame. Then stillness.
>
> Razumov hung over, breathing the cold raw air tainted by the evil smells of the unclean staircase. All quiet. (p. 63)

Haldin's descent into 'the deep black shaft', with its sounds sinking away 'into the depths' and 'the tiny flame' disappearing in shadow, becomes for Razumov an image of his descent to death. And what Razumov breathes into his deepest being is an air which is 'tainted' not so much by 'the evil smells of the unclean staircase' as by the corruption of betrayal.

III

When Razumov begins to attend lectures again after the betrayal, he is said to be 'quite sufficiently self-possessed for all practical purposes', but 'his new tranquillity' in fact is 'like a flimsy garment' that seems 'to float at the mercy of a casual word' (p. 71), exposing his more profound loss of self-possession. Almost at once he begins to be plagued by dreams which reveal his unconscious perception of what he has brought on himself by the betrayal:

> Still-faced and his lips set hard, Razumov began to write. When he wrote a large hand his neat writing lost its character altogether – became unsteady, almost childish. He wrote five lines one under the other.
>
> > History not Theory.
> > Patriotism not Internationalism.
> > Evolution not Revolution.
> > Direction not Destruction.
> > Unity not Disruption.
>
> He gazed at them dully. Then his eyes strayed to the bed and remained fixed there for a good many minutes, while his right hand groped all over the table for the penknife.
>
> He rose at last, and walking up with measured steps stabbed the paper with the penknife to the lath and plaster wall at the head of the bed. This done he stepped back a pace and flourished his hand with a glance round the room.
>
> After that he never looked again at the bed. He took his big cloak down from its peg and, wrapping himself up closely, went to lie down on the hard horse-hair sofa at the other side of his room. A leaden sleep closed his eyelids at once. Several times that night he woke up shivering from a dream of walking through drifts of snow in a Russia where he was as completely alone as any betrayed autocrat could be; an immense, wintry Russia which, somehow, his view could embrace in all its enormous expanse as if it were a map. But after each shuddering start his heavy eyelids fell over his glazed eyes and he slept again. (p. 66)

When Razumov writes his manifesto (which so impresses Councillor Mikulin), he formulates a mature, intellectual justification of the betrayal, but the 'almost childish' hand in which it is written reveals the emotional immaturity in which the betrayal is rooted. The quoted passage is further suggestive of the way in which a secret sharer makes subversive comments on his conscious intentions. When Razumov 'stabs' the paper to the lath and plaster, he pins his colours to the wall, so to speak, with a gesture which defiantly proclaims both his acceptance of responsibility for having disposed of Haldin, who had lain on the bed, and the finality of the deed, for 'after that he never [looks] again at the bed'. But his dream indicates that Haldin is not so easily disposed of. In evoking the totality of his isolation in the immense Russia for which he has betrayed Haldin, it expresses more than his unconscious perception of the degree to which he has cut himself off from his fellows by his own act; since it is he – the man who has just spelt out his anti-revolutionist position – who is 'as completely alone as any betrayed autocrat could be', the dream is also an early intimation that, in betraying Haldin, he has in fact betrayed himself. It is precisely at this point in the narrative that the narrator draws attention to the necessity of finding a 'key-word' as an aid 'to the moral discovery' which, he says, 'should be the object of every tale'; thinking of Russia as a whole, he advances the word 'cynicism' since he sees it as 'the mark of Russian autocracy and of Russian revolt' (p. 67), but the moral discovery Razumov slowly makes is that betrayal means self-betrayal, which is as good a key-word as any in his story.

During his first interview with Mikulin, Razumov experiences a waking dream which is further revelatory of the implacability of his unconscious vision:

At that moment Razumov beheld his own brain suffering on the rack – a long, pale figure drawn asunder horizontally with terrific force in the darkness of a vault, whose face he failed to see. It was as though he had dreamed for an infinitesimal fraction of time of some dark print of the Inquisition. . . .
He was indeed extremely exhausted, and he records a remarkably dream-like experience of anguish at the circumstance that there was no one whatever near the pale and extended figure. The solitude of the racked victim was particularly horrible to behold. The mysterious impossibility to see the face, he also notes, inspired a sort of terror. . . . (p. 88)

This experience links up with one that immediately follows Haldin's departure from his rooms when, with 'his mind [hovering] on the borders of delirium', Razumov suddenly hears himself saying, 'I confess' – 'as a person might do on the rack' – and thinks to himself, 'I am on the rack' (p. 65). The two experiences are an accurate if appalling forecast of the mental torture to which he has condemned himself, a self-torture which continues until a confesssion is indeed wrung from him – his confession of the betrayal to Natalia. The vision in Mikulin's office, moreover, vividly communicates the main causes of his suffering. As in his earlier dream of the wintry Russia, the fact of his solitude, his apparent abandonment by those who might have been near him, is a specific cause of anguish; but though this is 'particularly horrible', it does not seem to be as terrible as his inability 'to see the face' of the figure on the rack (though he knows it is 'his own brain suffering' there, for this inspires 'a sort of terror'. Ironically, he has lost face neither with the revolutionists nor the government officials, but the loss of face is his own harsh judgement on himself, and points to his loss of even a tenuous identity which is one of the most damaging consequences of his loss of the full possession of himself. When he betrays Haldin, he ceases to be the man he was, as is quietly dramatized in his encounter with a friendly professor, whom he used to visit: 'How is it we never see you at our Wednesdays now, Kirylo Sidorovitch?' the professor asks; and he is 'too astonished to be offended' when Razumov meets his advance 'with odious, muttering boorishness' (p. 299). Realizing he has attracted 'the eye of the social revolution', Razumov consciously envisages the possibility that 'he no longer [belongs] to himself' (p. 301). This is true in more ways than he realizes; and it is not without significance that the narrator (on the day of Razumov's confession) remembers his 'extraordinary hallucined, anguished, and absent expression' (p. 320).[8]

Initially, however, he simply tries to deny the change. He is most himself at home, though the narrator notes his room might have been expected to be 'morally uninhabitable'. He sets to work again, 'at first, with some success', and his 'repaired watch' (dropped on the night of the betrayal), which is to be heard 'faintly ticking on the table by the side of the lighted lamp', seems to assert the continuity of the life he has taken up again at the point Haldin interrupted it – just as the lamp would seem to banish the vision of the dark staircase. But his 'unwillingness' to leave the place where he is 'safe from Haldin' grows so strong that in the end he ceases 'to go out at all', thus demonstrating that, if betrayal is a denial of the bonds of fellowship, its logical consequence is complete isolation. And indeed whenever he has previously gone out, he has 'felt himself at once closely involved in the moral consequences of his act', for it is 'abroad' that 'the dark prestige of the Haldin mystery' falls on him, clinging to him 'like a poisoned robe it [is] impossible to fling off' (pp. 299–300). That Razumov is implicitly associated with Hercules here suggests he is the victim of his own poison: once he becomes habituated to keeping up false pretences with the friends and sympathizers of Haldin, he is morally ready – sufficiently poisoned – for the role Mikulin wishes him to play. Mikulin, indeed, who asks the unanswerable question 'Where to?' by way of answer to Razumov's announced intention 'to retire' (p. 99), believes he is in effect made ready by the betrayal itself. He points out to Razumov that his desire to return to his old way of life, to assert 'his attitude of detachment', is untenable, given the kind of commitment he has made (p. 294). Having asserted the primacy of the state over the individual where Haldin was concerned, Razumov cannot claim exemption for himself in this respect; and, if the moral consequence of the betrayal is further betrayal, both of himself and of those on whom he will be set to spy, the political consequence is his transformation into a secret agent. It is Razumov's loss of self that leaves room, as it were, for the false self that is foisted on to him.

But his loss of self also makes room for other visitants, it being a capacious gap that has to be filled, and (after he has confessed to Natalia) Razumov shows in his journal that he is fully aware of what happened to him spiritually as a result of the betrayal:

> I was given up to evil. I exulted in having induced that silly innocent fool [i.e. Kostia] to steal his father's money. He was a fool, but not a thief. I made him one. It was necessary. I had to confirm myself in my contempt and hate for what I betrayed. . . . (p. 359)

Razumov analyses his own condition here in terms both of a psychology and a theology. The gullible Kostia, naively ready to do his bit for the Revolution and so for the gallant Razumov, is savagely exploited by him. Razumov sees clearly that he was led to corrupt Kostia, to make him (and anyone else connected with Haldin) contemptible, in order to justify his own behaviour to himself, and so to enable him not only to live with the betrayal of Haldin but undertake further betrayals as a spy. The fact that he 'exulted' in Kostia's corruption, however, suggests that it was not psychological need alone that drove him; and he sees that he behaved as he did also because he was 'given up to evil', that, in giving Haldin up, he had in effect given away his soul. In a manner that is reminiscent of Kurtz, Razumov must be seen as having abandoned himself to a passion of evil: 'Natalia Victorovna,' he writes in his journal, 'I embraced the might of falsehood, I exulted in it – I gave myself up to it for a time' (p. 360). Razumov, that is to say, is not possessed by the rage of self-preservation alone; having given himself to falsehood, he comes to think of himself in a more traditionally orthodox way as having been 'possessed'. He confesses in his journal that he was tempted to steal Natalia's soul by setting out to win her love:

> Perhaps no one will believe the baseness of such an intention to be possible. It's certain that, when we parted that morning, I gloated over it. I brooded upon the best way. The old man you introduced me to insisted on walking with me. I don't know who he is. He talked of you, of your lonely, helpless state, and every word of that friend of yours was egging me on to the unpardonable sin of stealing a soul. Could he have been the devil himself in the shape of an old Englishman? Natalia Victorovna, I was possessed! . . . (pp. 359–60)

Razumov is also taken up, of course, with his spying. But on the day he writes his first report to Mikulin he experiences a strong revulsion from the kind of existence that has been forced on him:

The futility of all this overcame him like a curse. Even then he could not believe in the reality of his mission. He looked round despairingly, as if for some way to redeem his existence from that unconquerable feeling. He crushed angrily in his hand the pages of the notebook. 'This must be posted,' he thought. (p. 316)

The 'curse' by which Razumov is overcome here would seem to be not so much the 'futility' of spying as the spiritual despair into which his life as a spy has driven him – and which imprints itself in his looks when he drops his guard. But if his sense of futility is 'unconquerable', his feeling of despair is not, for though he looks round 'despairingly', it is 'as if for some way to redeem his existence'. Conrad's depiction of a way to redemption is the crowning triumph of the novel.

IV

Even before he has actually betrayed Haldin but after he has decided to do so, Razumov is held for a moment by the possibility of confession. In order to escape from the terrible 'moral solitude' in which he finds himself, he '[embraces] . . . the delirious purpose of rushing to his lodgings . . . to pour out a full confession in passionate words that would stir the whole being of [Haldin] to its innermost depths'; and he imagines how such a confession would end in 'embraces and tears' and in 'an incredible fellowship of souls – such as the world had never seen' (pp. 39–40). It is the fellowship that Razumov craves, and it is unfortunate for both Haldin and himself that 'the glimpse of a passing grey whisker' at this point evokes for him the image of Prince K— since it deflects the craving to him – and his only access to the Prince is by way of the betrayal.

The contact with the Prince is short-lived, but it leads to his meeting with Mikulin. After his first meeting with the councillor Razumov suddenly begins to think of him as a unique fellow-soul – and he once again envisages confession as a means of cementing a relationship:

Go back! What for? Confess! To what? 'I have been speaking to him with the greatest openness,' he said to himself with perfect truth. 'What else could I tell him? That I have undertaken to carry a message to that brute Ziemianitch? Establish a false complicity and destroy what chance of safety I have won for nothing – what folly!'

Yet he could not defend himself from fancying that Councillor Mikulin was, perhaps, the only man in the world able to understand his conduct. To be understood appeared extremely fascinating.

On the way home he had to stop several times; all his strength
seemed to run out of his limbs; and in the movement of the busy
streets, isolated as if in a desert, he remained suddenly motionless for
a minute or so before he could proceed on his way. He reached his
rooms at last. (pp. 297–8)

Razumov's sense of his moral solitude is excruciating: at best, we
remember, he is 'as lonely in the world as a man swimming in the deep
sea'; now, after the betrayal, and with less apparent chance of survival, he
is 'isolated as in a desert'. When he stops in the street and 'all his strength
[seems] to run out of his limbs', it is to despair that he momentarily
succumbs, his condition once again recalling that of Jim on board the
Patna, for after Jim has decided there is nothing he can do in the emergency, this seems 'to take all life out of [his] limbs'. It is the intensity of
his need for human contact that accounts for the irrationality of Razumov's
urge to return to Mikulin and confess to him. It turns out to be significant
that in these two initial instances the idea of confession should be associated with something like sudden abandon.

In the absence of vital human relationships Razumov begins to keep a
journal, which the narrator describes as 'the pitiful resource of a young
man who had near him no trusted intimacy, no natural affection to turn
to', but it is perhaps even more to the point that he calls the journal a
'mental and psychological self-confession' (pp. 308–9). Razumov, that is
to say, is in the end driven to self-communion, and even this is assayed
by way of confession. But the journal is more than a pitiful resource:

The record, which could not have been meant for any one's eyes but
his own, was not, I think, the outcome of that strange impulse of
indiscretion common to men who lead secret lives, and accounting
for the invariable existence of 'compromising documents' in all the
plots and conspiracies of history. Mr. Razumov looked at it, I
suppose, as a man looks at himself in a mirror, with wonder, perhaps
with anguish, with anger or despair. Yes, as a threatened man may
look fearfully at his own face in the glass, formulating to himself
reassuring excuses for his appearance marked by the taint of some
insidious hereditary disease. (p. 214)

The self-communion, we see, is in fact, a self-scrutiny, a necessary part of
Razumov's self-discovery; and if he looks in the glass to reassure himself,
he does at least register the fact of the insidious disease. We may regard
the journal, indeed, as the one place in which he relaxes his repressive
hold on his secret sharer, the shadow (it will be recalled) that informed
his dreams, and which he quickly dispels when it otherwise rises into his
conscious mind: after he has left Peter Ivanovitch and his 'painted

Egeria', for instance, he feels 'as though another self, an independent sharer of his mind', is able 'to view his whole person very distinctly indeed'; though he formulates 'his opinion of it' – presumably, his person, that is – in the 'mental ejaculation: "Beastly!" ', his 'disgust' quickly vanishes 'before a marked uneasiness', and he simply concludes it is 'an effect of nervous exhaustion' (p. 230).

The journal, furthermore, is the means by which he composes himself:

> Alone in his room after having posted his secret letter [i.e. his first report to Mikulin], he had regained a certain measure of composure by writing in his secret diary. He was aware of the danger of that strange self-indulgence. He alludes to it himself, but he could not refrain. It calmed him – it reconciled him to his existence. . . . (p. 339)

Razumov's calmness and composure suggest that in his writing of the journal he regains a modicum of the self-possession he has lost. Since this would seem to be the product of his self-confession, it is clearly intimated how he might reconcile himself to his existence not alone in his secret writing but in the public world outside his room. And his self-possession, we note moreover, seems also to be the product of his readiness to let go, to relax the tight hold on himself that, as a spy, he has successfully managed to maintain, for he is 'aware of the danger of that strange self-indulgence', but cannot and does not refrain from it.

The person who sparks his confession in the outside world is, of course, Natalia. She reports to the narrator how Razumov was 'quite overcome' and 'positively reeled' when they met for the first time:

> 'I was grateful to him for that emotion, which made me feel less ashamed of my own lack of self-control. Of course I had regained the power of speech at once, almost. All this lasted not more than a few seconds. "I am his sister," I said. "Maybe you have heard of me." '
>
> 'And had he?' I interrupted.
>
> 'I don't know. How could it have been otherwise? And yet . . . But what does that matter? I stood there before him, near enough to be touched and surely not looking like an impostor. All I know is, that he put out both his hands then to me, I may say flung them out at me, with the greatest readiness and warmth, and that I seized and pressed them, feeling that I was finding again a little of what I thought was lost to me for ever, with the loss of my brother – some of that hope, inspiration and support, which I used to get from my dear dead . . .' (pp. 172–3)

The intensity of Razumov's emotion when he chances on Natalia, the degree to which he is overcome, suggests something more than the shock which he might be expected to feel in such a situation; it would seem to be expressive, rather, of a quite involuntary and genuine feeling of remorse. He may be taken to imply later that, when he thereupon flings his hands out at her, he launches his exercise in Satanism, for he confesses in his journal that it was then he finally decided to steal her soul: 'When we met that first morning in the gardens, and you spoke to me confidingly in the generosity of your spirit, I was thinking, "Yes, [Haldin] himself by talking of her trustful eyes has delivered her into my hands!" If you could have looked then into my heart, you would have cried out aloud with terror and disgust' (p. 359). Razumov may well have felt that his best defence against Natalia's trusting innocence was to attack and violate it, but the 'readiness and warmth' with which he puts out his hands to her are patently sincere and betoken, rather, his own deep desire for human connection in response to what her emotion seems to proffer.

Razumov, that is, falls in love with Natalia despite himself – as is quite apparent by the night of his confession:

> He raised his face, pale, full of unexpressed suffering. But that look in his eyes of dull, absent obstinacy, which struck, and surprised everybody he was talking to, began to pass away. It was as though he were coming to himself in the awakened consciousness of that marvellous harmony of feature, of lines, of glances, of voice, which made of the girl before him a being so rare, outside, and, as it were, above the common notion of beauty. He looked at her so long that she coloured slightly. (pp. 342–3)

His love, we see, has grown to such an extent that it seems to fill his inner emptiness, for it dispels the 'absent' look in his eyes. And love's alchemy would seem, too, to posit that the lost self may find itself, for it is as though he 'comes to himself' in his feeling for her. The narrator realizes Razumov has discovered that he 'needs' her (p. 347), but that creates another need, the need, in the fullness and sincerity of his love, to confess his betrayal of her brother – and renounce her: 'I felt,' he writes, 'that I must tell you that I had ended by loving you. And to tell you that I must first confess. Confess, go out – and perish' (p. 361).

Razumov's confession, however, is actually triggered by his one and only meeting with Haldin's mother, during which he makes some further discoveries:

> The fifteen minutes with Mrs. Haldin were like the revenge of the unknown: that white face, that weak, distinct voice; that head, at first turned to him eagerly, then, after a while, bowed again and motionless . . . had troubled him like some strange discovery. And there seemed to be a secret obstinacy in that sorrow, something he could

not understand; at any rate, something he had not expected. Was it hostile? But it did not matter. Nothing could touch him now; in the eyes of the revolutionists there was now no shadow on his past. The phantom of Haldin had been indeed walked over, was left behind lying powerless and passive on the pavement covered with snow. And this was the phantom's mother consumed with grief and white as a ghost. . . . He had said all he had to say to her, and when he had finished she had not uttered a word. She had turned away her head while he was speaking. The silence which had fallen on his last words had lasted for five minutes or more. What did it mean? Before its incomprehensible character he became conscious of anger in his stern mood, the old anger against Haldin reawakened by the contemplation of Haldin's mother. And was it not something like enviousness which gripped his heart, as if of a privilege denied to him alone of all the men that had ever passed through this world? It was the other who had attained to repose and yet continued to exist in the affection of that mourning old woman, in the thoughts of all these people posing for lovers of humanity. It was impossible to get rid of him. 'It's myself whom I have given up to destruction,' thought Razumov. 'He has induced me to do it. I can't shake him off.'

Alarmed by that discovery, he got up and strode out of the silent, dim room with its silent old woman in the chair, that mother! He never looked back. It was frankly a flight. But on opening the door he saw his retreat cut off. There was the sister. . . . (pp. 340–341)

The 'strange discovery' Razumov makes as he confronts 'that figure of sorrow' (p. 340), as he takes in the fact of a 'mother consumed with grief', has such a forceful effect on him because it is of something he has never known – the power of a mother's love. It is in that enduring love, he suddenly realizes, that Haldin – though walked over and dead – 'continues to exist', as he does too 'in the thoughts' of the revolutionists, despise them though he may; and this realization brings with it the bitter reflection that it is he himself who is 'given up to destruction', that it is he – in his unmitigated isolation – who will be utterly destroyed. This discovery is followed by another, to which he is led by Mrs. Haldin's 'incomprehensible' silence. She has intuitively divined that he is lying – the narrator tells us later that 'she had not believed him' (p. 372) – and her silence, not understood but quite unexpected, unnerves him. He has come to speak to Mrs. Haldin and her daughter only after having been informed of Ziemianitch's suicide and having heard Sophia Antonovna's explanation of it, an explanation which fortuitously clears him of all suspicion 'in the eyes of the revolutionists'. Finding Mrs. Haldin alone, he attempts finally to lay the ghost of Haldin, secure in the belief that 'nothing [can] touch him now', but her silence denies him the confirmation of his safety. Instead, as his 'old anger against Haldin' stirs in response, he is made sharply aware that 'the phantom of Haldin' has in fact not been 'left behind', that indeed he cannot 'shake him off', that his corpse is still hanging round his neck. If Razumov's departure is 'frankly a flight', it is as much from his own insights as from that intimidating silence that he flees, from the devastating sense of his isolation and from the knowledge that he will always have to bear the burden of the betrayal. When his 'retreat' is 'cut off' by the advent of Natalia, he stands firm, but – facing up to his new knowledge – gives in to an overwhelming need to shake the corpse from his neck and break out of his isolation. 'You are going, Kirylo Sidorovitch?' she asks, and he answers: 'I! Going? Where? Oh yes, but I must tell you first . . .' (p. 346). Razumov's 'Where?' recalls Mikulin's 'Where to?' and suggests that, if the logic of betrayal leads in political terms to his spying, it leads – in spiritual terms – to his confession. It leads, that is, since he is safe from all suspicion when he confesses, to what is actually a self-betrayal (though it proves to be redemptive), thus symbolizing what has been implicit all along. It leads also, in the end, to an affirmation of that need for a human bond which was tacitly repudiated in the betrayal: 'Do you know why I came to you?' Razumov asks Natalia. 'It is simply because there is no-one anywhere in the whole great world I could go to. Do you understand what I say? Not one to go to. Do you conceive the desolation of the thought – no-one – to – go – to?' (pp. 353-4).

Strung up to the point of confession, Razumov cannot easily bring the painful words to his lips; and as he struggles both to make the confession and keep it back, it is a moot question whether his urge to let go will prove stronger than his will to hold on:

> The convulsive, uncontrolled tone of the last words [Razumov has just told Natalia that she is 'a predestined victim', and added that this is 'a devilish suggestion'] disclosed the precarious hold he had over himself. He was like a man defying his own dizziness in high places and tottering suddenly on the very edge of the precipice. Miss Haldin pressed her hand to her breast. The dropped black veil lay on the floor between them. Her movement steadied him. He looked intently on that hand till it descended slowly, and then raised again his eyes to her face. But he did not give her time to speak.
> 'No? You don't understand? Very well.' He had recovered his calm by a miracle of will. . . . (pp. 349-50)

To Razumov confession is like a dizzying plunge to death because he knows that it must mean the giving up of Natalia, who alone has seemed to hold out to him the hope of life, and because he knows too that it must mean the end of his present existence. It must mean, furthermore, an abrogation of identity, an irrevocable loss of face in relation to the person (so admiring of him) that he cares for most; and as he totters 'on the very edge of the precipice', our minds are taken back to Captain Allistoun of the *Narcissus*, who – standing firm at all costs once he has confined Jimmy to his cabin – will not expose himself to a far less demanding reversal. We are taken even further back to Willems, who – it will be recalled – is said to be 'like one who, falling down a smooth and rapid declivity that ends in a precipice, digs his finger nails into the yielding surface and feels himself slipping helplessly to inevitable destruction'. A great gap divides the tortured Russian from the outcast of the islands or the tight little captain, but the resemblance is sufficiently striking to suggest that the path trod by Conrad in fifteen years of intense creative activity, though taking in larger and larger areas of experience, is circular and returns – at the end of this great period – to a point not far removed from that from which he started. But this is misleading, for if the novelist does come back to such a point, he sets off at once in a very different direction.

Willems lets himself slip – and falls to destruction. At first it seems as if Razumov, though he manages to steady himself on the very edge of the precipice, is to follow a similar fate:

'This man is deranged', I said to myself, very much frightened.

The next moment he gave me a very special impression beyond the range of commonplace definitions. It was as though he had stabbed himself outside and had come in there to show it; and more than that – as though he were turning the knife in the wound and watching the effect. That was the impression, rendered in physical terms. One could not defend oneself from a certain amount of pity. But it was for Miss Haldin, already so tried in her deepest affections, that I felt a serious concern. Her attitude, her face, expressed compassion struggling with doubt on the verge of terror.

'What is it, Kirylo Sidorovitch?' There was a hint of tenderness in that cry. He only stared at her in that complete surrender of all his faculties which in a happy lover would have had the name of ecstasy.
(pp. 350–1)

At this stage Razumov no longer totters, struggling to keep his hold, but lets go. When he does so, he gives in – the images in this passage vividly suggest – to an abandon that is comparable to the abandon of suicide, for it is as though he has 'stabbed himself' and is 'turning the knife in the wound', and also to the abandon of passion, for it is as though he has surrendered, like 'a happy lover', to 'ecstasy'. To let go, it would seem, is to die, is indeed to lose possession of the self, but the lover's ecstasy, at least, suggests that this may be a happy preliminary to the restoration of self. And this, though 'rendered in physical terms' (as I remarked of 'The Secret Sharer'), is evocative of what happens to Razumov in his spiritual crisis.

When Razumov finally confesses by pressing 'a denunciatory finger to his breast with force' and saying that his story 'ends here – on this very spot', he remains looking at Natalia 'with an appalling expressionless tranquillity' (p. 354). It is his apparent lack of feeling that the narrator finds appalling, but his outer tranquillity is the first indication that he has recovered possession of himself. In his journal Razumov seems to grasp this paradox:

It is only later on that I understood – only today, only a few hours ago. What could I have known of what was tearing me to pieces and dragging the secret for ever to my lips? You were appointed to undo the evil by making me betray myself back into truth and peace. You! (p. 358)

This passage brings to mind Donne's appeal to his three person'd God to break, blow, burn and make him new; for if Razumov is torn to pieces by the secret that is finally dragged to his lips, it is not he that is undone but the evil, and he too is made anew. Or, rather, he recovers the self he has lost, for he is betrayed 'back into truth and peace'. If he finally allows himself to slip over the precipice, it is not to destruction that he falls, for – as he realizes – he is 'saved' by Natalia and by the confession she inspires 'from ignominy' and from the 'ultimate undoing' which the exploitation of her love would have meant (p. 361). In refusing to take advantage of her love and in deliberately and selflessly renouncing her, Razumov not only affirms that need for integrity in personal relations which he had denied in his betrayal of Haldin but demonstrates his own newly achieved wholeness, an integrity of being.

Razumov persists in believing that, after the confession, 'perdition is [his] lot' and that he has 'done with life' (p. 362), but this is not what the journal indicates:

Suddenly you stood before me! You alone in all the world to whom I must confess. You fascinated me – you have freed me from the blindness of anger and hate – the truth shining in you drew the truth out of me. Now I have done it; and as I write here, I am in the depths of anguish, but there is air to breathe at last – air! And, by the by, that old man sprang up from somewhere as I was speaking to you, and raged at me like a disappointed devil. I suffer horribly, but I am not in despair. There is only one more thing to do for me. After that – if they let me – I shall go away and bury myself in obscure misery.

In giving Victor Haldin up, it was myself, after all, whom I have betrayed most basely. . . . (p. 361)

The 'one more thing' Razumov says he still has to do is, of course, to make his public confession to the revolutionists, going to them – like Jim to Doramin – to take responsibility for what he has done and court physical retribution. But, unlike Jim, he does not abandon himself to despair – he is 'not in despair' despite his anguish – and his spirit remains firm within him. It is true that in the event his body takes rough punishment, for he is first deafened by Necator and then crippled by the tramcar he does not hear, thus having the marks of his experience emblematically imprinted on him, as it were, his deafness to Haldin's appeal for help having been the prelude to another sort of crippling – but none of this can efface what he gains from the confession to Natalia. His confession to her is, first of all, a liberation, for it 'frees' him from 'the blindness of anger and hate' and marks his 'escape from the prison of lies' (p. 363). And this, in turn, is a release into renewed life, for 'there is air to breathe at last', whereas 'the choking fumes of falsehood' had previously 'taken him by the throat' (p. 269). It is a release, furthermore, from that which has possessed him – from a preoccupation with self-preservation, as his readiness to expose himself to the revolutionists shows; and from the grip of a demonic evil, as the curious reference to the narrator's having raged at him 'like a disappointed devil' suggests, for when he first felt himself possessed, we recall, it was to wonder whether the devil had not taken the shape of the 'old Englishman'. Finally, Razumov (like the captain-narrator in 'The Secret Sharer') comes to the sort of self-knowledge that is the condition and reward of a full possession of self – and that to some degree mitigates the miserable existence which is left him. But it is, after all, no more than a miserable existence; and it confronts us with the austere bleakness of Conrad's vision which, though it sees how a Jukes or the captain-narrator may win through to a steeled heart amid the turmoil of the sea, seems able to envisage the deprivation of a redeemed Razumov – or a Monygham – as the only sort of triumph to be wrested ashore from an engulfing darkness of the spirit.

Razumov, however, is nevertheless the most impressive exemplar in Conrad of a self-possession that, paradoxically, may accrue from a readiness to let go. It is a paradox, as I have tried to show, that is at the heart of Conrad's work; and, if in the course of this discussion I have had occasion to make comparisons in one way or another between Razumov and characters in every one of the works analysed in this study – between him and Captain Allistoun, and Kurtz, and Jim and Jukes; between him and Nostromo and Decoud, and Verloc, and the captain-narrator in 'The Secret Sharer' – it is because in *Under Western Eyes* Conrad has brought accumulated wisdom to bear on his most complex character. It is wisdom which is the product of his art and runs against one of his own most cherished beliefs: at the end of his ordeal Razumov may violate 'the first condition of good service', but as a result he is spiritually qualified for it.

Notes

1 'A Familiar Preface' to *A Personal Record*, p. xix.

2 R. W. Stallman, 'Conrad and "The Secret Sharer"', *The Art of Joseph Conrad: A Critical Symposium*, ed. R. W. Stallman (Michigan, 1960), p. 277. The essay was originally published in *Accent*, 9 (Spring, 1949).

3 *Joseph Conrad: Achievement and Decline* (Cambridge, Massachusetts, 1957), p. 11.

4 *Conrad the Novelist* (Cambridge, Massachusetts, 1958), p. 48.

5 *Joseph Conrad's Fiction: A Study in Literary Growth* (Ithaca, N.Y., 1968), p. xv.

6 *The Last Twelve Years of Joseph Conrad* (London, 1928), p. 32.

7 *Joseph Conrad: A Psychoanalytic Biography* (Princeton, N.J., 1967), pp. 49–50.

8 *Conrad's Models of Mind* (Minneapolis, 1971), pp. 130–1. Cf. C. B. Cox, who believes Conrad suffered from 'a basic uncertainty about his own identity'. *Joseph Conrad: The Modern Imagination* (London, 1974) p. 6.

9 'Author's Note' (1920) to *'Twixt Land and Sea*, pp. vii–viii.

10 *Joseph Conrad*, p. 220.

11 ibid.

12 ibid.

13 'Author's Note' (1919) to *The Mirror of the Sea*, p. vi.

14 Going by dates of publication, Moser fixes on the year 1912 as the dividing line, though he says that it 'should not be thought of as a definite watershed. It is simply a convenience. In that year "The Secret Sharer", the last first-rate Conrad, appeared in book form [though written before the completion of *Under Western Eyes*], and *Chance*, the first clearly second-rate work that pretended to be of major importance, began to appear as a serial in the New York Herald.' *Joseph Conrad*, p. 8.

15 ibid., p. 51.

16 Conrad explicitly connects only two of these phenomena: in *Chance* Marlow posits a direct link between panic and suicide in his analysis of

what must have impelled Flora de Barral towards self-destruction: 'That dread of what was before her . . . flamed up into an access of panic, that sort of headlong panic which had already driven her out twice to the top of the cliff-like quarry. She jumped up saying to herself: "Why not now? At once! Yes. I'll do it now – in the dark!" (p. 229). From the start, however, Conrad began implicitly to establish other relations among these cardinal points, steadily moving to a strong sense of their interconnectedness.

In this respect C. B. Cox has commented interestingly on the part played in Conrad's life by his 'urge to self-destruction'. *Joseph Conrad*, p. 3.

Chapter Two **The Nigger of the 'Narcissus'** *pages 26–50*

1 'To My Readers in America', 1914. This note is not included in the Dent Collected Edition, but may readily be found in the Signet Classic edition of *Typhoon and Other Tales*, from which the quotation is taken, p. 17.

2 Morris Beja, commenting on the fact that Conrad 'stresses the "moment of vision" ', a phrase used elsewhere in the preface, as 'an essential aspect of his view of both life and art', says that he has 'an affective view of aesthetic experience: art makes the person perceiving it do something. In effect, he says, that in the greatest literature the reader experiences epiphanies'. *Epiphany in the Modern Novel* (London, 1971), p. 52.

3 See, notably, Albert J. Guerard, *Conrad the Novelist*, p. 107; and Ian Watt, 'Conrad Criticism and *The Nigger of the "Narcissus"*, *Twentieth Century Interpretations of The Nigger of the 'Narcissus': A Collection of Critical Essays*, ed. John A. Palmer (Eaglewood Cliffs, N.J., 1969), pp. 80–2. The essay was originally published in *Nineteenth-Century Fiction*, 12 (1958).

4 *The Metaphysics of Darkness: A Study in the Unity and Development of Conrad's Fiction* (Baltimore and London, 1971), p. 5. There would accordingly seem to be more to Conrad's use of the two images than Marvin Mudrick is willing to give him credit for: '. . . occasionally, at least, [Conrad's] choice of metaphor seems calculated rather to impress us with his ingenuity than to illuminate his subject. A particular simile – the storm as madman – strikes him as so ingenious that he uses it twice, obtrusively, in the course of a few pages during the storm episode. . . . The effect is to distract picturesquely, to diminish and make doubtful our sense of cosmic magnitude, which is being superbly established by a sequence of images not attentive to themselves but subordinated and integral to the great complex image of the storm.' 'The Artist's Conscience

and *The Nigger of the "Narcissus"* ', *Twentieth Century Interpretations*, ed. John A. Palmer, pp. 73–4. The essay was originally published in *Nineteenth-Century Fiction*, 11 (1957).

5 'Jimmy Wait and the Dance of Death: Conrad's *Nigger of the "Narcissus"* ', *Twentieth Century Interpretations*, ed. John A. Palmer, p. 42. The essay was originally published in *Critical Quarterly*, 7 (Winter 1965).

6 *Joseph Conrad's Letters to R. B. Cunninghame Graham*, ed. C. T. Watts (Cambridge, 1969), pp. 56–7.

7 See Ian Watt, 'Joseph Conrad: Alienation and Commitment', *The English Mind*, ed. Hugh Sykes Davies and George Watson (Cambridge, 1964), p. 259; Cecil Scrimgeour, loc. cit., p. 41; and Avrom Fleishman, *Conrad's Politics: Community and Anarchy in the Fiction of Joseph Conrad* (Baltimore, 1967), p. 27.

8 Letter of 4 September 1892. *Letters of Joseph Conrad to Marguerite Poradowska, 1890–1920*, tr. from the French and ed. John A. Gee and Paul J. Sturm (New Haven, 1940), p. 45.

9 The analogy between a ship's voyage and the journey of life comes naturally to Conrad. In writing of 'Landfalls and Departures' in *The Mirror of the Sea*, the two sorts of journey coalesce as he recalls the last visit he paid to an ailing captain under whom he had sailed: 'Was he looking out for a strange Landfall, or taking with an untroubled mind the bearings for his last Departure?' (p. 12). And when the *Narcissus* finally makes its landfall and is berthed, 'she [ceases] to live' (p. 165).

10 Letter of 7 April 1924 to Henry S. Canby. G. Jean-Aubry, *Joseph Conrad: Life and Letters* (London, 1927), II, 342.

11 G. Jean-Aubry, *Life and Letters*, I, 84.

12 In an essay written in 1918 Conrad maintains that the necessity to hold together makes men rise above themselves: 'The mysteriously born tradition of sea-craft commands unity in a body of workers engaged in an occupation in which men have to depend upon each other. It raises them, so to speak, above the frailties of their dead selves.' 'Well Done', *Notes on Life and Letters*, p. 183. And Bruce Johnson has remarked that 'if Conrad's work – especially *Nostromo* – has established anything, it must be that many of us really have no name, that most of us are in one way or another somebody else's man, and that self-possession, while it is the only source of value in an absurd universe or at least in a cosmos where man has only an absurd role, depends almost mystically on a sense of human solidarity'. *Conrad's Models of Mind*, p. 15.

13 Cf. Conrad's comment in a letter of 26 August 1901 to William Blackwood on Admiral Sir William Robert Kennedy's account of a shipwreck in *Hurrah for the Life of a Sailor: Fifty Years in the Navy*: 'A wrestle with wind and weather has a moral value like the primitive acts

of faith on which may be built a doctrine of salvation and a rule of life.'
Joseph Conrad: Letters to William Blackwood and David S. Meldrum,
ed. William Blackburn (Durham, North Carolina, 1958), p. 133.

14 *Joseph Conrad: The Making of a Novelist* (Cambridge, Massachusetts, 1940), pp. 148–9.

15 *Joseph Conrad*, p. 33.

16 'Conrad Criticism and *The Nigger of the "Narcissus"* ', loc. cit.,
p. 93. It is Jimmy's fear of death, I take it, that explains Conrad's description of him (in the note 'To My Readers in America') as being 'the centre of the ship's collective psychology' (p. 17).

17 *Conrad the Novelist*, p. 109.

18 'Conrad Criticism', loc. cit., p. 94.

19 With the significant exception, of course, of Singleton. He tells Jimmy straight out to 'get on with' his dying and not to 'raise a blamed fuss' with the crew 'over that job', for they cannot help him. It is because death, for Singleton, is a 'job' like any other, to be accepted as part of the business of living, that he can see clearly what the others cannot; and when asked whether he thinks Jimmy will die, he answers 'deliberately': 'Why, of course he will die' (p. 42).

20 Letter of 16 November 1897 to Stephen Crane. 'The Letters of Joseph Conrad to Stephen and Cora Crane', ed. Carl Bohnenberger and Norman Mitchell Hill, *The Bookman* (New York), 69 (May 1929), 230.

21 Cecil Scrimgeour suggests that this acceptance also marks a release for the men; and, though he seems to me to give more weight to a cry of Belfast's than it can bear, his view is phrased in terms which link it suggestively to that advanced in this chapter: 'In this world of pitiless nature and human illusions acceptance of death is the first step towards liberation and health of spirit. When Belfast cries to Jimmy's corpse that seems so reluctant to slip down the board into the sea: "Be a man! . . . Go, Jimmy go" he voices the crew's desire to be relieved for good of their burden and responsibility; but he also expresses what they all know in their hearts. They now know that the meaning of life is to be found in the way a man asserts his own manhood, and that he is released to take possession of himself most completely when he ceases evading the reality of death and accepts it.' 'Jimmy Wait and the Dance of Death', loc. cit., p. 53.

Chapter Three 'Heart of Darkness' *pages 51–76*

1 See, for instance, Albert J. Guerard, *Conrad the Novelist*, p. 37; and Douglas Hewitt, *Conrad: A Reassessment* (London, 1952), p. 18. John A. Palmer maintains that 'in all the works in which he appears'

Marlow is the 'protagonist', but this would hardly appear to be the case in *Lord Jim* and *Chance*. See *Joseph Conrad's Fiction*, p. 18.

2 I do not think there is any reason to believe, as C. T. Watts maintains (*Joseph Conrad's Letters to R. B. Cunninghame Graham*, p. 119) that Marlow is being ironic here. A few pages later Marlow refers to 'a large shining map' of Africa, 'marked with all the colours of a rainbow', that he sees in the Company's offices in the sepulchral city, and comments: 'There was a vast amount of red – good to see at any time, because one knows that some real work is done in there . . .' (p. 55).

3 On occasion Marlow refers explicitly to continuing obscurities; cf. p. 72, for instance.

4 A similar view of African savagery is taken in the earlier story, 'An Outpost of Progress': 'All night they were disturbed by a lot of drumming in the villages. A deep, rapid roll near by would be followed by another far off – then all ceased. Soon short appeals would rattle out here and there, then all mingle together, increase, become vigorous and sustained, would spread out over the forest, roll through the night, unbroken and ceaseless, near and far, as if the whole land had been one immense drum booming out steadily an appeal to heaven. And through the deep and tremendous noise sudden yells that resembled snatches of songs from a madhouse darted shrill and high in discordant jets of sound which seemed to rush far above the earth and drive all peace from under the stars.' *Tales of Unrest*, pp. 98-9.

5 Support for such a reading is provided by a passage in 'An Outpost of Progress': 'Few men realize that their life, the very essence of their character, their capabilities and their audacities, are only the expression of their belief in the safety of their surroundings. The courage, the composure, the confidence; the emotions and principles; every great and every insignificant thought belongs not to the individual but to the crowd: to the crowd that believes blindly in the irresistible force of its institutions and of its morals, in the power of its police and of its opinion. But the contact with pure unmitigated savagery, with primitive nature and primitive man, brings sudden and profound trouble into the heart . . .' (p. 89).

6 Conrad directly described the activities of the modern Romans in Africa as 'the vilest scramble for loot that ever disfigured the history of human conscience and geographical exploration'. 'Geography and Some Explorers', *Last Essays*, p. 17.

7 Cf.: 'These essays . . . suggest that [Conrad] is misty in the middle as well as at the edges, that the secret casket of his genius contains a vapour rather than a jewel; and that we need not try to write him down philosophically, because there is, in this particular direction, nothing to write.' Review of *Notes on Life and Letters*, 1920, reprinted as 'Joseph Conrad: A Note', *Abinger Harvest* (New York, 1955), p. 131.

8 See Stephen A. Reid, 'The "Unspeakable Rites" in *Heart of Darkness*', *Modern Fiction Studies*, 9 (Winter 1963–4) for an interesting specification of the unspeakable.

9 Cf. 'An Outpost of Progress': 'Once Carlier shot a hippo in the river. They had no boat to secure it, and it sank. When it floated up it drifted away, and Gobila's people secured the carcase. It was the occasion for a national holiday, but Carlier had a fit of rage over it and talked about the necessity of exterminating all the niggers before the country could be made habitable' (p. 108).

10 *Conrad the Novelist*, pp. 39, 41.

11 'The Ultimate Meaning of "Heart of Darkness" ', *Nineteenth-Century Fiction*, 18 (June 1963), p. 45.

12 Letter of 31 May 1902. *Letters to William Blackwood*, ed. William Blackburn, p. 154.

13 Thomas Moser, *Joseph Conrad*, p. 79.

14 Florence H. Ridley, 'The Ultimate Meaning of "Heart of Darkness" ', loc. cit., pp. 51–2.

Chapter Four A. Lord Jim   *pages* 77–103

1 J. Hillis Miller, 'The Interpretation of *Lord Jim*', *The Interpretation of Narrative : Theory and Practice*, ed. Morton W. Bloomfield (Cambridge, Massachusetts, 1970), p. 228.

2 Douglas Hewitt, *Conrad*, pp. 37, 38.

3 Letter of 18 July 1900. *Letters to William Blackwood*, ed. William Blackburn, p. 106.

4 See pp. 31, 36, 37, 39, 42, 45, 48, 50, 51, 56, 66, 67, 68 (two references), 79, 80, 81 (two references), 82, 83, 84, 97 (three references), 107, 111, 121, 134 (two references).

5 See pp. 346, 347, 348, 349, 351.

6 Letter to Garnett of 12 November 1900. *Letters from Joseph Conrad*, ed. Edward Garnett (Indianapolis, 1928), p. 171.

7 *Joseph Conrad*, pp. 171–2.

8 It is perhaps worth noting that, though Conrad based the *Patna* episode on what happened to the *Jeddah*, keeping fairly faithfully to the real-life story, he invented the detail of the submerged wreck. The *Jeddah* was abandoned when it appeared likely to sink in a bad and prolonged storm. See Jerry Allen, *The Sea Years of Joseph Conrad* (Garden City, N.Y., 1965), pp. 120–4; and Norman Sherry, *Conrad's Eastern World* (Cambridge, 1966), p. 48.

9 See Note 1 to Chapter One above (p. 210).

10 For an interesting discussion of the motif of beetles and butterflies

in the novel, see Tony Tanner, 'Butterflies and Beetles – Conrad's Two Truths', *Chicago Review*, 16 (Winter-Spring 1963), 123–40. The essay has been reprinted in *Twentieth-Century Interpretations of Lord Jim: A Collection of Critical Essays*, ed. Robert E. Kuehn (Englewood Cliffs, N.J., 1969), pp. 53–67.

11 Dorothy Van Ghent, though not referring to this passage, comments in related terms on the unconscious force which seems to direct Jim: '. . . because [Jim's jump] is a paradigm of the encounters of the conscious personality with the stranger within, the stranger who is the very self of the self, the significance of Jim's story is *our own* significance, contained in the enigmatic relationship between the conscious will and the fatality of our acts'; and: 'In contrast with the captain of "The Secret Sharer", Jim repudiates the other-self that has been revealed to him; at no time does he consciously acknowledge that it *was* himself who jumped from the *Patna* – it was only his body that had jumped . . .' 'On *Lord Jim*', *The English Novel: Form and Function* (New York, 1953), pp. 229, 233.

12 It is similar to Jung's description of man's 'worst enemy': '[Man] imagines his worst enemy in front of him, yet he carries the enemy within himself – deadly longing for the abyss, a longing to drown in his our source, to be sucked down to the realm of the Mothers. His life is a constant struggle against extinction, a violent yet fleeting deliverance from ever-lurking night. This death is no external enemy, it is his own inner longing for the stillness and profound peace of all-knowing non-existence, for all-seeing sleep in the ocean of coming-to-be and passing away. Even in his highest strivings for harmony and balance, for the profundities of philosophy and the raptures of the artist, he seeks death, immobility, satiety, rest.' I owe this passage from *Transformation* to Elliot B. Gose, who cites it in relation to Jim's actual death at the end of the novel in 'Pure Exercise of Imagination: Archetypal Symbolism in *Lord Jim*', P.M.L.A., LXXIX (March 1964), 146.

13 It is striking that Conrad's view should at the same time be parallel to another system, for the sexual overtones of 'the blessed stiffness' do not only evoke a sexual vitality as opposed to the impotence of despair but 'the sexual or life instincts' which Freud thinks of as countering 'the ego or death instincts'. He distinguishes 'two kinds of instincts: those which seek to lead what is living to death, and others, the sexual instincts, which are perpetually attempting and achieving a renewal of life'; and he suggests that 'Eros operates from the beginning of life and appears as a "life instinct" in opposition to the "death instinct" which was brought into being by the coming to life of inorganic substance.' *Beyond the Pleasure Principle*, tr. James Strachey, ed. Gregory Zilboorg (New York, 1967; first published in German in 1920), pp. 79, 82, 106.

14 Though Bernard C. Meyer takes a rather one-sided view of Jim's jump, it accords – in the upshot – with that advanced here: 'In the certain expectation that the leaky *Patna* will sink, he scuttles his seaman's code of conduct, and gripped by the instinct for self-preservation, he jumps overboard.' *Joseph Conrad*, p. 159.

15 This links up with Robert Penn Warren's view, in a most interesting account of the passage, that man 'should, to follow the metaphor, walk on the dry land of "nature", the real, naturalistic world, and not be dropped into the waters he is so ill-equipped to survive in.' He has previously said that 'by the dream Conrad here means nothing more or less than man's necessity to justify himself by the "idea", to idealize himself and his actions into moral significance of some order, to find sanctions'. 'On *Nostromo*', *The Art of Joseph Conrad: A Critical Symposium*, ed. R. W. Stallman, p. 218. The essay was originally published as an introduction to the 1951 Modern Library edition of *Nostromo*.

16 The decline in the power of the writing in this section is probably partly attributable to the fact that it also contains 'the story of [Jim's] love' (p. 275), and Conrad is no more successful than usual at handling such a story. At all events, it is a strange phenomenon of such good novels as *Lord Jim* and *Under Western Eyes* that they should contain weak middle sections, almost lacunae, though these come between exceptionally fine opening and closing sections. Albert J. Guerard also finds the middle part of *Lord Jim* to be weak: '[Chapters 22–35 do] not bear much rereading. The later chapters (36–45), though "adventurous" and "romantic", are very moving; they recover the *authenticity in depth* of the first part. . . . And I think this points to the serious weakness of Chapters 22–35: that the adventures . . . have nothing to do with the essential Jim. . . . We may add that a characteristic mediocrity sets in with the introduction of Jewel in Chapter 28 . . . But Chapters 25–27 (on the defeat of Sherif Ali) seem the weakest of all on later readings.' *Conrad the Novelist*, p. 168.

17 Gustav Morf, for instance, says that 'Jim's final and deadly mistake, the permission to let Brown and his men go away *in possession of their arms*, is due to the paralysing influence of [his] identification [with Brown]'. *The Polish Heritage of Joseph Conrad* (London, n.d. [1929?]) p. 157. See, too, Albert J. Guerard, *Conrad the Novelist*, p. 149.

18 Though Tony Tanner says that Jim 'dies to vindicate a superior Ideal', he concedes that 'his martyrdom is also a suicide, for he refuses to fight and escape from the angry natives as Tamb' Itam and Jewel urge him to do. His death is an easy way out. It is the final relapse into peace, the merciful release from the world of action. It is the end of his flight from a ghost, the last shutting of eyes that never again need be reopened, and escape into an immobility which can never be disturbed. Jim has been

true to his weaknesses as well. . . .' *Conrad : Lord Jim* (London, 1963), p. 55.

19 *Chance*, p. 183.

Chapter Four B. 'Typhoon' *pages* 104–12

1 Letter of 14 February 1899 to David Meldrum. *Letters to William Blackwood*, ed. William Blackburn, p. 56.

2 In the Author's Note to the *Typhoon* volume of stories, Conrad recounts the genesis of the tale: 'I . . . was casting about for some subject which could be developed in a shorter form than the tales in the volume of "Youth" when the instance of a steamship full of returning coolies from Singapore to some port in northern China occurred to my recollection. Years before I had heard it being talked about in the East as a recent occurrence. It was for us merely one subject of conversation amongst many others of the kind' (p. v).

3 *Joseph Conrad*, p. 162.

4 Albert J. Guerard, *Conrad the Novelist*, p. 294.

5 Douglas Hewitt, *Conrad : A Reassessment*, p. 112.

6 Later on Jukes dimly perceives 'the squat shape of his captain holding on to a twisted bridge-rail, motionless and swaying as if rooted to the planks' (p. 81) – but MacWhirr's rootedness is clearly of a different order: rooted in the moral imperatives of the seaman's code of conduct, he is impressively sustained by it, and it is his firm determination to live up to that code that in part ensures his enviable stability.

Chapter Five Nostromo *pages* 113–43

1 *Conrad the Novelist*, p. 211.

2 In regard to the timing of the Montero revolt, Conrad is neither as careless nor perverse as Albert J. Guerard assumes him to be. He intends the revolt to have been going on for about a year by the time the Monterist forces reach Sulaco, as is indirectly indicated much later by the reference to Pedrito Montero's having 'expected to find comfort and luxury in the Intendencia after a year of hard camp life, ending with the hardships and privations of the daring dash upon Sulaco . . .' (p. 392).

3 This is revealed when Gould is allowed to say: 'I had no idea that [Hirsch] was still in Sulaco. I thought he had gone back overland to Esmeralda more than a week ago. He came here once to talk to me about his hide business and some other things. I made it clear to him that nothing could be done' (p. 381). Gould says this to Dr. Monygham on

the morning after Sotillo's arrival, and we know, therefore, that Hirsch in fact came to speak to him only three nights previously, on the night of the reception following Barrios's departure.

4 See Thomas Moser, *Joseph Conrad*, p. 43; and Albert J. Guerard, *Conrad the Novelist*, p. 175.

5 ibid.

6 *Conrad: A Reassessment*, pp. 66, 68. Albert J. Guerard has also commented on the way the reader's expectations are frustrated 'from beginning to end of the first part' of the book, but he does not offer an explanation of the significance of this. See *Conrad the Novelist*, p. 215.

7 'On *Nostromo*', *The Art of Joseph Conrad*, ed. R. W. Stallman, p. 222.

8 Douglas Hewitt also refers to this passage, but he views the telegraph wire as a symbol of 'the enslavement of the country'. See *Conrad: A Reassessment*, p. 54.

9 *The Metaphysics of Darkness*, p. 116.

10 'Autocracy and War', *Notes on Life and Letters*, p. 86.

11 Richard Curle, Introduction to *Nostromo*, p. viii.

12 *Notes on Life and Letters*, p. 107.

13 F. R. Leavis has commented suggestively on 'the presence of Decoud and Nostromo in the lighter as it drifts with its load of silver and of Fear (personified by the stowaway Hirsch) through the black night of the gulf...' 'Joseph Conrad', *The Great Tradition* (London, 1948), p. 197.

14 *Conrad: Nostromo* (London, 1969), p. 34.

15 See Chap. III, p. 56 above.

16 Avrom Fleishman makes a similar connection between Gould and the Professor: 'This remarkable passage [i.e. that which asserts Gould has "something . . . of the spirit of a buccaneer"] suggests . . . the image of the nihilist, like the Professor of *The Secret Agent* or Jörgenson of *The Rescue*, who would rather bring everything down with him than accept partial or temporary defeat'. *Conrad's Politics*, p. 181. Gould, moreover, in the inner emptiness of his 'cold and overmastering passion' for the mine is a striking prefiguration of Gerald Crich in *Women in Love*.

17 *Joseph Conrad*, p. 87.

18 Cf. C. B. Cox, *Joseph Conrad*, p. 79.

19 *Conrad the Novelist*, pp. 199, 200.

Chapter Six **The Secret Agent**   *pages* 144–70

1 *Joseph Conrad: A Critical Biography* (London, 1960), p. 340.

2 Conrad frequently referred to the ironic method as a distinguishing feature of the novel. In a letter of 7 November 1906 to Algernon Methuen,

he said, 'I confess that in my eyes the story is a fairly successful (and sincere) piece of ironic treatment applied to a special subject – a sensational subject if one likes to call it so.' G. Jean-Aubry, *Life and Letters*, II, 38. And in a letter to Marguerite Poradowska of 20 June 1912, he wrote, 'The book is not very characteristic of me, but I am fond of it because I think that in it I managed to treat what is after all a melodramatic subject by the method of irony. This was the artistic aim I set myself . . .' *Letters to Marguerite Poradowska*, ed. John A Gee and Paul J. Sturm, p. 116.

3 Letter of October 1907. *Letters from Joseph Conrad*, ed. Edward Garnett, p. 204.

4 *A Reader's Guide to Joseph Conrad* (New York, 1960), p. 194. See too F. R. Leavis, *The Great Tradition*, pp. 210–11; Claire Rosenfield, *Paradise of Snakes: An Archetypal Analysis of Conrad's Political Novels* (Chicago, 1967), p. 90; Donald C. Yelton, *Mimesis and Metaphor: An Inquiry into the Genesis and Scope of Conrad's Symbolic Imagery* (The Hague, 1967), p. 85; and C. B. Cox, *Joseph Conrad*, p. 93.

5 Conrad himself thought highly of it. J. H. Retinger reports that when he once asked him 'which of his books he considered the best, he answered without hesitation: "*Nostromo* and *The Secret Agent* because in those I accumulated the most difficult technical obstacles and I overcame them most successfully." ' *Conrad and His Contemporaries* (London, 1941), p. 91. F. R. Leavis makes the same valuation: '*The Secret Agent* . . . is . . . indubitably a classic and a masterpiece, and it doesn't answer to the notion at all – which is perhaps why it appears to have had nothing like due recognition. . . . *The Secret Agent* is truly classical in its maturity of attitude and the consummateness of the art in which this finds expression . . . [*The Secret Agent* and *Nostromo*], for all the great differences between them in range and temper, are triumphs of the same art. . . .' *The Great Tradition*, pp. 209–10.

6 See *Dickens and the Art of Analogy* (London, 1970).

7 *A Set of Six*, p. 77.

8 Letter of 12 March 1897. *Letters from Joseph Conrad*, ed. Edward Garnett, p. 94.

9 I am indebted to Avrom Fleishman's stimulating discussion of *The Secret Agent*, though, approaching the novel from the standpoint of 'the organic community', he takes a different view of the nature of the social forces that are threatening disintegration and of the imagery that points to it: '[The imaginative] perspective is a vision of the modern world in a state of fragmentation – as if by explosion. It is an ironic vision because Conrad's fundamental social value was the organic community, while the present status of men is that of isolation from each other, alienation from the social whole, and, in consequence, loneliness and self-destruction. The dramatic action presents this vision simultaneously in

two plots, one in the public, political realm and the other in the private, domestic one. The two plots, and the social sectors they represent, are welded together not as much by their point of contact in Verloc as by the imagery, which is maintained throughout the novel in both plots. This imagery is the symbolic equivalent of the theme of fragmentation, and takes the varied forms of personal self-enclosure (secrecy, ignorance, foolishness, madness, etc.) and of physical dismembering (explosion, butchering, islands, etc.).' *Conrad's Politics*, pp. 188–9.

10 Though *Women in Love* was written in 1916, it is set in pre-war England.

11 Letter to John Galsworthy of 12 September 1906. G. Jean-Aubry, *Life and Letters*, II, 37.

12 Letter to Algernon Methuen of 7 November 1906. Ibid., p. 38.

13 Cf. C. B. Cox, *Joseph Conrad*, p. 99.

14 Paul L. Wiley is one of the few critics to point to a connection between the attitudes of the lady patroness and those of the anarchists: 'The causes for unrest Conrad attributes . . . to the anarchistic spirit throughout the social order. The proclaimed anarchists . . . are inherently no more vicious than the elderly patroness of Michaelis, who believes in the complete economic ruin of the system which permits the indulgence of her eccentricities . . .' *Conrad's Measure of Man*, p. 110.

15 Letter of 7 October 1907. *Letters to R. B. Cunninghame Graham*, ed. C. T. Watts, p. 170.

16 John Hagan has made an interesting connection between Conrad's view here and that in the Malay novels: '. . . one of Conrad's purposes is to show that complacency, self-interest, dissension, and moral indifference exist among the forces of law and order as among those bent upon the disruption of those forces. The final impression is of a society analogous to those which Conrad depicted in his earlier novels dealing with the East: societies torn by dissension between natives and their white exploiters, and by dissension within the ranks of both.' 'The Design of Conrad's *The Secret Agent*', *E.L.H.*, XXII (June 1955), 158.

17 'Poland Revisited', *Notes on Life and Letters*, pp. 143–44.

18 Irving Howe, 'Conrad: Order and Anarchy', *Politics and the Novel* (New York, 1957), p. 96. Part of the essay has been reprinted in Ian Watt, ed., *Conrad: The Secret Agent*, a Macmillan casebook (London, 1973).

Chapter Seven A 'The Secret Sharer' *pages* 171–83

1 In the case of 'The Secret Sharer' and *The Shadow-Line*, Carl Benson also points to their common exploration of the theme of initiation. See 'Conrad's Two Stories of Initiation', *P.M.L.A.*, LXIX (March 1954), 45–56.

2 Jocelyn Baines, *Joseph Conrad*, pp. 345, 355, 359.

3 ibid., p. 485.

4 He too was an untried captain, having held his command 'for less than a year'. See Jerry Allen, *The Sea Years of Joseph Conrad*, p. 114.

5 Norman Sherry also believes that the incident in 'The Secret Sharer' is based on this episode. See *Conrad's Eastern World*, p. 267.

6 *Conrad the Novelist*, p. 26.

7 Guerard elaborated the implications of the 'broad concern' of the story in this way in an earlier and well-known introduction to the Signet Classic edition of '*Heart of Darkness*' and '*The Secret Sharer*' (New York, 1950), p. 9. Donald C. Yelton follows him in maintaining Leggatt 'embodies a dark potentiality of the self'. *Mimesis and Metaphor*, p. 280.

8 'Legate of the Ideal', *Conrad: A Collection of Critical Essays*, ed. Marvin Mudrick (Englewood Cliffs, N.J., 1966), p. 81. The essay was originally published in *Conrad's 'Secret Sharer' and the Critics*, ed. Bruce Harkness, 1962.

9 Letter to John Galsworthy, dated 'Monday, 1913.' G. Jean-Aubry, *Life and Letters*, II, 143–4.

10 *Conrad's Short Fiction* (Berkeley & Los Angeles, 1969), p. 151.

11 Previously unpublished letter of 14 June 1917 to Mr. A. T. Saunders. Norman Sherry, *Conrad's Eastern World*, p. 295. It is interesting that Conrad should have got the date of the *Cutty Sark* incident wrong and changed the transfer to the American ship into a swimming ashore. Sherry suggests he was 'probably trying to put [Saunders] off the track' in his literary detective work. *Conrad's Eastern World*, p. 254.

12 'Legate of the Ideal', loc. cit., p. 79.

13 *Conrad the Novelist*, p. 25.

14 In exclusively registering the captain's irresponsibility, critics seem to me to fail to do justice to the tension of opposites evoked by the scene. Cf. Porter Williams, who says the captain's risking of his ship goes 'beyond an absolute limit for any responsible mariner, even though it involved an act of compassion'; and notes that what is not explained is 'why Conrad leaves us with the impression that there is no need to condemn what appears as the shocking behavior of reaching the point where the loss of the ship and much of its crew seemed so nearly certain'. 'The Matter of Conscience in Conrad's *The Secret Sharer*', *P.M.L.A.* LXXIX (December 1964), 626, 628. Donald C. Yelton maintains that 'whatever we may make of [the captain's] earlier behavior, his action in risking his ship and all hands . . . cannot by any license be said to illustrate a maturity of either professional or moral judgement; nor can it . . . be said to furnish him with valid rational grounds for "self respect and confidence". In short,

his self respect and confidence are irrationally grounded; he has, as it were, made a wager – with himself, with "Fate" – and he has won it.' *Mimesis and Metaphor*, p. 289.

Chapter Seven B. **Under Western Eyes** *pages* 184–209

1 Conrad certainly thought of an earlier version of the novel in these terms. In a letter to John Galsworthy of 6 January 1908 he wrote:

The student Razumov, meeting abroad the mother and sister of Haldin falls in love with that last, marries her and, after a time, confesses to her the part he played in the arrest of her brother.

The psychological developments leading to Razumov's betrayal of Haldin, to his confession of the fact to his wife and to the death of these people (brought about mainly by the resemblance of their child to the late Haldin), form the real subject of the story.

G. Jean-Aubry, *Life and Letters*, II, 65.

2 It is a dilemma to which a contemporary of his was to give vivid expression in 1939 when it had its bearing on life in England: 'I hate the idea of causes, and if I had to choose between betraying my country and betraying my friend, I hope I should have the guts to betray my country.' E. M. Forster, 'What I Believe', *Two Cheers for Democracy* (Penguin, 1965), p. 76.

3 Jocelyn Baines takes a similar view, maintaining that Razumov is 'the most considerable character that Conrad created'. *Joseph Conrad*, p. 362.

4 Conrad disliked Dostoevsky – Jocelyn Baines quotes him as referring to the Russian as 'the grimacing, haunted creature' (ibid. p. 360) – but a Polish critic, Wit Tarnawski, has shown the numerous ways in which *Under Western Eyes* is indebted to *Crime and Punishment*: 'Poleska [another Polish critic] quotes the fundamental resemblance, that the heroes of both novels are students psychically shattered by a crime they committed. To this we may add that love is a factor arousing the consciences of both and leading them to the confession of guilt. Resemblances in detail are still more striking: the roles of mother and sister in both novels, the mental derangement of both mothers at the end of the novels, the curious illness of both heroes after committing the crime, the identical roles played by the sledge-driver Ziemianitch and the house-painter, both suspected and at the same time relieving the hero of suspicion. Finally both writers create a similar final situation for their heroes – freeing them of suspicion so that their confessions may arise from their own free will.' Quoted (from a translation) by Eloise Knapp Hay, *The*

Political Novels of Joseph Conrad: A Critical Study (Chicago and London, 1963), p. 280.

5 Leo Gurko has pointed out that Razumov is 'goaded by his threatened and resentful egotism' into plunging 'into the web of rationalization that finally persuades him to identify his own interests with the established Russian power'. *Joseph Conrad: Giant in Exile* (New York, 1962), p. 188. Bruce Johnson also remarks that 'there is so much selfish rationalization in Razumov's suddenly intensified conservatism that we can hardly accept it at face value'. *Conrad's Models of Mind*, p. 147.

6 Razumov has frequently been compared to Jim, though usually on the grounds of his being portrayed in a similar drama of guilt and atonement. The most interesting statement of this view is that of André Gide in a journal entry: 'Much interested by the relationship I discover between *Under Western Eyes* and *Lord Jim*. (I regret not having spoken of this with Conrad.) That *irresponsible* act of the hero, to redeem which his whole life is subsequently engaged. For the thing that leads to the heaviest responsibility is just the *irresponsibilities* in a life. How can one efface that act? There is no more pathetic subject for a novel, nor one that has been more stifled in our literature by belief in Boileau's rule: that the hero must remain, from one end to the other of a drama or a novel "such as he was first seen to be".' Quoted from the Justin O'Brien translation of the Journals by R. W. Stallman, ed., *The Art of Joseph Conrad: A Critical Symposium*, p. 5.

7 Conrad's art here is so sure that he can even afford an undercutting irony while presenting Razumov with the greatest seriousness. Razumov may long to wield a stick with a stern hand, but the stick he has used to beat Ziemianitch has broken in his hands and been flung away, a mute intimation of the futility and vanity of authoritarian pretensions. Not that those of the revolutionists are viewed any less ironically:

> I do not remember now the details of the weight and length of the fetters riveted on [Peter Ivanovitch's] limbs by an 'Administrative' order, but it was in the number of pounds and the thickness of links an appalling assertion of the divine right of autocracy. Appalling and futile too, because this big man managed to carry off that simple engine of government with him into the woods. . . . It was the end of the day; with infinite labour he managed to free one of his legs. Meantime night fell. He was going to begin on his other leg when he was overtaken by a terrible misfortune. He dropped his file.
> 'All this is precise yet symbolic . . .' (pp. 120–1).

Revolutionary activity, it is indicated, is a filing away in the dark at the fetters of autocracy; moreover, since the revolutionists are not fit for 'the gift of liberty' (which the file is said to be (p. 121)), they let it slip through their fingers.

8 Cf. Osborn Andreas, who says Razumov must 'force the image of himself that he presents to the world and the image of himself which he possesses in his own mind to coalesce and become one. He feels that he can no longer endure a situation in which his true self is like a disembodied and invisible ghost which, instead of inhabiting his visible body, merely accompanies him wherever he goes.' *Joseph Conrad: A Study in Non-conformity* (New York, 1959), p. 134.

Index

Characters are indexed under the names by which they are commonly referred to.